Controversial Issues in Criminology

Controversial Issues in Criminology

Edited by

John R. Fuller
State University of West Georgia

Eric W. Hickey
California State University, Fresno

Series Editor

Steven A. Egger
University of Illinois at Springfield

ALLYN AND BACON
Boston • London • Toronto • Sydney • Tokyo • Singapore

Editor-in-Chief, Social Sciences: Karen Hanson
Series Editorial Assistant: Heather Ahlstrom
Marketing Manager: Susan E. Ogar
Sr. Editorial Production Administrator: Susan McIntyre
Editorial Production Service: Ruttle, Shaw & Wetherill, Inc.
Manufacturing Buyer: Megan Cochran
Cover Administrator: Jenny Hart
Electronic Composition: Omegatype Typography, Inc.

Copyright © 1999 by Allyn and Bacon
A Viacom Company
160 Gould Street
Needham Heights, MA 02494
Internet: www.abacon.com

Library of Congress Cataloging-in-Publication Data
Controversial issues in criminology/edited by John R. Fuller, Eric
   W. Hickey.
      p.   cm.
      Includes bibliographical references.
      ISBN 0-205-27210-X
      1. Criminology–United States.   2. Criminal justice,
   Administration of–United States.   I. Fuller, John R.   II. Hickey,
   Eric W.
HV6025.C626   1998   98–18866
364.973–dc21   CIP

Printed in the United States of America
10   9   8   7   6   5   4   3   2   1   04   03   02   01   00   98   99

Contents

Controversial Perspectives

Controversial Policies

About the Editors

John R. Fuller, Ph.D.

John R. Fuller is Professor of Criminology and Sociology at the State University of West Georgia in Carrollton. His book, *Criminal Justice: A Peacemaking Perspective* (Allyn & Bacon, 1998), an introductory criminal justice textbook, is the result of over twenty-five years of working in, learning about, and teaching about the criminal justice system.

Dr. Fuller has earned a Bachelor of University Studies from the University of New Mexico and a Master of Science and Doctor of Philosophy from the School of Criminology at Florida State University. He has been teaching at the State University of West Georgia for seventeen years and is the coordinator of the criminology program. He has also worked as a probation and parole officer and a criminal justice planner in south Florida.

Dr. Fuller maintains a Web page devoted to the theme "peacemaking and crime" at http://www.westga.edu/~jfuller/peace.html.

Eric W. Hickey, Ph.D.

Currently teaching criminal psychology at California State University, Fresno, Dr. Hickey also serves as Adjunct Professor for Fresno City College and the California School of Professional Psychology. Dr. Hickey has considerable field experience working with the criminally insane, psychopaths, sex offenders, and other habitual criminals. Internationally recognized for his research on multiple homicide offenders, Dr. Hickey has published and lectured extensively on the causes of violence and serial crime.

His book, *Serial Murderers and Their Victims,* now in its second edition, is used as a teaching tool in colleges and universities in studying criminal personalities. This research became the basis for the Learning Channel documentary *To Kill and Kill Again,* an in-depth analysis of the life and crimes of Jeffrey Dahmer. Dr. Hickey's research is often the subject of newspaper, radio, and television interviews, including *Newsweek,* National Public Radio, CNN's *Burden of Proof* and *Larry King Live,* the BBC's *Channel 24,* and ABC's *This Week, Good Morning America,* and *20/20.*

As a consultant to various law enforcement and private agencies, Dr. Hickey testifies as an expert witness in various criminal cases. He also served as a consultant to the UNABOM Task Force during the hunt for the Unabomber. Dr. Hickey conducts training seminars for community and government agencies involving the profiling and investigating of sex crimes, arson, and homicide cases, as well as cases of stalking and workplace violence. His latest research examines the psychology of stalking, the classification of stalkers, intervention and deterrence strategies for potential offenders, and modes of victim assistance.

Preface

One of the characteristics of scientific development that most plagues historians is the enormous diversity of viewpoints that continue to persist long after it appears that a consensus has been reached. The difficulty arises not only because consensus is never total, but also because of the fact that consensus always means the consensus of a particular community. Scientists make up many communities, and these communities vary by subject, by methodology, by place, and by degree of influence. Science itself is a polyphonic chorus. The voices in that chorus are never equal, but what one hears as a dominant motif depends very much on where one stands. At times, some motifs appear dominant from any standpoint. But there are always corners from which one can hear minor motifs continuing to sound.

—Evelyn Fox Keller, 1983 (p. 174)

It is our intent as editors of this volume on *Controversial Issues in Criminology* to give voice to some of the minor motifs sounding from the corners of the discipline. Therefore, we have omitted some topics one might expect to find in such a volume on controversial issues, such as debates on capital punishment and drug legalization. Although these are certainly controversial issues, they are at the forefront of the criminal justice policy conversation, and most students are well familiar with them and have already formed opinions. We offer instead fourteen debates covering a broad range of issues that lack consensus and inspire sometimes heated rhetoric and fascinating reasoning on what are the most effective and least inhumane criminal justice policies.

Criminology is a dynamic field because it speaks to the heart of the human condition. There are individuals who commit heinous behaviors, but there are questions as to what is responsible for those behaviors, what theories best explain them, and what policies and practices the criminal justice system can adopt that would address the unwanted behaviors without sacrificing the precious legal, civil, and human rights of everyone. In short, there is very little consensus not only on what works in addressing criminal behavior, but also on what policies are worth the unintended consequences they carry as baggage.

We have invited some of the leading scholars in the field to address controversial issues as well as some of the new, promising individuals who demonstrate some fresh approaches to thinking about crime. We are proud of the contributions they make here. Writing for the controversial issues volume placed some severe restrictions on our contributors. We asked them to take positions that may be more extreme than they would normally espouse. For the sake of teasing out the boundaries of these controversial issues, the authors were asked to forego their normal reluctance to present their material in an unbalanced manner. By having opposing viewpoints in which each author is given the opportunity to present a rejoinder to his or her counterpart, we trust the structure of the volume provides the balance of opinion. The reader will be the ultimate judge as to whether this goal is achieved. In any event, the contributors should not be faulted for their partisan views. They were asked, as part of an intellectual exercise, to argue their side as eloquently as possible, even to the extent that they might go beyond their own thinking on the subject. For their willingness to do this, the editors are extremely grateful.

Finally, we wish to acknowledge the work of Stephanie Benmimoune and Amy Hembree in helping us to coordinate the effort of dealing with thirty authors spread across the country. With so many individuals involved, these types of efforts have been likened to "herding cats," and we are thankful for the help provided to us.

John R. Fuller and Eric W. Hickey

Reference

Keller, E. F. (1983). *A feeling for the organism: The life and work of Barbara McClintock*. New York: W. H. Freeman.

Controversial Issues in Criminology

Should Prostitution Be Legalized?

Robert P. McNamara, Ph.D., is Assistant Professor of Sociology at Furman University. He is the author of several books, including *Crime Displacement: The Other Side of Prevention; The Times Square Hustler: Male Prostitution in New York City; Sex, Scams and Street Life: The Sociology of New York City's Times Square; Police and Policing* with Dr. Dennis Kenney; *The Urban Landscape: Selected Readings* with Dr. Kristy McNamara; and *Crossing the Line: Interracial Couples in the South* with Maria Tempenis and Beth Walton. Dr. McNamara has also written numerous articles on a variety of topics and has been a consultant for state, federal, and private agencies on topics such as AIDS, drug abuse, urban redevelopment, homelessness, policing, and gangs.

Jacqueline Boles, Ph.D., is Professor of Sociology at Georgia State University. One of her major interests is deviant occupations. Over a six-year period, she and Kirk Elifson interviewed and drew blood from male, female, and transvestite prostitutes and their customers for the Centers for Disease Control. She is currently writing a book on show business.

YES

ROBERT P. McNAMARA

Some experts contend that our society is undergoing a number of changes that are transforming our basic orientation toward sexuality and causing us to fundamentally question what is appropriate with regard to sexual behavior. Although many forms of sexual deviance exist, prostitution, homosexuality, and pornography are the three main types in our society. For the purposes of this discussion, I will constrain my remarks to prostitution, particularly its legalization, a concept that raises several interesting and thought-provoking questions about our society as well as how we regulate the conduct of others.

Prostitution: A Brief History of Acceptance

Prostitution presents a paradox. Throughout America's history, commercialized sex has been illegal; yet we often tolerate and employ prostitutes anyway. Throughout the nineteenth century, for instance, officials in nearly every large city permitted brothels and red-light districts, such as the Storyville section in New Orleans, which contained as many as 230 brothels at one time. Although prohibited by law, prostitutes in red-light districts were allowed because they were segregated from the "respectable" population and because the restrictions simplified their control (Conklin, 1980).

This geographical isolation minimized the likelihood that prostitution would annoy citizens. As long as prostitutes stayed in their place, they were easy to ignore. But this arrangement between officials and brothels did not last. During the first decade of this century, there was a crusade against vice. Prostitution was publicly denounced as a destroyer of innocent helpless women. It was also alleged that the activity was a primary source of venereal disease, and it was said to corrupt people's morals in general (Conklin, 1980).

Organizations such as the American Social Hygiene Association called for the abolishment of segregated vice areas and efforts to be made to rehabilitate prostitutes. By 1918, approximately two hundred cities had closed their districts. However, rather than eliminating prostitution, the shutdown only forced the prostitutes into bars and onto the streets (Conklin, 1980). Currently, Nevada is the only state that has legalized prostitution; all other states have legislation that outlaws it.

How successful are these laws? Although, in some instances, they may limit the outlets for prostitution by closing down bars and massage parlors, it is doubtful that they have deterred prostitution in any significant way. As an illustration, prostitution accounted for 76,754 arrests in 1996, according to the Uniform Crime Reports, and it is estimated that this industry earns roughly $173 billion per year (Adler, Mueller, & Laufer, 1996). Typically, prostitution is considered a misdemeanor punishable by a fine or a short jail sentence. Most of the women (and men) are back on the street shortly after their arrest. Many prostitutes have had multiple arrests. However, in terms of law enforcement response, not only is prostitution lacking in priority, but it is also generally seen as a nuisance. Many law enforcement officials contend that if the public wants this type of activity, then so be it. However, these officials are still subject to public opinion and must do something to give the appearance of controlling the problem. What has been done? In larger cities, we have again reverted to the district zone strategy. In an effort to reach some sort of compromise among all parties, certain cities have designated areas in which prostitutes can operate with relative impunity. In San Francisco, it is the Tenderloin district; in New York, it is the Times Square area; and in Boston, it is the Combat Zone.

We have not only come full circle with regard to dealing with the problem, but also not considered the most important implication: Should we allow people to engage in acts of sex for money? Additionally, as mentioned earlier, a number of problems surface when dealing with prostitution. That is, are we using valuable resources that could (and should) be targeted elsewhere?

A Case for the Legalization of Prostitution

Although I am not advocating the legalization of prostitution per se, I am suggesting that we consider the issues; by doing so, we may very well conclude that legalization is a possible solution to the concerns of many people about this activity. When asked why prostitution should remain illegal, many people's responses focus on the moral implications of the activity. Some argue that prostitution contributes to the long-term disintegration of society. That is, prostitution is not a victimless crime. The victim is society, because activities such as prostitution cause society to lose its ability to influence people to adhere to the norms and expectations required of all members. Other opponents contend that prostitutes often victimize clients and are involved in drug trafficking or other crimes. For these reasons, prostitution must remain illegal.[1]

In general, in examining whether prostitution should be legalized, advocates stress the following five main points, among others.

Prostitution and Civil Rights

One of the most ardent claims by proponents of legalization has to do with the rights and freedoms of individuals in their pursuit of happiness. In other words, what rights should two consenting adults have to engage in any behavior of their choosing, particularly in private? Does the government have the right to decide how, when, and in what ways two people enjoy themselves sexually? If so, what are the compelling societal reasons for this? Advocates of legalization argue that laws against prostitution violate a number of fundamental freedoms central to a democratic society. One might argue in response that society is threatened in some way by this behavior. But if this is so, say legalization proponents, why has the government been unable to clearly articulate them, aside from a moral or religious basis? In general, then, prostitution should be legalized because it flies in the face of an individual's pursuit of life, liberty, and happiness.

Prostitution and Feminism

Related to the first reason are the rights of women in society. Proponents of legalization argue that there are far too many inconsistencies in the way we think and act, particularly when it involves women's behavior. For instance, if a woman sleeps with many men for free, she is considered promiscuous, but not a criminal. If a man has a series of sexual relationships, he is lauded for his prowess with women. Furthermore, if a man purchases gifts for a woman (or a woman purchases gifts for a man) in an attempt to seduce her (or him), this is considered part of the mating ritual in our society (where the norms of reciprocity are clearly seen—you have to give to get). Why, then, is the exchange of cash, even a single dollar, a deciding factor in determining whether one act is romantic and the other criminal?

Second, the rights of women to choose what to do with their bodies has been upheld in the courts as well. A pregnant woman, for example, is able to decide whether she wants to keep her baby. Although there is much less controversy over whether a woman has a right to choose to have sex for money, the issue of choice remains dubious for one issue and not for the other.

Legalizing Prostitution Would Reduce Utilization

Some people have argued that if prostitution became legal, many who now avoid this activity because it is illegal would begin to engage in it. Thus, not only would the incidence of people employing prostitutes increase, the size of the sex market would grow, thereby lowering the price and making it attractive to still more people. In response, proponents of legalization assert that it could also be the case that prices may increase because of the constraints the government would place on prostitutes. Ironically, they say, it may very well be that legalization of the trade might price many customers out of the market. That is, the increases in costs would drive prices up, which would prevent many people from using the services of a prostitute—which is exactly what opponents want in the first place.

Regulating Prostitution as a Business

Perhaps the most common assertion by proponents of the legalization debate relates to controlling prostitution in the same way as other small businesses—through taxation, regulation, and supervision. Concerns about human immunodeficiency virus (HIV) and acquired immune deficiency syndrome (AIDS) issues among prostitutes is also covered here. The government can take steps to ensure that there is adequate screening and testing for sexually transmitted diseases as well as provide HIV counseling.

Essentially, the idea is that, by regulating prostitution as a business, the government can oversee the process and make certain there is a considerable amount of safety, to the client as well as the provider. In addition, society benefits from legalization through the taxation of these activities—revenue we currently do not receive. Moreover, by regulating it like a small business (or even defining it as private consulting), the government can curtail the extent of prostitution: it can limit when, where, and under what circumstances the activity occurs. This means that for those who continue to think prostitution is unacceptable and do not want to be exposed to it (much in the same way as exotic dance/gentlemen's clubs have been regulated), the presence of streetwalkers in their neighborhoods is not a constant reminder to them wherever they go. Restrictions such as these also simplify the control of the problem, as in the aforementioned red-light districts of the past and present.

Legalization Resolves Problems in the Criminal Justice System

Legalization advocates also point to the problems of enforcing prostitution laws as well as their costs to society. McWilliams (1997) contends that the costs involved in regulating consensual activities such as prostitution are exorbitant. If prostitution were made legal, the clogged dockets of courtrooms around the country could be greatly alleviated. Prostitution offenders are also problematic for correctional agencies. Do we really want our prisons filled with people who have engaged in consensual sex with another person? Is that really our main priority?

If we decide that it is, consider the costs of building new prisons as well as the rising costs of caring for an offender while she (or he) is incarcerated. The other option, of course, is to instead use the prison space based on the threat the offender poses to society. In this way, say advocates of legalization, it is hard to imagine that a street-walking prostitute is more threatening to us than, say, an armed robber or a rapist. And the fact that so many of us employ the services of prostitutes suggests that we do not mind having them around. If this is true, then what kind of a threat do they really pose, and should we be wasting valuable resources in this manner?

Finally, a substantial amount of resources are used by the police to enforce prostitution laws. Undercover, or sting, operations are very expensive and time-consuming and prevent officers from targeting other, more pressing needs in the community.

Discussion

Given all that has been said, can we ever really accept the idea of legalizing prostitution? Probably not. The truth is, our moral inconsistency about many activities is exemplified in the case of consensual sex for money. This phenomenon is described by many sociologists as the distinction between abstract norms and statistical ones. In other words, a distinction exists between the kinds of things that we think should be illegal and whether we actually engage in them. Additionally, our ideas about morality (e.g., right and wrong, good and bad, legal and illegal) have been socialized in such a way that we may never be able to accept the idea that something as offensive, as wrong, as despicable as prostitution could ever be legitimated in our society. What is particularly fascinating is our failure to realize that although we have socially constructed prostitution as a deviant and illegal activity (see, for instance, Berger & Luckman, 1968), we have also chosen to ignore the stigma associated with it by participating in the activity. Thus, it is offensive only because we have designated it as such, not because it is intrinsically wrong, and even then we still participate on a fairly regular basis.

Some people might be willing to consider an alternative to our current policy on prostitution, but not by legalizing it. Others simply state that legalization is the only effective way to solve the problem. Is there some middle ground? The short answer is yes. First, most people who advocate legalization are not in favor of a wide-open, sex-for-everyone, environment. Rather, they say society would be better served by a thoughtful set of enforceable laws that reduces the costs to prostitutes, clients, and society. Simply put, there is a need for boundary setting with prostitution, as with most activities. For instance, to drive an automobile, a certain set of rules apply. If these rules are followed, the person is allowed to legally drive and use the roads. Similarly, prostitution must also have a number of parameters to follow. One example occurs in England, where prostitutes are allowed to operate but cannot solicit people in public. Additionally, English law prohibits pimps from participating in the trade (Reynolds, 1986). Even in Nevada, where prostitution is legal, there are limits to where members of the trade can operate.

One way to minimize the effects of the collateral problems presented by prostitution is to target more law enforcement officers to that type of activity. For instance, a greater law enforcement emphasis could be placed on those individuals who take advantage of or victimize clients rather than on prostitution in general. Another way to target the problem would be to increase the penalties to prostitutes who steal, assault clients, or engage in narcotics trafficking. A victim might be more willing to file charges against a prostitute if he or she knows that the penalties are more severe for this kind of activity. Still another strategy might include less police pressure on massage parlors, brothels, or hotels while increasing it on streetwalkers. This would severely limit the sex trade to those areas. The symbolic message sent by these types of crackdowns (see Sherman, 1990) would clearly demonstrate to the participants in the trade when and where prostitution is tolerated by local law enforcement.

Thus, there are many reasons to consider legalizing prostitution. Economically, it can be an added resource for a community; socially, it makes an already common activity acceptable, it can be more adequately addressed as a public health problem, and, at the same time, it can help us prioritize our resources as they relate to fighting crime. The main reason not to legalize prostitution, it seems, centers on moral or religious grounds—some people believe it is wrong and will not consider other alternatives.

However, while recognizing the proposed benefits of legalization, many people have not considered one issue: We expect prostitutes to simply accept the changes and the boundaries created by legalization. In other words, we assume that prostitutes will accept the introduction of the government into their lives without question or dispute. This is dubious, because prostitutes are used to violating the constraints set out by society, not abiding by them. There is no reason to believe that they will not simply ignore the stipulations that would turn this activity into a legitimate industry, even though complying with them might benefit prostitutes at some level. In all likelihood, should they choose to ignore the rules regulating the trade—such as failing to submit to physical examinations or failing to pay taxes—our response would be to punish them for violating these laws, which would put them in the exact position in which they currently find themselves—violating the law and being punished for it. Thus, one has to wonder whether legalization, or any type of legal constraint, would not simply result in a form of displacement (see McNamara, 1994a; 1994b).

In sum, legalization of prostitution has many advantages, particularly because, in many instances, our behavior generally reflects an attitude of acceptance or indifference toward it. Although we say in principle that it should be illegal, our behavior forces us to consider the practical realities of how this activity can be controlled for the greater good of society. In many ways, some form of legalization or decriminalization may actually be a more effective way of solving the problem than our current efforts. Perhaps we should examine the Nevada situation more closely to see whether what allows it to be successful can be duplicated in other states. Above all else, we must recognize that we cannot ignore this problem: it will not simply go away on its own, and we must take steps to contain it to acceptable levels. As frustrating as that may seem, the realities of the situation are that it is here and we must deal with it—the question then becomes how.

NOTE

1. In response to these claims, proponents of legalization assert that prostitution remaining illegal has not prohibited many people from engaging in it. With regard to the second point, advocates of legalization agree that these types of additional crimes do occur, but they are not attributable to the activity itself—they are collateral effects of prostitution that can be addressed without prohibiting the sex trade.

REFERENCES

Adler, F., Mueller, G., & Laufer, T. (1996). *Criminology.* New York: McGraw-Hill.

Berger, P., & Luckman, T. (1968). *The social construction of reality.* New York: Doubleday.

Conklin, J. (1980). *Criminology.* New York: Macmillan.

McNamara, R. P. (Ed.). (1994a). *Crime displacement: The other side of prevention.* New York: Cummings and Hathaway.

McNamara, R. P. (Ed.). (1994b). *The Times Square hustler: Male prostitution in New York City.* Westport, CT: Praeger.

McWilliams, P. (1997). Why laws against consensual activities are not a good idea. http://www.mcwilliams.com/books/aint/205.htm

Reyonds, H. (1986). *The economics of prostitution.* Springfield, IL: Charles Thomas.

Sherman, L. S. (1990). Police crackdowns: Initial and residual deterrence. In M. Tonry and N. Morris (Eds.), *Crime and justice: A review of research;* Vol. 12. Chicago: University of Chicago Press.

Rejoinder to Dr. McNamara   JACQUELINE BOLES

There are a number of reasons why legalization is not the preferred solution to the problem of prostitution. Prostitution, like consensual sex, is not the government's business. Adult men and women do not need the government's permission to engage in free or bartered sex: Take me to a nice restaurant, and after dinner, we'll see. Why should any government be involved in the exchange of sex for money? If commercial sex workers (CSWs) are licensed, regulated, and taxed, then the government is, however indirectly, in the prostitution business.

Even if prostitution were legalized, prostitutes would still be stigmatized as they are today. Many CSWs would not register as prostitutes because they would fear public exposure. For example, it is difficult to recruit female prostitutes to join prostitute rights groups such as Hooking Is Real Employment (HIRE) and Call Off Your Old Tired Ethnics (COYOTE) because they are afraid that their families or ex-husbands will find out what they are doing. Many of these women have children and know that they will lose custody if their occupation becomes known. Consequently, many CSWs will not register, defeating one of the purposes of the law.

Also, prostitutes who are underage, sick, or heavy users of illicit drugs will not register because they fear exposure. In our interviews with CSWs, we (Boles & Elifson, 1994) discovered that a large number of them knew that they were HIV-positive, but they did not intend to get treatment because they wished to continue prostituting. In sum, legalizing prostitution will not bring all prostitutes into the fold, and those who are at greatest risk (young mothers, HIV-positive, underage) will be the least likely to come forth.

The money that CSWs would pay in licensing fees would probably not recompense whatever government agency had the unenviable job of trying to register and collect money from prostitutes. How would fees be set and the monies collected? The range of income among CSWs is wide; call women and men and escorts may make thousands of dollars per week, whereas, for a streetwalker, two hundred dollars per week might be considered good. Can we safely assume that CSWs will keep an honest set of books and willingly pay their fair share? The underground economy is fueled by the large number of people who work off the books: for example, exotic dancers, day laborers, drug dealers, independent craftsmen, and other personal service providers.

Established businesses such as the brothels in Nevada are easier to regulate, license, and collect fees from. Currently, sex shops of one kind or another are granted business licenses and pay taxes. The legalization of prostitution elsewhere would probably lead to an increase in brothels and other sex shops, a development that many people would reject because of the general unsightliness of these establishments.

Finally, in considering the legalization of prostitution, let us consider the point of view of those who disapprove of prostitution on moral or ethical grounds. Although many condemn prostitution on religious grounds, others view prostitution as dehumanizing and exploitive. Some see it as akin to slavery. Feminists have mixed reactions to prostitution. Most support the right of women (and men) to engage in prostitution, but they see the institution as exploitive of the CSW. For those who find prostitution immoral or dehumanizing and exploitive, the legalization of prostitution would mean that the government sanctions and supports that institution.

In the United States today, our approach to prostitution is schizophrenic. Our politicians mouth moral pieties about sin and vice, while they often condone the behavior in private. Ordinary citizens want prostitution out of sight and, thus, out of mind. Those who live in convention cities acknowledge that prostitution is good for the convention business. Many of us pray for the souls of CSWs but object to the use of tax monies to help these people make a new start. What is the answer?

It is not legalization but rather decriminalization. Get the government out of the sex business. Allow CSWs to conduct their business as they see fit, and also allow health workers, job counselors, and others of good will to intervene when possible to improve the quality of life for male and female sex workers.

REFERENCE

Boles, J., & Elifson, K. (1994). The social organization of transvestite prostitution and AIDS. *Social Science and Medicine, 19*(1), 85–93.

NO

JACQUELINE BOLES

In every major city in the world, male, female, and transgender (transvestite and transsexual) prostitutes ply their trade. Whether in port cities along the great rivers of central Africa or the rialto districts of San Francisco, Bangkok, New York, London, and Moscow, sex workers seek and find willing customers. In most of these areas, the government is involved in the regulation of prostitution, sometimes taxing the brothels, taverns, and bars where prostitutes work; in other cases, the prostitutes themselves are licensed and taxed. In the United States, in every state except Nevada, prostitution, in one form or another, is against the law. Usually, a number of laws exist regarding prostitution: loitering for the purpose, soliciting, masturbation for hire, and so on. Some laws penalize those whose income derives from prostitution: pimps, panderers, and bawdy-house owners. In certain counties in Nevada, prostitution is legalized; that is, brothels (which are mostly trailers sitting in the desert) are licensed by the county. In those counties, the brothels pay taxes, and the sex workers are checked regularly for sexually transmitted diseases (STDs).

In general, then, most jurisdictions choose either to legalize or to criminalize prostitution; often, of course, they do both. They legalize some behaviors or locations and criminalize others. For example, it may be legal to work in a brothel but illegal to work on the street. Why do governments seek to regulate prostitution? The three primary reasons are money, morality, and monstrousness, that is, it is ugly, shocking, or revolting. For some, prostitution is lucrative; the brothel, bar, pimp, or prostitute may make a lot of money, which the government can tax. In some Nevada counties, brothels are the primary economic activities. Second, some people believe that prostitution is immoral; therefore, for *moral* communities, laws are needed that prohibit prostitution and other assorted behaviors, often those dealing with sex, such as adultery, fornication, and sodomy.

However, for many, prostitution is not so much immoral as it is unattractive. Several years ago, Delores French, founder of Hooking is Real Employment (HIRE), and I were on the Mayor's Task Force on Prostitution (MTFOP), which had been established by then-mayor Andrew Young to do something about prostitution in midtown. Several upper-middle-class folks, mostly white, had moved into this newly trendy neighborhood. Most of the older neighborhood residents were night people such as prostitutes, drug dealers, entertainers, and hustlers. The new residents complained to the mayor about the many unattractive features associated with prostitution: gaudy female and garish transvestite sex workers, tasteless sex shops, and overdressed men lurking in shadows. We were told, "You have to get those prostitutes out of midtown; they're ruining the neighborhood."

There is an alternative to legalization or criminalization: decriminalization. I argue that the best strategy for dealing with prostitution is to decriminalize it, that is, to take it out of the legal system altogether. Decriminalizing prostitution would make it legal but unregulated.

In the following sections I offer reasons that decriminalization is the preferred solution to the problem of prostitution.

The Money Issue

Yes, prostitution pays, at least for some. Many prostitutes and those that live off their efforts often make a lot of money, and that money does not always fall into the clutches of the Internal Revenue Service. Most prostitution is "off the books," and prostitutes and pimps are not strongly motivated to pay their fair share to Uncle Sam. It is difficult to estimate the amount of money generated by illegal prostitution in the United States. In 1982, an estimated half million prostitutes operated in the United States, and if each of those made, on average, $40,000 a year, their combined gross incomes would total $20 billion a year (Simon & Witte, 1982). Helen Reynolds (1986) offers one of the few studies of the economics of prostitution. She argues from a microeconomic perspective that prostitutes, like nonprostitutes, seek to maximize utility under constraint. Humans guide their economic behavior in terms of their perceptions of the incentives and disincentives open to them under any economic system. Reynolds points out that no matter what system is developed to control prostitution, that is, control or legalization, prostitutes will attempt to maximize their income. For example, Clark County, Nevada (where Las Vegas is located) has not legalized prostitution; yet, prostitution flourishes there because of the large number of affluent customers. In the 1980s, Boston tried to limit prostitution to a so-called combat zone. That worked well for a while, until customers stopped going to the area because it was both unsightly and dangerous; consequently, sex workers started frequenting other locales, including convention hotels.

In sum, both control and legalization strategies entail spending considerable sums of money on police enforcement and incarceration without significantly controlling the activity. In a cost–benefit analysis, Reynolds (1986) argues, prostitution regulation costs the government more than the income that might be generated from taxes. Furthermore, there is always the problem of possible law enforcement corruption. Police, judges, and correctional officers often solicit sexual favors from prostitutes and payoffs from their pimps (Atkinson & Boles, 1977).

Decriminalization will eliminate the need for police to focus on catching prostitutes and allow them to concentrate on more serious offenses that may be associated with prostitution, such as rape, robbery, and assault. The act of prostitution may be a victimless crime, but certainly there are often victims. While Kirk Elifson and I were interviewing transvestite prostitutes, three were murdered in drive-by shootings (Boles & Elifson, 1994). In Toledo, Ohio, recently, two prostitutes were murdered and four were raped (Crimes on Prostitutes Increasing, 1997). Johns, too, are assaulted and robbed. Neither prostitutes nor johns are likely to report being crime victims because prostitution is illegal, and they believe that the police will show little interest in apprehending their assailants.

In sum, if prostitution is decriminalized, government will save money, and the police can concentrate on serious offenses, including those committed against sex workers or their customers.

Morality

Many citizens consider prostitution immoral, but an increasing number have come to believe that the constitutional guarantee of privacy should extend to sexual acts committed by consenting adults. Essentially, whether a particular behavior is moral or immoral cannot be argued logically, proved by a preponderance of evidence, or decided by a majority of the electorate. Most of our beliefs about morality are derived from our religious heritages and are not susceptible to proof.

Moral entrepreneurs seek to influence legislation affecting personally held moral beliefs. They are especially vigorous in the area of sexuality, supporting legislation that criminalizes adultery, fornication, sodomy, and prostitution. In a heterogeneous society such as our own, laws that serve no purpose other than supporting one group's moral convictions have no place. The criminal justice system is not the arena for adjudicating conflicting belief systems.

In 1973, the United States Supreme Court affirmed the right of women to terminate pregnancies, basing their decision on right of privacy as found in the Fourth Amendment. To date, the Supreme Court has yet to affirm the right to exchange sex for money.

In the mid-1970s, prostitutes began to organize, first in Lyons, France, and then in the United States. Margo St. James founded Call Off Your Old Tired Ethics (COYOTE) in 1973, and that organization and its affiliates continue to lobby for decriminalization. COYOTE has argued that prostitutes provide a sexual service and that prostitutes, like other women, should have control over their own bodies. Male prostitutes have been less organized and active than their female counterparts; however, the Coalition for Safer Hustling (CASH, now defunct) was an organization founded to provide health services to and advocate for male prostitutes (Boles & Elifson, 1997). CASH also advocated the decriminalization of prostitution. These prostitute rights organizations have argued that, however one feels about the morality of prostitution, in a free society adults who freely choose prostitution are protected by the Constitution: (1) due process clause—Fourteenth Amendment; (2) freedom of speech and association—First Amendment; and (3) the right to privacy—Fourth Amendment. Those who choose to engage in prostitution should have the same rights and protections as those who make X-rated films, sell alcohol or cigarettes, or engage in other legal commercial activities and transactions.

Monstrousness

Within prostitution, there is a prestige hierarchy. At the top are the call boys and girls, who operate out of their homes. They are circumspect and discrete, and usually not even their neighbors know what they do for a living. Escorts usually work for an agency that advertises in phone books and local papers. The escort is called at home and usually meets the client at a restaurant or bar. Some sex workers hang out in certain bars that are prostitute-friendly. Hustlers frequent gay bars; and women, so-called hooking bars, which are known to taxi cab drivers, hotel bellhops, and others who, for a fee, refer conventioneers to them. Currently, in the United States, only Nevada has legal brothels; however, several cities in Europe still allow brothels. In many U.S. cities, there are a variety of sex shops that advertise their services, such as "Photograph our Models" and "Get a Massage from One of our Beautiful Models." The monumental unattractiveness of most sex shops, including brothels, is illustrated from this guide to Nevada's brothels (Engle, 1973):

> The Green Lantern consists of several oversized house trailers. Two pea-green jobs, one a double, are connected by a corridor, With a third trailer crossed at the back to complete the arrangement.... a black vinyl sofa completes the public room furnishings.

At the bottom of the prostitute pecking order is the streetwalker or crack whore. In most cities, areas where male, female, or transvestite sex workers conduct their strolls are easily identified. Crack whores usually stay around crack houses and exchange crack cocaine for sex.

Most complaints about prostitution focus on streetwalkers and sex shops (Hobson 1987). In midtown Atlanta, citizens continuously complained to the mayor about the sleazy streetwalkers and garish sex shops that blighted their neighborhood. MTFOP was created for the purpose of eliminating those eyesores. In most political jurisdictions in the United States, laws that purport to control prostitution are enacted because of citizen complaints directed at street prostitution and sex shops.

Efforts to improve the appearance of neighborhoods by either legalizing or criminalizing prostitution have not been successful. Once again, prostitutes, like other economic actors, seek to maximize financial gain within the constraints placed on them. If the police clamp down on street prostitutes in one area, they will simply move to another. At one time, most of Atlanta's street hustlers worked on one small street contiguous to Peachtree Street. In preparing the city for the Democratic Convention, the police set up roadblocks across this street, completely disrupting traffic. The hustlers moved to a new location, and within two weeks their customers found them. After the convention, the police left, and the hustlers returned.

In 1974, Boston created an official Adult Entertainment District in a neighborhood that had been given the unofficial name *Combat Zone*. In this district, merchants could put up moving and flashing signs and display and sell pornographic materials. Though street solicitation continued to be illegal, the police had considerable discretion in making arrests. Most street prostitution was ignored, and some public officials charged that the police were paid off to ignore it (Reynolds, 1986). Eventually, many of the prostitutes left the Combat Zone because there was too much competition for a declining number of customers. As in Nevada, the strategy of trying to contain prostitution in one geographic area will almost always fail.

Removing blight associated with prostitution is a difficult but not insoluble problem. Here are my recommendations:

1. Decriminalize prostitution. This will free police to redirect their efforts toward serious offenses and eliminate one source of corruption. If prostitution is not illegal, sex workers may be more motivated to declare their income to the IRS, particularly if they are able to become property owners.
2. Enact zoning laws that limit the locations where sex shops can operate. Furthermore, restrict the outward appearance of these shops so that they are not so glaringly unattractive.
3. Do not obstruct the growth of escort and call services, because these services are unobtrusive and do not contribute to community blight.
4. Offer health and social services to sex workers. Educate sex workers about STDs and encourage them to behave responsibly. They will be more willing to submit to tests for STDs if they know that their work is legal and that they will not be harassed for pursuing it. Encourage those who have alcohol or drug problems to get treatment.
5. Develop and make available job training programs for sex workers who wish to leave the life. One cannot practice sex work forever.
6. Provide educational materials about STDs and safe sex practices at locations such as bars, where potential customers of sex workers congregate. Inform customers where they can be tested for HIV and other STDs.

Sex work is work and should be treated as such. Sex workers provide a service; if they did not, they would be out of business. When the sex worker and customer are both adults, their activities are not the law's business. We should implement strategies that will protect sex workers and their customers from harm and minimize community blight. We should provide information that will encourage both sex workers and customers to behave responsibly and provide services for those sex workers who choose to leave the life.

REFERENCES

Atkinson, M., & Boles, J. (1977). Prostitution as an ecology of confidence games: The scripted behavior of prostitutes and vice officers. In C. Bryant (Ed.), *Sexual deviancy in a social context,* (pp. 219–231). New York, NY: Franklin Watts.

Boles, J., & Elifson, K. (1997, May 13–16). *Out of Cash: The rise and demise of a prostitute's rights organization.* Presented at the International Conference on Prostitution, Van Nuys, CA.

Boles, J., & Elifson, K. (1994). The social organization of transvestite prostitution and AIDS. *Social Science and Medicine, 19*(1), 85–93.

Crimes on prostitutes increasing. (1997, September 22). *Ohio State Lantern,* p. 9.

Engle, R. (1973). *Brothels of Nevada.* Los Angeles: Melrose Publishers.

Hobson, B. (1987). *Uneasy virtue: The politics of prostitution and the American reform tradition.* New York, NY: Basic Books.

Reynolds, H. (1986). *The economics of prostitution.* Springfield, IL: Charles C. Thomas.

Simon, C., & Witte, A. (1982). *Beating the system.* Boston: Auburn House Publishers.

Rejoinder to Dr. Boles

ROBERT P. MCNAMARA

Professor Boles's argument in favor of decriminalizing prostitution has been given support by many scholars and community activists. Specifically, Professor Boles points to three main issues that surround the debate: the economic issue, the morality related to prostitution, and what she refers to as monstrousness, which I take to mean the idea that prostitution as an act and prostitutes as individuals are perceived as inherently wicked. I would like to address each of these points briefly and focus on her recommendations to alleviate the problems related to the trade.

First, Dr. Boles states that the best strategy for dealing with prostitution is to decriminalize it, that is, to take it out of the legal system altogether. As Erich Goode (1997) points out, many scholars and experts are not clear in their definitions of decriminalization and legalization. As he states, the terms *legalization* and *decriminalization* refer to a range of different practices. The main distinction, it seems to me, is that one behavior is no longer considered a criminal act but would still be considered deviant to many. Legalization is the more definitive stance in that we are declaring the act, in a legal sense, appropriate. Unfortunately, in Professor Boles's description, determining the distinction between the terms is left to the reader.

Second, Dr. Boles calls for the decriminalization of prostitution because of the collateral damage it causes to the integrity of the law enforcement community. That is, because prostitution remains illegal and profitable, the risk of police corruption remains. Should the restrictions on prostitution be relaxed, this possibility is greatly diminished. Although it is true that police corruption exists with regard to this activity, we have to ask whether our inability to control corruption is a sufficient reason to decriminalize a particular act. It is even possible, given this logic, to imagine claims that we should decriminalize all types of behaviors in which police corruption has been discovered. Should we decriminalize organized crime activities because corrupt officers are involved in this activity? Should we eliminate traffic violations because some officers take bribes from motorists? At what point do we draw the line? Moreover, the presence of corruption does not invalidate the argument that prostitution is immoral.

With regard to the morality issue, Professor Boles and I agree on one point: As any competent sociologist will assert, there is indeed a paradoxical distinction between what people say and what they do. In professional parlance, this is sometimes referred to as the distinction between abstract norms and statistical ones. People say prostitution should be illegal, but so many people employ this service that it raises the question of whether the opposition to it is real.

Professor Boles then goes on to cite constitutional protections that are ignored when it comes to two consenting adults who wish to exchange money for sexual pleasure. Specifically, she cites the Fourteenth Amendment's due process clause, the First Amendment protections of freedom of speech and association, and the Fourth Amendment's protection of privacy. It seems to me that the only amendment that applies here is the protection of privacy. It is not clear why the Fourteenth Amendment, which states that people accused of a crime are entitled to a fair hearing, is germane to the discussion. It also seems to me that no First Amendment violations are evident here either: freedom of speech is not being violated, nor is it an absolute protection. If the speech threatens the society, such as yelling "fire" in a crowded theater, it is not considered constitutionally protected. Similarly, freedom of association is not violated either—the laws do not say you cannot associate with prostitutes; they do not even say you cannot have intimate relations with them. Rather, they are saying you cannot have sex in exchange for money. Essentially then, we are left with the privacy issue—that what two consenting adults want to do in private is not, and should not be, the purview of the government. There is some truth to this point, although I think a compelling argument could be made that public health issues should be addressed, which make it reasonable for the government to become involved.

Fourth are issues relating to the monstrousness claim. What I think is important to understand here is that streetwalking prostitution, whether we care to admit it or not, transcends simple morality concerns. There are many economic considerations as well. While decriminalization could increase tax revenues (if prostitutes decided to pay their taxes), the community has an overriding interest and responsibility to ensure that property values and other concerns are protected.

Because I have already addressed several of Professor Boles's recommendations, I will limit my comments to the remaining ones. It seems to me her fourth, fifth, and sixth recommendations also raise more questions than they answer. For instance, as I mention elsewhere (see McNamara, 1994a), educating sex workers does not reduce risk behaviors. This is particularly true in the sex trade, where workers can charge additional fees for sex without protection. Additionally, decriminalizing prostitution will not necessarily encourage those addicted to drugs or alcohol to seek treatment. There are many people in "normal" professions who refuse to get help regardless of the level of encouragement they receive. In her sixth recommendation, Professor Boles suggests distributing material in public places so that people can become more informed about STDs and HIV/AIDS testing. I argue that it is highly unlikely that someone (customer or client) in a bar is going to pick up a brochure on HIV testing. Clients and workers are acutely aware of their public behavior and are very concerned about the possibility that someone will observe them and think they have an STD. Thus, the likelihood of success with this strategy is limited and overly optimistic.

Professor Boles's fifth recommendation also presents a number of obstacles. Given the criminal records of many prostitutes, as well as the limited education and skills of many streetwalkers, what types of job training programs would really work? She is correct in that one cannot practice sex work forever, but that practice will severely limit future employment opportunities.

Finally, Professor Boles believes that sex work is work and should be treated as such. However, it seems clear that even if we treat it as work and not as a criminal activity, parameters must be followed. In any occupation a series of obligations and responsibilities must be observed. If Professor Boles wants sex workers to be treated like other employees, then she must also accept that with this change in status comes a host of other responsibilities. In short, if prostitutes want the freedom to ply their trade, they must also accept some form of regulation by the government. And if violations occur, the workers should expect sanctions. However, in doing this, we really have not solved the problem—we have only displaced it. Now the workers will be arrested for violating the laws governing their occupation rather than for prostitution. As a parting shot, Professor Boles calls for strategies that will protect sex workers and minimize urban blight. The problem is that this is simply not possible for streetwalkers. Their very presence contributes to the economic decline of a community. Although we could revert to the old red-light districts of previous eras, policy makers and public planners are increasingly discovering the value of revitalizing these sections of cities. As we have seen in the Times Square section of New York City, we can no longer afford to "write off" a section of the city simply for vice-related activities (McNamara, 1994b). In short, streetwalking, by its very nature, contributes to community blight, and we are hard pressed to find a place where it can occur with relative impunity.

REFERENCES

Goode, E. (1997). *Between politics and reason: The drug legalization debate.* New York: St. Martin's.

McNamara, R. P. (1994a). *The Times Square hustler: Male prostitution in New York City.* Westport, CT: Praeger.

McNamara, R. P. (1994b). *Sex, scams, and street life: The sociology of New York City's Times Square.* Westport, CT: Praeger.

Are Stalking Laws Effective?

Ronnie Harmon, M.A., is Administrative Director of the Bellevue Hospital Center Forensic Psychiatry Clinic. Ms. Harmon is a Fellow and former Vice President of the American Academy of Forensic Sciences and a recipient of both its Psychiatry and Behavioral Sciences Section Award for Outstanding Contributions and its General Section John R. Hunt Award. She is a member of the National Advisory Board of Survivors of Stalking, Inc., and a Ph.D. candidate in criminal justice at the City of New York's John Jay College.

N. Jane McCandless, Ph.D., is Associate Professor of Sociology at the State University of West Georgia. Her teaching is within the areas of social inequality and women's studies, and her current research focuses on violence against women.

YES

RONNIE HARMON

In 1989, actress Rebecca Schaeffer was shot to death at her California home by a mentally disturbed, obsessed fan who had been stalking her. At the same time, there were reports in the Los Angeles area of several noncelebrity stalking victims. As a consequence of these events, the California state legislature passed the first stalking legislation in the United States in 1990. Since that time, stalking legislation has been enacted in all fifty states, the District of Columbia, and at the federal level. Although the first statutes were passed hurriedly and contained flaws regarding constitutional safeguards, they represented major progress over what had come before. Since then, a second generation of legislation aimed at overcoming judicial objections has continued to improve the criminal justice system's ability to manage this problem.

What Is Stalking?

Stalking victims can be celebrities or ordinary individuals, men or women. The motives for harassment range from unrequited love to termination of employment.

The stalker's relationship with the victim and the stalker's motive in pursuing the victim are important issues in the management and understanding of stalking behavior. Whether they were intimate (a spouse, a lover, or a close family member), were acquaintances (coworkers, casual dates, or professional clients), or had no relationship (a celebrity or another stranger) may have some impact on how aggressively or dangerously the stalker behaves. Because there may be more than one type of motive for stalking behavior, the ways to discourage stalkers may differ. Some stalkers are obsessed with being in love with their target or angry over rejection (the jealous rage of the former lover and the delusional erotomanic fan fall into this category.) Stalking behavior also can be triggered by the feeling that the stalker has been harmed in some way by the target, possibly physically or financially. Terminated employees, disgruntled tenants, and patients who feel betrayed by their therapists may exemplify this type of stalker. Such individuals can be motivated by revenge and anger. Antiabortion activists who follow and harass the medical workers from abortion clinics also can be classified with this group.

Stalking is different from most other crimes because it involves a series of actions instead of one, clearly defined act. Telephone calls, letters and gifts, and visiting the home or office, activities that are welcome in many situations, can become frightening symbols of unwelcome aggression. In the past, victims have reported having difficulties convincing law enforcement personnel that these attentions were an unwelcome source of distress.

Preexisting Legal Tools

Before state legislatures drafted laws specifically protecting individuals against stalking, local law enforcement had limited tools for use against this type of behavior. Following someone, telephoning, and even threatening him or her were for the most part not against the law. Frequently, arrests could not be made until after the stalking had escalated to violence. These approaches can still be used to supplement stalking laws.

1. Restraining or Protective Orders: Civil restraining orders were among the few options open to victims before 1990, but were too limited to be effective

(Diacova, 1995; Lingg, 1993; Woods, 1993). Because they were primarily designed for victims of domestic violence, restraining orders often had "relationship requirements." Targeted individuals requesting protection through the civil courts had to be related by blood or marriage, or be involved in a close relationship with the person against whom the order was requested. There were also requirements that threats, attempts, or occurrences of physical abuse or property damage be made. A request for such an order had to be initiated by the victim, often with filing fees, legal procedures, and delays (although emergency orders were available under some circumstances). Generally, such orders were good for a maximum of one year, and the violation of a restraining order was usually a misdemeanor. Finally, enforcement of restraining orders often proved to be a problem. Many stalkers ignore restraining orders, and there are numerous horror stories reported in the media of women being assaulted or killed while in possession of such orders. In a recent survey of victims of domestic violence, researchers from the National Center for State Courts (Keilitz et al., 1997) reported that although some types of abusers curtailed their behavior after the issuance of civil protection orders, stalking incidents actually increased. They concluded that, in particular for violent abusers, criminal prosecution might be needed. With increased attention to stalking and domestic violence, state and federal laws have been modified to strengthen protective orders. The 1994 Violence Against Women Act required states to enforce each other's orders of protection and made it a federal offense to cross state lines to violate such orders. In 1996, the penalty for violating this law was increased to a felony. States have expanded protections to nonrelated individuals and have reduced or eliminated filing fees.

2. Assault: Although the ultimate threat is that stalking will escalate into violence, estimates are that a large proportion of stalking behavior does not lead directly to physical assault. Law enforcement authorities would prefer to have effective tools to control stalking behavior before it gets to that point.

3. Trespassing: Trespassing statutes might be useful if the stalker approaches the property of the targeted individual, either to leave items or to confront the victim. They are probably not effective if the stalker has a claim of ownership on the property (as may be the case with spousal stalking), if the stalking is not at the home (e.g., in a public place, at the workplace). Trespassing statutes also often require that there be a threat to harm the individual or the property.

4. Terrorism: Some states have statutes that prohibit terrorist activities. The definition of terrorism may encompass some forms of stalking behavior. In California, a terrorist is someone who "willfully threatens to commit a crime which will result in death or great bodily injury which…is so unequivocal, unconditional, immediate and specific…that it would cause a person to be in reasonable fear for his or her own safety or the safety of his or her immediate family"

(Diacovo, 1995). This statute has been used against stalkers, but the requirement that there be an "immediate" threat poses problems.

5. Annoyance Calls: In many states, it is a misdemeanor to make threatening or obscene phone calls with the intent to annoy. The problem in stalking cases is that the victim must know the identity of the caller. The statute also only addresses telephone-based stalking and cannot be used to contain other types of stalking.

Deficiencies in Early Stalking Legislation

As a result of the rush to appear responsive to an identified need, much of the initial legislation was flawed in ways that subjected it to legal challenges. Some laws were thought too broad to pass constitutional muster, but others were so narrowly drawn as to provide little additional protection for victims. Early stalking statutes have been challenged in at least nineteen state courts, primarily for vagueness and overbreadth (Boychuck, 1994; Lingg, 1993).

1. Vagueness: The Constitution requires that the definition of illegal behavior be clearly stated. Laws must be unambiguous enough for reasonable people to understand what is prohibited, and so that law enforcement is not arbitrary.

2. Overbreadth: This type of problem occurs when legislation written to control stalking also has the effect of prohibiting constitutionally protected behavior (e.g., picketing, free speech, lawful assembly). Some courts have interpreted stalking legislation so that, if the statute is primarily designed to prevent actions rather than speech, it is not considered unconstitutional. It has been argued that there is no constitutional protection for making threats. In most states, the legislation contains specific language exempting constitutionally protected activities from the provisions of the statute.

The New Generation of Laws

Court problems with the statutes frequently have been because of the absence of clear definitions of terms. Recent revisions have been directed at correcting these deficiencies. In most statutes, stalking is characterized as the act of willfully and repeatedly following or harassing another individual or that individual's immediate family, and a stalker is one who makes a credible threat, or intentionally or knowingly engages in a pattern or continuing course of conduct that would cause any reasonable person to suffer emotional distress or fear of death or great bodily harm. Definitions of these terms have evolved as a response to judicial decisions about the constitutionality of the original laws:

1. Harassing: The California Penal Code (Sec. 646.9[e]) defines harassment as "a knowing and willful course of conduct directed at a specific person that seriously alarms, annoys, torments, or terrorizes the person, and that serves no legitimate purpose." The definition implies that the stalking has taken place on more than one occasion and that the stalking behavior is deliberate.

2. Immediate Family: This has been defined as persons living in the same household as the victim, not necessarily related by blood or marriage. This definition is improved over previous versions, which did not include anyone but the primary victim. Stalkers frequently target individuals who are close to their objects, either because they perceive them as standing between them and their loved ones or because they are using them as a way to get even with the target individual.

3. Intentionally or Knowingly: Legislative definitions of these terms reflect the problem the original laws had contending with erotomanic stalkers, who may not intend to harm or frighten their victims. If stalkers know or should know that their behavior frightens their target, then in many states they can be prosecuted. In some cases, the intent to commit the action that has caused the fear is enough to substantiate charges. In other instances, the issuance of an order of protection has been assumed to provide notice to the stalkers. Courts have grappled with whether laws written with the phrase "intentionally following and harassing" are specific enough to be clear. In general, they have concluded that the adjective "intentionally" modifies "following," and that although a police officer may have difficulty telling whether someone is "intentionally harassing" someone else, "intentionally following" is not ambiguous.

4. Pattern or Continuing Course of Conduct: This is defined as a series of actions over time. Prohibitions against specific actions such as telephoning, following, trespassing, damaging property, and placing someone under surveillance have been replaced with this more general term. There is some debate (Ward, 1994) regarding whether being more specific about prohibited actions would reduce judicial concerns about vagueness or would limit law enforcement's ability to prosecute unspecified acts.

5. Repeatedly: This is related to the definition of "pattern or course of conduct." *Repeatedly* has usually been defined as "more than twice," but occasionally as "more than once."

6. Emotional Distress or Fear of Death or Great Bodily Harm: Some statutes specify that there must be fear of death or great bodily harm for a charge of stalking to be lodged. Lesser fear or emotional distress can be charged as harassment. In most states, varying levels of offense associated with stalking behavior exist. Orders of protection provide a first level of defense. Criminal charges for harassment and stalking range from misdemeanors through serious felonies, depending on both the seriousness of the offense and the presence of compounding factors (which may include multiple convictions for the stalking or harassment, violation of a restraining order, use of a weapon, and harassment of a minor). The ability to charge stalkers with different crimes gives police additional latitude in detaining and arresting stalkers. Some states have also specified the possibility of fear of sexual assault. Victims can prove that they have been caused distress by taking actions to protect themselves, such as changing a phone number, moving, or hiring a bodyguard.

7. Reasonable Person: Problems have arisen in the courts regarding whether the victim's fear is real. The issue is whether a person can be charged with a criminal offense based on the victim's subjective experience of the activity as frightening. The legislative response has been to use a "reasonable person" standard. Would any reasonable person see the actions of the stalker as threatening or frightening? Many states require not only that any reasonable person would be afraid under the circumstances, but also that the particular individual being stalked is actually afraid.

8. Credible Threat: Many stalkers do not threaten their targets. In states that still use the term *threaten,* threats often do not have to be direct or specific; threatening actions or gestures suffice. In California and Alabama, the actions of the stalker can be used to demonstrate an implicit threat. An Illinois court found that an act could be threatening even if it did not result in violence.

Other Issues

The greater awareness of the problem of stalking, created by the new legislation, has stimulated other improvements in the management of the problem.

1. Several states have implemented provisions for the mental health screening and treatment of stalkers. Although it is recognized that not all stalkers are mentally ill, and that mental health treatment of this population is difficult at best, there is some indication that this treatment may be effective for stalkers whose obsession is based on a delusional mental illness. Some states mandate the screening of stalkers for the presence of mental illness, followed by appropriate treatment when indicated. Participating in such treatment can be made a condition of probation or parole. The Bureau of Justice Assistance has recommended additional research into the connection between stalking and mental illness, with particular attention to substance abuse.

2. It has become clear that the passage of legislation by itself cannot effectively curtail stalking behavior without the active involvement of local law enforcement and judicial personnel. In 1994, the National Criminal Justice Association held a series of seminars around the country designed to advise local officials on how to best implement stalking codes. Police officers, prosecutors, and judges need to be sensitized and informed on an ongoing basis about the special issues associated with stalking cases. Some jurisdictions now have special Domestic Violence Courts with trained personnel that manage some stalking cases.

Conclusion

Although not perfect, current stalking legislation represents a great improvement over related laws existing before 1990. The victim of stalking has access to a wider range of resources and solutions than ever before.

REFERENCES

Boychuck, K. M. (1994). Are stalking laws unconstitutionally vague or overboard? *Northwestern University Law Review, 88*(2), 769–802.

Diacovo, N. (1985). California's anti-stalking statute: Deterrent or false sense of security? *Southwestern University Law Review,* (24). 389–421.

Keilitz, S., Davis, C., Efkeman, H. S., Flango, C., & Hannaford, P. (September, 1997). Research preview: Civil protection orders: Victims' views on effectiveness. National Center for State Courts, NIJ Grant Number 93-IJ-CX-0035. *National Institute of Justice Journal.* 23–24.

Lingg, R. A. (Spring, 1993). Stopping stalkers: A critical examination of anti-stalking statutes. *Saint John's Law Review.* 347–381.

Ward, C. (June 1994). Minnesota's anti-stalking statute: A durable tool to protect victims from terroristic behavior. *Law and Inequality: A Journal of Theory and Practice.* 613–647.

Woods, L. T., Jr. (1993). Note: Anti-stalker legislation: A legislative attempt to surmount the inadequacies of protective orders. *Indiana Law Review, 27,* 449–473.

Rejoinder to Ms. Harmon
N. JANE McCANDLESS

Ms. Harmon and I are arguing two different sides of the same issue, but I believe that we have some points of agreement. First, Ms. Harmon and I both agree that the revisions made to laws that target stalking behaviors are a significant improvement over the laws that were initially, and sometimes hurriedly, enacted. Indeed, early stalking laws were challenged on grounds of vagueness and overbreadth. In response to these challenges, and with guidance from experts in the field, stalking statutes have been greatly improved. Ms. Harmon and I also agree that the passage of stalking legislation alone cannot effectively end this criminal activity. We both agree that the involvement of law enforcement agencies and judicial personnel is vitally important. As I argued, far too many victims are faced with building a case of stalking without professional guidance or the assurance that their local law enforcement agencies are educated on this issue. Furthermore, many victims who spend time building their cases do so without the guarantee that the prosecution of the stalker will proceed smoothly, if even at all.

Although Ms. Harmon and I share some points of agreement, there remain several points of disagreement. First, I continue to question the overall effectiveness of the revised stalking statutes. A test of effectiveness might be whether such laws are sufficient when dealing with criminal activity. Ms. Harmon argues that preexisting legal tools, such as restraining orders or protection from abuse orders, might be used to supplement existing stalking laws. However, if supplementing a stalking law is necessary, then surely the law itself is deficient in some respect. The fact remains that if stalking laws were completely effective, restraining orders and protection from abuse orders would be redundant at best.

A second point of disagreement is in reference to the language used in these laws. Although I believe the language within the stalking statutes has certainly improved over the past few years, problems remain. Consider again the statutes that require a "credible threat." Even Ms. Harmon notes that many stalkers do not threaten their victims, and thus she indirectly supports my contention that a "credible threat" requirement is an imposition that leaves many victims without legal recourse.

Although Ms. Harmon argues that victims have, in the past, had difficulties convincing law enforcement personnel that the attention from the stalker was an unwelcome source of distress, yet I maintain that this situation has not significantly improved. I argue that law enforcement personnel remain unfamiliar with the stalking legislation and often lack comprehensive training on the issue. Furthermore, far too many victims never see their stalkers prosecuted, convicted, and sentenced. Additionally, societal attitudes remain problematic when attempting to convince law enforcement personnel that the victim is not responsible for what is happening to her or him.

Consider too the penalties imposed on the convicted stalker. Ms. Harmon argues that understanding the stalker's motives is an important issue in the management of stalking behavior. I agree. However, only a minority of states have provisions for mental health screening and treatment. I would once again ask how the criminal justice system plans on dealing with a stalker who suffers from a psychological disorder, such as erotomania. In the first sentence of her argument, Ms. Harmon addresses the mentally disturbed fan who stalked and then killed Rebecca Schaeffer, costar of the television series *My Sister Sam.* It seems to me that psychological disorders are best dealt with by those in the therapeutic setting, not the prison system.

Finally, though Ms. Harmon carefully reviews the recent revisions in the stalking statutes, we cannot automatically assume that these revisions have improved the overall effectiveness of the stalking legislation. Clarifications of relevant terms within such statutes may appear, on the surface, as an improvement. On closer scrutiny, we are left to wonder whether these clarifications will make the prosecution of the stalker easier for the victim and less confusing for law enforcement agents. Will the clarification of the term *following* ensure that the criminal justice system, as well as the larger society, will respond immediately and effectively to this victimization of women and men?

I agree with Ms. Harmon that stalking laws are necessary. Yet I maintain that these laws, as they currently exist, are not effective when dealing with our right to be left alone.

NO

N. Jane McCandless

Since the early 1990s, stalking laws have been developed and passed in all fifty states, and most recently stalking has risen to the level of a federal felony offense. The general purpose of these laws is to protect a person who is being subjected to another person's repeated following, harassing, or threatening behaviors. Generally speaking, stalking includes a series of willful and intentional acts that are unwanted, nonreciprocal in nature, and cause some physical or emotional distress for the victim. In the state of California, the first state to enact a stalking law, stalking constitutes:

> Any person who willfully, maliciously, and repeatedly follows or harasses another person and who makes a credible threat with the intent to place that person in reasonable fear of death or great bodily injury or to place that person in reasonable fear of the death or great bodily injury of his or her immediate family is guilty of the crime of stalking. (California Penal Code 646.9)

Best estimates suggest that one in twelve American women and one in forty-five men are stalked at least once (Stalking numbers 1997). Stalking laws now give these estimated 8.2 million women and 2 million men legal remedies and provide law enforcement agents the opportunity to intervene before the victim is physically injured or even killed. Although "it is not known how frequently stalking turns into homicide, according to some estimates, 90 percent of women killed by husbands or boyfriends were stalked before they were murdered" (O'Malley, 1996).

Before the advent of stalking laws, there was little law enforcement could do for a victim of stalking. Beyond a civil protective order, which is limited by a lack of enforcement and light penalties, or a protection from abuse order, which is often restricted to domestic partners, the "victims of stalking (were) virtually remediless in protecting themselves against this form of behavior" (Sohn, 1994). Thus, proponents of stalking legislation have argued that stalking laws are not only a necessary but an effective measure to curb stalking behaviors and prevent others from doing the same. "Generally, anti-stalking legislation is designed to promote the safety of citizens and protect basic rights to privacy" (Bjerregaard, 1996).

The arguments of those in favor of stalking legislation can be contrasted with others who believe that stalking laws may be necessary but are, in fact, ineffective. I maintain that stalking laws are currently ineffective and offer the following arguments to support my position.

The Language Used in Stalking Laws Is Problematic

According to Bjerregaard (1996), "the doctrines of void-for-vagueness and overbreadth are both of particular relevance to the current stalking legislation." The void-for-vagueness doctrine "requires that a statute give fair notice of forbidden behavior" (Boychuk, 1997). That is, this doctrine requires legislatures to "define criminal behavior sufficiently to put a potential offender on notice that his or her conduct is prohibited and remove police discretion to enforce the law in an arbitrary way" (Boychuk, 1997).

In reference to stalking statutes, some critics have noted that "these laws do not sufficiently distinguish stalking from innocent behavior and therefore give the police too much discretion in deciding when to make arrests" (Tucker, 1993). For example, the term *following,* frequently found within the stalking statutes, is not always defined. Is it then possible for a reporter to be arrested for the crime of stalking if, in fact, she or he is actively following a person who is seeking election to a public office? In sum, "the lack of a definition of *following* makes most stalking laws vulnerable to vagueness challenges" (Boychuk, 1997).

Because stalking laws have been criticized for being vague, so too have they been criticized for being too broad. In this case, a statute may be challenged as overbroad when it is directed at conduct that is constitutionally protected (Tucker, 1993). Consider the issue of individual civil liberties, such as our First Amendment right to freedom of expression. "If a statute is overly broad, individuals may be intimidated and therefore may be reluctant to exercise their right to engage in constitutionally protected speech" (National Criminal Justice Association, 1993). Is it then fair to assume that an individual who is exercising her or his right to speech is also guilty of stalking, if in fact another person defines that speech to be harassing? In cases in which the language was vague, "the state attorney's office has refused to pursue stalking charges because of the probability that a court will dismiss them" (Tucker, 1993).

Stalking laws also have been criticized for being so narrow in definition that some of the common behaviors of the stalker are excluded. A recurrent theme found in the accounts of those who have been victimized by a stalker is that the stalker frequently uses the telephone as a means of contact. In fact, several dozens of phone calls are often made throughout the course of a single day. But not all stalking laws protect the victim from these endless calls. A narrowly defined stalking law then allows the savvy stalker "to avoid the laundry list of no-nos while continuing to terrorize their victims" (Simakis, 1996).

Another criticism is that stalking laws often rely on a "credible threat," which requires that the stalker makes an actual threat that would place the victim in fear of death, bodily harm, or assault. To avoid prosecution, some stalkers stop short of making a "credible threat" and leave the victim without legal recourse. As pointed out by Sohn (1994) "if a perpetrator wants to terrorize his victim he can find other ways to do it than by (violating) stalking (laws)."

Finally, we might simply argue that stalking laws are unnecessary. All states have laws that govern behaviors associated with the crime of stalking. With laws prohibiting such activities as trespassing, invasion of privacy, harassment, and infliction of emotional distress, stalking laws are simply redundant.

The Criminal Prosecution of the Stalker Is Laden with Burdens for the Victim

Though stalking laws allow victims to seek legal recourse, the process of prosecution is difficult at best. When victims have concluded that they are being stalked, they must build a case. "Stalking victims are often put in the position of having to first prove their case to a law enforcement official before being afforded the opportunity to prove their case before a court of law" (Infolink, 1995). If the victim lives in a city where there is a task force created specifically to deal with stalking cases, such as the Threat Management Unit (TMU) in Los Angeles, California, guidance and professional support are offered. "Throughout Los Angeles, cops know they should refer potential stalking cases to the TMU, which generally responds within 24 hours" (Simakis, 1996).

Unfortunately, far more victims live in areas where there are no such task forces nor agencies that offer professional guidance. It is therefore the victim's responsibility to keep all written correspondence; document every sighting of the stalker that is of such frequency that the meeting cannot be one of "chance"; determine the origins of all gifts; save recorded messages; and file police reports in cases of vandalism or threats. Stalking is indeed a "paper crime," and without such evidence it is almost impossible to begin the task of prosecution.

Even with documented evidence, there still is no guarantee that the prosecution of the stalker will proceed smoothly. Only some victims have the financial resources to seek private legal counsel and bring civil charges against their stalker.

Most states have common law actions, allowing victims to sue their stalker for invasion of privacy, trespassing, or intentional infliction of emotional distress.

Victims quickly learn that actively pursuing a civil case is time consuming and often becomes emotionally costly as well. We must remember that the stalker also can seek legal counsel and challenge the victim's interpretation of each and every act or behavior in question. Stalkers commonly reinterpret their actions and behaviors, and sometimes during the process, actually assume the role of the victim. Meloy and Gothard (1995) found a clear tendency for some stalkers to use projection and attribute obsessional following, and even threatening behavior, to the person they were stalking. We also must recognize that civil remedies do not "adequately redress the victim's injuries" (Tucker, 1993), nor do such remedies serve as a deterrent to prevent future stalking behaviors (Guy, 1993).

When a civil suit is not an option, the victim can seek criminal charges through the local district attorney's office. However, according to Simakis (1996), "nationwide, most victims who report their stalkers never see them prosecuted." The simple reason is that stalking cases are not a district attorney's highest priority when such cases are found within a docket filled with more serious crimes.

Another problem that plagues the prosecution of the stalker is that "stalking laws are fairly new, and victims cannot always be certain that law enforcement officials, prosecutors, or even judges are aware of these laws" (Infolink, 1995). It often takes time for law enforcement personnel to become familiar with new laws and learn how to assist the victim. Even today, very few police departments have had comprehensive training on the issue of stalking. In some states, such as in the state of Florida, "a lack of detailed training on the stalking law has inhibited the enforcement of the law" (Tucker, 1993). In light of such circumstances, it is not unusual for authors to advise the victim to take a copy of their state's stalking law with them to their law enforcement agencies. However, if law enforcement agents are not aware of such laws, how can we expect the victim to be so informed that she or he knows how to obtain a copy of the law, provide a legal interpretation of the law, and then convince others that her or his pursuer is in violation of this law?

The Penalties Imposed on Stalkers Are Weak, and under Some Circumstances, Inappropriate

Stalking is most often classified as a misdemeanor, which means that the sanctions for violation of these laws are weak. Typically, the first conviction for stalking is punishable by a limited amount of jail time or fines. "In New York, the penalty for misdemeanor stalking remains the same as for beating a subway fare: a maximum of twelve months in jail or a minimum of probation, as determined by the judge" (O'Malley, 1996). However, even mandated separation is not a deterrent for all stalkers. Far too many victims have recounted how their stalkers continued to engage in obsessive behaviors from the confines of the county jail. Thus, jail time sometimes does little in offering the victim the knowledge that she or he can resume a normal life.

Another problem is that some stalkers have a psychological disorder, as in the case of the erotomanic stalker, or behavioral patterns that are not easily broken simply because the stalker is temporarily incarcerated. The *Diagnostic and Statistical Manual of Mental Disorders* (1987) lists erotomania as a specific subtype of delusional (paranoid) disorder and describes the erotomanic as an individual who has a delusional belief that they are passionately loved by someone else. In this case, stalkers are convinced that their victim is in love with them, and her or his preoccupation with the victim is paramount. According to some experts, the erotomanic will not respond to any legal intervention, and sometimes not even to psychological intervention, because "delusions are among the most difficult symptoms to treat" (Orion, 1997).

Other stalkers, classified as love obsessional (Zona, Sharma, & Lane, 1993), believe that if they pursue their victim long enough and hard enough, the victim will certainly reciprocate their affections. Sometimes stalkers fall within the classification of the simple obsessional stalker (Zona et al., 1993) and are stalking their victim because they are angry and want retribution or retaliation for a relationship that went bad. In either of these cases, the criminal justice system is not the best choice for the successful treatment of the stalker. If the law does not require that the stalker undergo psychological counseling, mandated jail time is a short-term response to a "long-term crime without a traditional crime scene" (Wright et al., 1996). Because most "state stalking laws fail to adequately address the rehabilitation of stalkers" (Tucker, 1993), "states should include some provision for reviewing the mental health of all persons charged with stalking violations" (Fritz, 1995).

Victim-Blaming and Stereotyping Interferes with the Enforcement of the Crime of Stalking

Societal attitudes are also a deterrent to the successful enforcement of stalking laws. For decades, "victim-blaming" has been quite common in the criminal justice system, suggesting that in some way the victim, especially if the victim is a woman, is responsible for what is happening to her; that in fact, she is to blame for the problem that she is experiencing. In the case of stalking, this victim-blaming attitude can fuel the belief that women should be flattered by unwanted attentions, or that the psychological warfare of the stalker is not as bad as she is making it out to be. Even worse, such attitudes often lead the victim to believe that she has done something to cause the behavior of the stalker and, if she changes something about herself, the stalking will cease.

In addition, it is wrongly believed that all stalkers are male. Indeed, three out of four stalkers are male. But women also engage in the crime of stalking, with estimates suggesting that as many as one-fourth of all stalkers are female.

However, the crime of stalking may not be taken seriously if the stalker is a woman and the victim is a man. No doubt, it would be easy to respond to this situation by concluding that it is difficult, if not impossible, for a woman to place a man in reasonable fear. The fact is that both victim-blaming and sex-role stereotyping can create a situation in which the crime of stalking may go unreported.

Stalking laws are necessary, and since their inception, many states have been amending these laws to include stronger penalties and mandated mental health evaluations. States are also struggling with the issue of "credible threat" and allowing the victim to seek damages for mental distress (National Victim Center, 1995). However, until all states reconsider such laws, these laws will continue to be challenged on the issue of effectiveness.

REFERENCES

Bjerregaard, B. (1996). Stalking and the First Amendment: A constitutional analysis of state stalking laws. *Criminal Law Bulletin, 32* (4), 307–342.

Boychuk, M. K. (1997). Are stalking laws unconstitutionally vague or overbroad? *Northwestern University Law Review, 88* (769), 1–53.

Diagnostic and Statistical Manual of Mental Disorders. (3rd ed.—rev.). (1987). Washington, DC: American Psychiatric Association.

Fritz, J. (1995). A proposal for mental health provisions in state anti-stalking laws. *The Journal of Psychiatry and Law, 23* (Summer), 295–318.

Guy, R. (1993). The nature and constitutionality of stalking laws. *Vanderbilt Law Review 46,* (991).

Infolink. (1995). *Stalking: Questions and answers.* (No. 43). Arlington, VA: National Victim Center.

Meloy, J. R., & Gothard, S. (1995). Demographic and clinical comparison of obsessional followers and offenders with mental disorders. *American Journal of Psychiatry, 52* (2), 258–263.

National Criminal Justice Association. (1993). *Project to develop a model anti-stalking code for states.* Office of Justice Programs: U.S. Department of Justice.

National Victim Center. (1995). *Stalking laws.* Arlington, VA: Author.

O'Malley, S. (1996). Nowhere to hide: Why the new stalking laws still do not protect women. *Redbook, 1* (1), 120–123+.

Orion, D. (1997). *I know you really love me.* New York: Macmillan.

Simakis, A. (1996). Why the stalking laws aren't working. *Glamour, 94* (5), 244–247+.

Sohn, E. (1994). Antistalking statutes: Do they actually protect victims? *Criminal Law Bulletin, 30* (3), 203–242.

Stalking numbers reported. (1997, November 14). *The Atlanta Journal/The Atlanta Constitution,* C-1.

Tucker, J. (1993). Stalking the problems with stalking laws: The effectiveness of Florida Statutes Section 784.048. *Florida Law Review, 45,* (609), 1–107.

Wright, J. A., Burgess, A. G., Burgess, A. W., Laszlo, A. T., McCrary, G. O., & Douglas, J. E. (1996). A typology of interpersonal stalking. *Journal of Interpersonal Violence, 11* (4), 4876–502.

Zona, M. A., Sharma, K. K., & Lane, J. (1993). A comparative study of erotomanic and obsessional subjects in a forensic sample. *Journal of Forensic Sciences, 38* (4), 894–903.

Rejoinder to Dr. McCandless   Ronnie Harmon

Dr. McCandless makes several cogent arguments for the ineffectiveness of stalking legislation. Fortunately for the victim of stalking, most of the issues she raises have already been taken up by state and federal legislators.

The Language Used in Stalking Laws Is Problematic

In response to recent litigation, specific revisions in state laws have been made to overcome the problems of vagueness and overbreadth when courts have found such revision necessary. It also must be noted that many state courts have ruled that the laws do withstand these challenges (Baty, 1996; Hueter, 1997).

As I pointed out in my article, legislative revisions have also substituted the phrase "continuing course of conduct" for the earlier laundry list of prohibited behavior. This takes some of the specificity out of stalking laws and makes it more difficult for stalkers to avoid prosecution by committing specific, not prohibited acts. Many states have done away with the requirement that a stalker threaten his or her target. For those that retain this provision, "threat" has usually been redefined so that an implicit threat is also prohibited.

Regarding whether other, preexisting laws can be used to control stalking behavior, I believe that my article has already addressed the limitations of these laws. Stalking legislation is more focused and allows law enforcement personnel to take action against activities that are not otherwise illegal.

The Criminal Prosecution of the Stalker Is Laden with Burdens for the Victim

Stalking is an unusual type of crime. Most criminal behavior is committed in one action (robbery, assault, rape, etc.), rather than in multiple incidents over the course of time. A crime such as stalking requires documentation by virtue of its nature. There does not appear to be any way to avoid this.

I grant Dr. McCandless her point that there is a need to educate law enforcement professionals about stalking and the new laws designed to combat it. This does not negate the validity or usefulness of the laws themselves.

Dr. McCandless considers the use of civil prosecution ineffective against stalking. I agree. That is why criminal laws are so necessary.

The Penalties Imposed on Stalkers Are Weak and, under Some Circumstances, Inappropriate

Many states use a multistage process to charge and penalize stalkers. Initial stalking behavior, which may not in itself be harmful to the physical person of the victim, is classified as a lesser offense. The continuation and escalation of such behavior, in the face of restraining orders or orders of protection, results in escalating penalties.

Regarding mandating some form of mental health intervention for stalkers, not all stalking behavior is caused by a diagnosable mental illness. Some form of treatment could be attempted for those individuals who might benefit. The problem is that it is not clear that an effective means of treating stalking behavior exits. Any proposed program should be monitored and evaluated to determine whether it is successful. It is also not clear that such a treatment program could be forced on a perpetrator, or that such forced participation in a program would be effective.

Victim-Blaming and Stereotyping Interferes with the Successful Prosecution of the Stalker

As with the law enforcement community, the public, including the victims of stalking, need to be educated about the issue and available remedies. There are some hotlines with victim support obtainable both by telephone and by Internet (Survivors of Stalking, The Stalking Victims' Sanctuary, the National Victim Center, and the Stop Harassment Now Web Ring). These services provide information, counseling, and assistance to individuals targeted by stalkers. Current and ongoing research is being made more accessible to the general public through popular works such as Dr. Doreen Orion's "I Know You Really Love Me," Linden Gross's "To Have or To Harm" (1994), and Michael Scott's "How to Lose Anyone Anywhere" (1998). Again, suggesting a need for such supplemental educational and support services does not per se mean that the current laws are inadequate. Without legislated prohibitions against stalking, support services would not be able to make meaningful recommendations to victims.

To conclude, I believe that Dr. McCandless' arguments, although having value at one time, have in many cases already been countered by revisions in stalking legislation. Her suggestions for supplemental services, although valid, do not negate the importance of the laws themselves as one component in combating the problem of stalking.

REFERENCES

Baty, J. A. (Fall 1996). Commentary: Alabama's stalking statutes: Coming out of the shadows. *Alabama Law Review, 48,* 229–250.

Francieweb.com/stalked [on line] with a link to the Stop harassment now web ring, an online discussion group. Retrieved November 12, 1977 from the World Wide Web: http://www.

Gross, L. (1994). *To have or to harm: True stories of stalkers and their victims.* New York: Warner Books.

Hueter, J. A. (January, 1997). Note and comment: Lifesaving legislation: But will the Washington stalking law survive constitutional scrutiny? *Washington Law Review, 72,* 213–240.

Orion, D. (1997). *I know you really love me: A psychiatrist's journal of erotomania, stalking and obsessive love.* New York: Macmillan.

Safety strategies for stalking victims. The National Victim Center [on line]. Retrieved November 12, 1997 from the World Wide Web: http://www.nvc.org/gdir/svsafety.htm.

The stalking victims' sanctuary [on line]. Retrieved November 12, 1997 from the World Wide Web: http://www.ccon.com/stalkvictim/

Scott, M. (1998). How to lose anyone anywhere. Kalamazoo, MI: Stealth Publishing; also [on line]. Retrieved November 12, 1997 from the World Wide Web: http://www.members.aol.com/besafenow/main.html.

Survivors of stalking. Retrieved November 12, 1997 from the World Wide Web: http://www.soshelp.org.

Multicide: Does Society Need the "Supersizing" of Murder?

Patricia Kirby is currently a doctoral candidate in sociology/justice at The American University in Washington, D.C. After spending time as a Baltimore City police officer and homicide detective, she joined the Federal Bureau of Investigation as a special agent. Her last assignment with the FBI was in the Behavioral Sciences Unit as a researcher and profiler.

Toni DuPont-Morales, Ph.D., is Assistant Professor in the School of Public Affairs at Penn State. She investigated and supervised predatory criminals before obtaining her doctorate in Law, Policy, and Society at Northeastern University in Boston, Massachusetts. She has published articles on violence, stalking, victimology, and accountability in government.

YES

PATRICIA KIRBY

Before discussing why society needs the supersizing of murder, a common understanding is needed of the concepts *supersizing* and *multicide*. The McDonalds' commercials have contributed to the coining of the term *supersize*. A businessman enters the fast food chain after a grueling day of subcompact rental cars and junior executive lodging and tells the person behind the counter: supersize me.

The perception of supersizing derived from this scenario is the enlargement or the increase in size and stature of something or someone. The combination of the terms *supersizing* and *murder* encourages thoughts of multiple murders with increasing numbers of victims and the magnification of these murderers in contemporary society.

The term *multicide,* from *multi*—meaning many, much, more than one or two—refers to the killing of many, or to a person who murders multiple victims. Included in the category of multicide are serial, mass, and spree killings. These three forms of multiple murder are often misperceived and incorrectly seen as interchangeable. Understanding the differences between these types of multiple murders facilitates comprehension of the phenomenon.

The element of time involved between murderous acts is primary in the differentiation of serial, mass, and spree murderers. Serial killers have a cooling off period between their murders, mass murderers kill their victims at one time, and spree killers operate within a short period of days or weeks.

A serial murderer is one who commits three or more murders over time, usually within weeks, months, or years. The motive for the murder is oftentimes not apparent, but the methods of murder and the selection of victims exhibit consistency with each murderous act (Hickey, 1991, 1997; Holmes & DeBurger, 1988; Keeney & Heide, 1994; Skrapec, 1994). The avoidance of detection and apprehension are paramount to the serialist, because his or her sole desire is to continue killing in a repetitive manner.

It is of importance that the number of victims of a serial killer is determined by forces outside his or her control and is a function of when he or she is apprehended. Because serial murderers are incapable of stopping their own behavior, the amount of time spent in a killing career depends on their success in eluding the police (Holmes and DeBurger, 1988; Ressler, Burgess, & Douglas, 1988).

Jeffrey Dahmer is an example of a serial killer. He is believed to have claimed the lives of more than a dozen boys over a period of years. While serving several sentences of life imprisonment without parole, he was murdered by a fellow inmate.

Spree killers commit multiple murders in a relatively short period. They will engage in the killing acts for days or weeks. The methods of murder and types of victims vary. The murders range from very violent overt attacks with knives and guns to more covert subtle acts such as poisoning. Victim selection appears random, without any particular distinct or discernible patterns.

Andrew Cunanan is classified as a spree killer. His reign of terror lasted several weeks before he committed suicide while hiding out on a houseboat in Florida. His known victim count within this period was five. His killing acts occurred in a serial manner as he traveled from California through the Midwest and down the East Coast to Florida.

Mass murder involves the killing of several victims, usually at one time in one location and in a short or prolonged period. The attack can occur for minutes or hours, with little concern or planning given to the avoidance of being captured (Fox & Levin, 1994; Holmes & Holmes, 1994). Oftentimes, mass murderers kill themselves, surrender, or allow police to kill them. The killer may attack totally innocent and unrelated people, such as students or customers in a restaurant. Domestic murders, workplace violence, and domestic and foreign terrorist attacks also are included under the umbrella of mass murder.

The execution-style behavior of mass murderers appears premeditated, and they seem prepared if necessary for a prolonged siege. The motives for the commission of mass murder, particularly domestic and foreign terrorism, appear as emotional and mental responses to the deeply held political and religious beliefs of the killer. A serious consequence of dealing with mass murderers is that it seems as though the less people value their own lives, the more difficult it is to appeal to their sense of survival and to assess their violent tendencies.

Domestic mass murder, the killing of one's family members, usually ends in murder–suicide. After venting the depression or rage on those closest to them, these murderers often complete the violent episode with suicide.

Workplace violence is a form of mass murder. Most of the selected victims are targeted as the causes or the responsible parties for the murderer's feelings of anger and frustration.

The prevention and detection of terrorist attacks prove an insurmountable undertaking. The fervor and unrealistic dedication of these individuals to irrational ideas ensure a degree of unpredictability in their behavior that makes logical and rational responses by law enforcement agencies and officials ineffective.

One of the more common examples of a mass murderer is Charles Whitman, a former Marine, who in 1966 climbed to the top of the bell tower at the University of Texas–Austin and shot and killed thirteen people. Another thirty-one were wounded during this single event. Whitman's selection of a public place is typical of mass murderers. The massacre was labeled the "crime of the century" because of the rarity of mass murder at that time (Fox & Levin, 1994). Other locations that have served as recent crime scenes for mass murders include schools, fast food restaurants, shopping malls, subway cars, and government and corporate buildings.

The Importance of Supersizing Murder

Although mass, serial, and spree murders occupy a very small portion of all criminal behavior in the United States and the world, these crimes receive more attention than any other form of illegal activity. Before the 1970s and the coining of the term *serial killing,* multicide was believed to be an isolated phenomenon of rare occurrence committed by mentally impaired or insane individuals.

People's fascination with the morose and frightening aspects of life and death created a market for the supersizing of murder. If it were not for people's insatiable desire to read and hear about murder, especially multicide, we would not be inundated with newspaper and magazine stories about serial killers, unabombers, and domestic terrorists.

The supersizing of murder raises our awareness of multiple homicides. The public thrives on the killings, no matter how brutal. Understanding what motivates an individual to kill in a serial, mass, or spree style assists in the apprehension of such persons, encourages preventive measures, and, most importantly, may save lives.

The greater awareness of serial murder by contemporary society and an increased willingness by U.S. law enforcement to exchange information and recognize links between murders may contribute to the appearance of serial murder as an American phenomenon (Jenkins, 1994; Newton, 1990). The attention by the press and the American public contributes to the perception that serial murder is an act endemic to our culture.

Society fosters the atmosphere for the creation and production of movies such as *Fatal Attraction, Copycat* and *Silence of the Lambs.* Crime books, novels, and television movies about the lives of Ted Bundy, John Wayne Gacey, Jeffrey Dahmer, Aileen Wournos, and others intrigue audiences of all ages. The media is interested in what sells; therefore, does society actually create the demand for information about multiple murderers?

To address the problem of multiple murder and to lessen the treatment of it as a rare violent occurrence or the behavior of a deranged lunatic who spontaneously erupts into a killing frenzy, we need to enhance our understanding of the complexities of the phenomenon. A healthy awareness and a comprehensive approach based on knowledge and understanding and a lack of fear is a beginning.

Serial murder has a different impact on society than mass murder. Although immediate but short-lived horror and panic follow the occurrence of a mass murder, the effects of serial murderers may be experienced for years. An example is the Green River Killer, who threatened the Pacific Northwest during the 1980s (Holmes & Holmes, 1994). Although task force and media attention were plentiful, the killer has never been identified nor apprehended.

Awareness and recognition of potentially violent individuals and situations are a product of supersizing murder. The press and the media have the power to sensationalize and publicize the phenomenon of multiple murder, but criminologists and law enforcement agencies have the responsibility to define, educate, and inform society about the murderers and their behavior. With the assistance of educators and law enforcement agencies, supersizing can be productive. The recent case of Theodore Kaczynski, the Unabomber, is a compelling example of a collaborative effort between the media and many agencies within the criminal justice system and federal government. The compilation and comparison of information concerning the victims and recipients of the explosive packages helped determine a profile of the bomber for apprehension and a profile of the type of selected victims for prevention of future violence. The United States Postal Service implemented numerous changes to scrutinize mailed packages. Law enforcement agencies, the Federal Bureau of Investigation, the Bureau of Alcohol, Tobacco, and Firearms, and local jurisdictions investigated and analyzed the ongoing evidence and data from each case. Task forces of criminologists and psychologists were established. During the years between the revelation of the existence of the Unabomber and his final apprehension, the continuous media coverage kept the public, law enforcement, and postal services informed and cautious about potentially violent problems.

Workplace violence seems to have developed as a 1990s crime. In recent years, the number of violent incidents in the workplace has escalated. This type of violence attracts immediate media attention. Yet the awareness created by the coverage has forced corporate America to become more sensitized to the safety of their workers and to the existence and treatment of ongoing employee problems. Training programs have been implemented to assist management and employees in dealing with the reality of workplace violence and the implementation of techniques to identify and react to these situations. Downsizing and layoffs are handled with greater concern and professional assistance today than ten years ago.

Knowledge is essential to solve most crimes, particularly multicide. The success of many past serial and spree murderers was founded on the inability of law enforcement to recognize that a particular murder was one in a series of killings rather than an isolated homicide. The greater the information about an individual and their murderous acts, the better the chance of apprehension of the criminal and prevention of the crimes. The term *linkage blindness* (Egger, 1984) relates to the lack of communication of information between law enforcement agencies within different geographic and legal jurisdictions.

The overemphasis of multicide by society and the media may draw some unwarranted attention to particular homicides. But to comprehensively address a phenomenon with the inherent complexities of multicide, increased knowledge and awareness at the investigative, apprehension, prosecution, and sentencing stages of the criminal justice process are essential. Change never seems easy and is usually not attempted without an immense amount of public and societal concern and outrage.

Today's multiple murderers are practically household names. They are the subjects of their own series of trading cards. And because of the hype and the extensive television and newspaper coverage of individuals such as Dahmer and Cunanan, many people erroneously believe that they are experts in the area of serial and mass murder. Oftentimes it is more difficult to debunk the false information than it is to educate society and disseminate accurate information. The real power and responsibility to teach and inform the public does not lie within the media's definitions of the phenomenon but in the writings of criminologists and researchers.

As society increases personal awareness and scholarship of the problems surrounding multicide, policy and legislative changes may be encouraged and emphasized. The more pressure exerted on the law enforcement responses, court proceedings, and sentencing procedures for change, the less frightened and more responsive society will become to the problems of multicide.

REFERENCES

Egger, S. A. 1984. A working definition of serial murder and the reduction of linkage blindness. *Journal of Police Science Administration, 12* (3), 348–357.

Fox, J. A. & Levin, J. (1994). *Overkill.* New York: Plenum Publishing Corporation.

Hickey, E. (1991). *Serial murderers and their victims.* Pacific Grove, CA: Brooks Cole.

Hickey, E. (1997). *Serial murderers and their victims* (2nd ed.). Belmont, CA: Wadsworth Publishers.

Holmes, R. M., & DeBurger, J. (1988). *Serial murder.* Newbury Park, CA: Sage.

Holmes, R. M. & Holmes, S. T. (1994). *Murder in America.* Thousand Oaks, CA: Sage.

Jenkins, P. (1994). *Using murder: The social construction of serial homicide.* New York: A. DeGruyter.

Keeney, B. T. & Heide, K. (1994). Gender differences in serial murderers: A preliminary analysis. *The Journal of Interpersonal Violence, 9* (3), 383–398.

Newton, M. (1990). *Hunting humans: The encyclopedia of serial killers.* New York: Avon Books.

Ressler, R. K., Burgess, A., & Douglas, J. (1988). *Sexual homicides: Patterns and motives.* Lexington, MA: Lexington Books.

Skrapec, C. (1994). The female serial killer: An evolving criminality. In H. Birch (Ed.). *Moving targets.* Berkeley: University of California Press.

Rejoinder to Ms. Kirby
TONI DUPONT-MORALES

My colleague's description of society's obsession with the differentiating factors between serial, spree, and mass murder is articulate and precise. The behavioral nuances, the time factors, the physical endeavors, and the sociopsychological profiles are vital to the evolution of comprehending and apprehending multicidal killers. The challenge is to transcend society's obsession with the morose and develop educational opportunities to address the development of multicidal killers.

If sensationalism created by spin doctors can sell murder, then sensationalism can sell intervention and prevention. Ego documentaries routinely feature investigators, prosecutors, judges, and academicians discussing the perpetrator's heinous acts. Is it so economically risky to extend these discussions to behaviors of concern in children, adolescents, and adults? Knowledge about the phenomenon of multicide should be linked to the complexities surrounding intervention and prevention.

Reiss and Roth (1993) have documented multidisciplinary research on the complexities of violent behavior and its control. Why then, has science policy concerning the development and control of violence not been linked to criminal justice policy and legal issues? Yes, the Unabomber, Ted Kaczynski's moniker, is a compelling example of collaboration by media and multilevel governmental agencies. During the seventeen-year history of the Unabomber, however, numerous changes implemented by the United States Postal Service to scrutinize mail for potential danger did nothing to identify and control the danger that existed for employees of the postal service.

With all the knowledge about violence and investigation of violence, the postal service missed opportunities to prevent and control violence in its own workplace. The criminal justice system needs to develop a curriculum to teach nonviolence. Give the task to the media spin doctors, and society will listen. For instance, news bites about the killings might be followed by public service announcements addressing violence, mental health services, mentoring, and antiviolence alternatives. The news coverage of the Kentucky school killings would have been an opportune time to air intervention service announcements directed toward adolescents. Hollywood and sports celebrities willingly donate their time and prestige.

Increased awareness about the investigation, apprehension, prosecution, and sentencing stages of the criminal justice process has occurred. Society has *Court TV, The People's Court, Nightline, 20/20, Dateline,* and *Burden of Proof,* to name a few, to educate about these processes. It would appear that most individuals can readily discuss the "plat de jour" legal issue. How can legal programming cultivate "an immense amount of public and societal concern and outrage" that will result in attitudinal changes toward societal and familial violence? Why has a balanced effort between prevention and apprehension never materialized in the criminal justice system? Aren't we suppose to learn about both from each incident of violence?

It is imperative that the processes involved in serial, spree, and mass murder be documented. However, the accumulation of data must serve more than an elite group of citizens or solely members of law enforcement. The acquired data must serve to enhance the prevention and early apprehension of such killers. This data also must be incorporated into our public policies and court decisions.

Consider the case of *Joshua Deshaney* v. *Winnebago County Department of Social Services* (489 U.S. 189 [1988]). Joshua was battered, returned to the batterer, and battered again until nearly brain dead, requiring institutionalization. All of this occurred while under the auspices of Winnebago County and a direct court order to social services to supervise Joshua's welfare. Winnebago County was sued on behalf of Joshua, citing the due process clause and a deprivation of liberty—freedom from abuse. The Supreme Court decided that the county had not acted to deprive Joshua of his due process although they had passively allowed a third party, his father, to do so. Furthermore, to find for nine-year-old Joshua would have brought child abuse into federal constitutional oversight. Governmental agencies cannot afford to be held liable for the violent behavior committed on children. We can afford, however, to build prisons and fight violence after it is committed.

If violence is a continuum, then a common perception might be that there exist opportune times in which to divert the individual. How do we measure the lifetime risk of engaging in violence? Is it possible that if we offer intervening services, overestimating this risk will not violate one's constitutional rights? Predictions about who will engage in violence or will escalate their violence have led to mandatory sentences and prison overcrowding. Offering supportive services before a perpetrator moves along the continuum of violence is one avenue to prevention.

Supersizing limits the analysis of violence to products of violence rather than the factors that influence the production of violence. Violence is collectively, individually, and communally developed. Criminologists can profile a person who robs and murders a convenience store clerk by analyzing the neighborhood, acquiring local demographics, and speaking to the patrolling officer. Investigators cannot do this for incidents of multicide unless the perpetrator is apprehended or there are repeated incidents. However, profiling the lifestyle interactions with aspects of violence is possible for both perpetrators.

We need information about the nexus between biological factors, psychological factors, employment factors, community factors, educational settings, family, and peers on the facilitation and development of violence (Pepler & Rubin, 1991). Some believe this is where the supersizing of murder should direct our inquiry. It is the isolationism offered by supersizing that fails to draw investigators, prosecutors, and judges back to intervention and prevention; it is the elitism that discourages academicians and researchers from making their findings practical.

REFERENCES

Pepler, D. J., & Rubin, K. H. (Eds.). (1991). *The development and treatment of childhood aggression.* Hillsdale, NJ: Erlbaum.

Reiss, A. J., Jr., & Roth, J. A. (Eds.). (1993). *Understanding and preventing violence.* The National Research Council. Washington, DC: National Academy Press.

NO

TONI DUPONT-MORALES

Serial, spree, and mass murder are categories of multicide that represent a logical rationalization of the killing of multiple human beings by one or more individuals (Cormier, Angliker, Boyer, and Merserau 1972; Gebreth, 1986). Although most multicides are committed by a single person, multiple offenders and involvement by both genders is not a rare phenomenon (Jenkins, 1990). This "supersizing" of murder fulfills a need to quantify aberrant killing techniques. Supersizing includes the production of ego documentaries, educational and entertaining profiles depicting the life, carnage, and mayhem caused by the killer. Society does not need the macro-efficiency and calculability provided by "supersizing" murder into categories of multicide (Ritzer, 1996).

Constructing Multicide

The supersizing of murder encourages the categorization and specialization of definition but not a genuine inquiry into causation. When these killers are analyzed, the presence of unremediated violent familial interactions and abusive social interactions during childhood, adolescence, and transition into adulthood are noted (Hickey 1997; Sampson & Laub, 1993). Until the pivotal "crossover"—the move from victim to victimizer, coupled with the move from fantasy to reality, the killer remains in control of his physical, social, and sexual violence.

The social and psychological resources that might have intervened in the crossing over to the formation of the violence, the fantasies of committing the violence, and the actual commission of the violence are often nonexistent. The perpetrator may not know how to access the necessary services to alleviate the emotional pain that is experienced. Often, the perpetrator may abuse substances as a means of self-medication. These substances dull the anxiety from the forming violence and the fear that results from such fantasies. Furthermore, there is little social scientific documentation about any effective nexus of psychological, sociological, and biological intervention in the sequencing of violence. Unfortunately, policy makers have determined that funding institutions to imprison or execute killers is preferable to funding preventive services for children, adolescents, or adults.

Practicing for Multicide

The killer engages in the stalking of a victim, a process of constructing and deconstructing predatory violence. Because a potential serial killer's victim is unaware of the predicament, nonroutine self-protective measures are not possible. For the multiple killer, interpreting his narcissistic self-image through a personal conception of violence is assisted by stalking behavior (Pollack, 1995). Stalking is an old behavior that often accompanies predatory violence. Until the stalking escalates, until the stalker penetrates the "comfort zone" of the victim, deviant thoughts are fantasies. The comfort zone is a spatial domain in which the victim engages in lifestyle activities, and it is within this domain that multicide occurs (Gottfredson, 1981; Holmes & Rossmo, 1996; Ressler, Burgess, & Douglas, 1988).

Once the killer's predatory rage is no longer controlled, the unfortunate victim crosses over into the comfort zone of the killer. Social science is the study of variations, and we have limited knowledge about how variations within crossover eventually facilitate these killings. The killer has the ultimate control, and it is the precarious balance of this control that may be the substantiating difference between three, twenty, or one hundred victims.

Society's Perception of Supersizing

Multicide frightens society. Even with well-documented profiles of victims and potential victims, societal fears are exaggerated. Serial killers and spree killers drive a wedge into civility between human beings. Individuals are frightened to say "good morning" or acknowledge the presence of a stranger. Because the killer is not notably different from those in the community, citizens assume that it is best to suspect everyone. They remember the disguises of Bundy and the chameleon ways of Cunanan.

With this fear, independence, solitude, and trust become liabilities. Cunanan's friends were some of his victims; Kemper admonished college coeds who trusted that he would take them to their destination; and Bundy killed those who helped a handicapped clean-cut young man politely requesting assistance. Gacy, a trusted leader of the business community, killed young men who were seeking employment, and McVeigh, a quiet young man who served in the military and loved his country, blew up a federal building during business hours.

Another negative aspect of supersizing murder is the innate ritual of seeking the culpability of the victims for their own victimization and blaming authorities for incompetency. Victim blaming irrationally confirms that victims are economically and politically marginalized people, criminally involved, social risk takers, and purveyors of aberrant sexual activities. It is important that they not be like us. If we travel in groups, speak and look at no one, remain aware of our surroundings, and let someone know where we are at all times, we will be safe. If we engage in moral and conservative behaviors, we will be safe. If we give law enforcement the money, the intrusive power, and the technology they need, we will be safe. Wrong (de Becker, 1997).

The Technology of Multicide

Offices within the U.S. Department of Justice and the Criminal Justice Center at Sam Houston State University in Huntsville, Texas, established the National Center for the Analysis of Violent Crime (NCAVC) in 1984. The NCAVC included four core programs: the Violent Criminal Apprehension Program (VICAP) located in the Behavioral Science Unit (BSU) of the Federal Bureau of Investigation (FBI) in Quantico, Virginia; Research and Development; Profiling and Consultation; and Training. Through these programs, the investigation and apprehension of individuals who commit multicide progressed from particularly astute investigators to the realm of technology.

Technology offers a catalyst for the media. Capitalizing on a frenzy to be first with the story, both the media and law enforcement rush to present the products of their technology and the touted profile of the killer. For law enforcement and prosecuting attorneys, multicide offers the opportunity to enrich their careers and increase their charisma for the public and potential voters. Careers are fast-tracked by involvement with multicide. Although isolated, these cases become celebrated.

Multicide quantifies murder for society without reflecting the human component of terror and suffering. It denigrates death to a sociopsychological profile, an organized or disorganized crime scene, physical evidence, and a geographical profile that can be entered into a database and converted into charts (Ressler & Shachtman, 1992). This quantification is more concerned with the processes within the NCAVC than with the social formation and impact of multiple murder on a community.

The inability of law enforcement to apprehend the killer, even when they know who it is, as with Andrew Cunanan, does little to demonstrate the efficiency of technology. We do not know what might have happened if Cunanan had not provided the police with their greatest break—his suicide.

A technological foundation for the investigation of multicide promotes the legitimization of profiling but only after at least three victims have been murdered or the perpetrator has been apprehended. Technology offers an illusion of control for those panicked by this type of killer. The use of computers, electronic databases, and investigative tools and techniques does not stop or apprehend these killers. Perhaps it is because those who engage in multicide do not contextualize the act of violence or the receivers of that violent act. Instead these killers are seeking the optimum setting, the specialized instruments, and the appropriate victims that will enhance their killing efficiency. They mirror the intensity and behaviors of their pursuers. The use of technology has not prevented multiple homicide; it has only added to its categories.

Also unaddressed by technology is the panic generated by the release of the killer's profile and the briefings detailing the future direction of the killer. These declarations by law enforcement during well-staged press conferences are conducted to alleviate community fear and increase a phantom sense of personal safety. Thus, the products of crime-fighting technology are electronically transmitted. News editors from the printed media, experts from respected institutions, and leaders in law enforcement will prognosticate on 24-hour news programs about the killer's motivation and techniques. However, these media rituals will not add to our understanding of the suffering endured by the victims or the numerous times some form of intervention might have prevented the violence.

Premonitions, visions, "getting into the mind of the killer," and profiles are now the dialogue of not only movies but also newspaper and magazine articles.

Media enhance their financial gain through the advances and exclusives they negotiate with families, friends, and acquaintances of the killer and the victims (Palmer, 1994). The media often become a petri dish for a contagion that will result in similar killings. After the frenzy dies down, the world of violence has been constructed by interpretation and policy, but it has not been controlled or prevented.

Perhaps the greatest concern is that law enforcement experts disagree with even the frequency of multiple homicides (Hickey, 1997). Estimations of fifty multicidal individuals to five hundred such individuals are discussed. Multicide is rare, common, or increasing in frequency, depending on the source. Such "exactness" exacerbates the fears of society and the perception of potential victimizations in the future.

Predicting Multicide

Rage appears to be a predictor of multicide. The term *postal* describes multicidal rage within the workplace. Perhaps the only supersizing of murder that has had some predictability has been the mass murder of employees by nonstrangers. Research, managerial training, and workplace violence prevention programs address disgruntled employees, spouses, significant others, and customers (Stage, 1997). The increase in workplace violence has insurers developing policies to prevent loss and cover the result of such violence (Esters, 1997). Responsible employers hire conscientiously, train supervisors, promote a positive physical and emotional environment, immediately investigate threats, and engage in remedial action to protect and assist victims because of potential liability (Williams, 1997).

Multicide involving nonstrangers is also reported in families in which domestic violence has gone from beyond the spouse or child to the extended family. Spouses, grandparents, parents, siblings, in-laws, children, uncles, aunts, and even pets have been murdered during one act of rage. However, in this situation, it appears that the killing rage was the end result of documented threats and lesser incidents of violence.

A similar ritual has been documented in educational environments, where the victims may be peers or teachers. The rage appears to be the answer to the killer's loss of control over a group of nonstrangers and the need to obliterate those perceived as responsible for this loss (Wood, 1996).

Multicide has been considered an American phenomenon, probably because the philosophy of supersizing and "bigger is better" is considered a cultural marker of the United States. However, statistics indicate that multiple homicide is a universal enigma. Caution must be taken to distinguish multicide from the numerous victims of political unrest, military action, genocide, and war. Worldwide multicide includes the same factors as those found in the United States. Multicide appears to release a contagion of rage and homicidal behaviors. Once the news releases chronicle the killings, it is not unusual for a grouping of these killings to occur (Methvin 1996).

What makes such fatal rage, and how do we control it? First, the rage is not always known. The declaration by law enforcement that an unassuming, unremarkable individual is the killer of multiple victims comes as a surprise to his neighbors, his coworkers, his family, or his community. Similarly, a declaration that "a loner," "an angry misfit," "a weirdo," or "an outcast" killed multiple victims enrages society because "the signs" were ignored by authorities, family members, or treatment agents. What factors distinguish a killing rage? Should society be paranoid about those who are paranoid, schizoid, or a borderline personality? Maybe the question should be, "Does society have a role in preventing such personalities from escalating to multiple homicide?"

Victimization and Multicide

The drive to distinguish the motivating factors resulting in multiple homicide are of questionable benefit for society. The perception that those who engage in such behaviors are evil or sick increases a perception of societal helplessness. When multiple killings occur, society engages in a number of adaptive behaviors up to a point of political or economic discomfort.

Gun control laws remain a contentious topic for politicians, emergency room physicians, conservatives, liberals, and citizens. The bumper sticker that reads: "They'll get my colt .45 when they pry it from my dead cold hands," ignores several important issues. What if those being killed are elementary school children in Scotland or high school children in Kentucky? Should all high school students carry guns, or should elementary schools have armed protection? Gun laws have done little to prevent such killings, but should society limit the manufacturing of guns and ammunition? Is the prevention of victimization worth intrusion into constitutional rights, the strengthening of gun laws, and the control of business activities?

Ironically, the existence of these killers provides a constraining factor for society. The potential that one might come across such a killer encourages modification of social behaviors. Is such self-regulation a boon or bane?

When one witnesses or sees the results of domestic violence, does this encourage the reporting of such violence in one's neighborhood? Are screams heard in the middle of the night and the sound of beatings enough to report a neighbor who goes to work, cuts his grass, and appears normal? Is the colleague who makes regular threats against the boss displaying a sarcastic wit or is he potentially dangerous? Is the regulation forbidding guns in the workplace, even when registered, an invasion of constitutional rights or a preventive policy?

Do human resource officers, school counselors, or industrial psychologists have the right to mandate treatment for disruptive individuals? Rage is developmental and requires intervention from kindergarten through adult life as a means of preventing victimization.

Conclusion

The rationality of classifying behaviors, the embracing of technology as a replacement for exemplary investigators, and the law enforcement jargon of "profiling," "spree," "serial," and "mass" have not changed the perception that society does not know how to prevent multiple homicide. Policy makers, social scientists, and law enforcement have not allotted the resources to formulate intervening and preventive programs. We can hunt down those who kill for profit, we can assassinate those who kill for political power, we can impose economic sanctions on those who commit genocide, but we are powerless to address those who commit multiple murders.

REFERENCES

Cormier, B. M., Angliker, C. C. J., Boyer, R., & Mersereau, G. (1972). The psychodynamics of homicide committed in a semispecific relationship. *Canadian Journal of Criminology and Corrections, 14,* 335–344.

de Becker, G. (1997). *The gift of fear: Survival signals that protect us from violence.* New York: Little, Brown & Company.

Esters, S. D. (1997, February 4). Workplace violence prompts policy. *National Underwriter, 10* (8), 3, 43.

Gebreth, V. J. (1986). Mass, serial and sensational homicides. *Law and Order, 34,* 20–22.

Gottfredson, M. R. (1981). On the etiology of criminal victimization. In J. L. Underwood (Ed.), *Victims of crime: A review of research issues and methods* (pp. 37–54). Washington, DC: National Institute of Justice.

Hickey, E. W. (1997). *Serial murderers and their victims* (2nd ed.). Belmont, CA: Wadsworth Publishing Company.

Holmes, R. M., & Rossmo, D. K. (1996). Geography, profiling, and predatory criminals. In R. M. Holmes & S. T. Holmes (Eds.), *Profiling violent crimes: An investigative tool* (2nd ed.) (pp. 148–165). Thousand Oaks, CA: Sage.

Jenkins, P. (1990). Sharing murder: Understanding group serial homicide. *Journal of Crime and Justice, 13* (2), 125–147.

Methvin, E. H. (1996, June 3). Bloody murderers. *National Review, 48* (10), 40–44.

Palmer, A. (1994, May 28). A dead clever way to make money. *The Spectator,* 9–11.

Pollack, P. H. (1995). A case of spree serial murder with suggested diagnostic opinions. *International Journal of Offender Therapy and Comparative Criminology, 39* (3), 258–268.

Ressler, R. K., Burgess, A. W., & Douglas, J. E. (1988). *Sexual homicide.* Lexington, MA: Lexington Books.

Ressler, R. K., & Shachtman, T. (1992). *Whoever fights monsters.* New York: St. Martin's Press.

Ritzer, G. (1996). *The McDonaldization of society: An investigation into the changing character of contemporary social life* (Rev. ed.). Thousand Oaks, CA: Pine Forge Press.

Sampson, R. J., & Laub, J. H. (1993). *Crime in the making: Pathways and turning points through life.* Cambridge, MA: Harvard University Press.

Stage, J. K. (1997, February 17). Attack on violence. *Industry Week, 246* (4), 15–18.

Williams, H. A. H. (1997, February). 10 Steps to a safer workplace. *HR Focus, 74* (2), 9–10.

Wood, C. (1996, April 15). Fatal rage. *Maclean's,* 32–33.

Rejoinder to Dr. Dupont-Morales

PATRICIA KIRBY

In her argument against the need to supersize murder, Dr. Dupont-Morales emphasizes that society does not know how to deal with nor how to prevent multicide. Her major objections to the supersizing of murder strongly reinforce her position by focusing on the following three areas: (1) that supersizing merely encourages the act of categorizing multiple murderers but does not initiate inquiry into the causation of these murders; (2) the use of law enforcement experts and technology have contributed very little to the prevention of multicide; and (3) rage is a predictor of multicide, and further victimization will be prevented when society begins to deal with the personal rage of individuals.

It is true that society does not know how to prevent multicide nor how to deal with the behavior of multiple murderers. This lack of knowledge creates a greater need for criminologists and sociologists to initiate research and encourage educational discourse about multicide. A comprehensive understanding of this phenomenon will generate ideas and measures that assist in earlier detection and apprehension of serial, mass, and spree killers.

The lack of inquiry into the human components of multicide discussed by Dr. Dupont-Morales is not a result of the supersizing of murder. The public is interested in why serial, spree, and mass murderers commit their acts, but the media's only responsibility in supersizing is to impart newsworthy information to the public. The legal, behavior, and law enforcement professionals are responsible for clarity about actions and issues of multiple murderers.

The categorization of multiple murderers does enhance our understanding of this phenomenon. By defining each category (serial, spree, and mass), we begin to label the actions of these individuals and elaborate on their criminal behavior and activity and to define causation, because individual motives are the catalysts for different types of behavior.

Dr. Dupont-Morales criticizes the law enforcement approach of degenerating death to the quantification of murders, by using technology, and geographic and psychological profiling. She further believes that the law enforcement experts and technological advancements have not aided in the prevention of multicide. I believe that the law enforcement experts and the psychological and geographic techniques are investigative tools to assist in apprehension of suspects and the prevention of further unnecessary deaths. These tools are not meant to be the only processes for dealing with multiple murders but rather part of an overall comprehensive approach toward understanding and resolving multicide. Analysis of the crime and the use of technology can provide information and assistance to save lives by earlier detection and apprehension, but it cannot change or prevent the initial behavior of the murderer.

Dr. Dupont-Morales believes that law enforcement officials could not catch Andrew Cunanan and that he provided the break in his case by his self-imposed death. I argue that Cunanan's suicide was a direct result of the supersizing and publicizing of his murders by law enforcement agencies and the media. An atmosphere was created in which he could no longer safely practice his killing acts. Fleeing the country unrecognized was impossible. Another option was to surrender and face life imprisonment or the death penalty. He selected the act of suicide as his escape, which was consistent with his personality.

Dr. Dupont-Morales's third point involving rage as a predictor of multicide is very viable. Yet I believe that her statement about society dealing with rage as prevention of further victimization is very naive. Rage contributes to many forms of deviant and undesirable behavior other than multiple murder. In the case of multicide, many of the murderers do not publicly or privately exhibit rage before their first criminal act. Thus, the identification and treatment of enraged individuals as a preventive measure is extremely difficult, if not impossible. Treatment would require that the individuals voluntarily solicit help and assistance for themselves. In individuals enmeshed in the psychological fantasies of serial murderers or the extreme emotional beliefs of terrorists, the probability of seeking self-treatment for their rage is very low. Therefore, society's first opportunity to treat and respond to this rage is at the onset of their criminal activity. Identification for treatment begins with apprehension, which is a product of investigative techniques and criminal analysis of the crime scene evidence.

Supersizing may encourage sensationalism and categorization rather than authentic inquiry, but until murderers are identified and apprehended, and their crime scenes are analyzed, we cannot begin to understand the causation behind their murderous acts. Identification and apprehension are key in the prevention of multicide.

Should Official (Government) Statistics Be the Primary Source for Research on American Terrorism?

Brent L. Smith, Ph.D., is Professor of Justice Sciences and Sociology and Chair, Department of Justice Sciences, at The University of Alabama at Birmingham. His research on terrorism has appeared in *Criminology, Justice Quarterly, Studies in Conflict and Terrorism, Terrorism: An International Journal,* and other scholarly publications. He has frequently provided congressional testimony to the Judiciary Subcommittee on Crime in hearings on American terrorism, and he was an invited discussant at the National Research Council's specially convened meeting on American terrorism in 1996. Dr. Smith is the author of *Terror in America: Pipe Bombs and Pipe Dreams,* State University of New York Press, 1994.

Mark Hamm, Ph.D., is Professor of Criminology at Indiana State University. His most recent books include *Apocalypse in Oklahoma: Waco and Ruby Ridge Revenged* and *Ethnography at the Edge: Crime, Deviance, and Field Research* with Jeff Ferrell. He continues his work on political violence.

YES

Brent L. Smith

This question is reminiscent of the debate between Edwin Sutherland and Paul Tappan over fifty years ago. At that time, Edwin Sutherland (1945) launched an initiative suggesting that government statistics on white collar (primarily corporate) crime were flawed: that they tended to grossly underrepresent the actual volume of white collar crime because most white collar offenses were handled by regulating agencies and rectified through administrative action. Sutherland advocated that these offenses be labeled, identified, and counted as white collar crimes. Tappan (1947), in contrast, argued that the definition of crime is provided by criminal law, and as such, criminologists are obligated to study what society defines as criminal, rather than to create or advance their own definitions regarding what should or should not be considered criminal. To some extent, the debate reflected differences of opinion regarding the role of criminology and criminologists— whether we were to be "activists" helping to shape the definitions of crime and criminality or whether we were to be detached empiricists studying crime and its causation for purely scientific reasons. Most students of this debate would have to acknowledge that Sutherland won.

Since that time, official statistics have come to be questioned extensively, and when used in contemporary empirical research, they always come with a caveat regarding their source and limitations. Our healthy distrust of "official" statistics, however, can occasionally lead us astray from an important source and method of studying crime. Governmental data on terrorism are classic examples of misplaced avoidance of the use of official statistics.

The problem with avoiding official statistics on terrorism is twofold. First, it creates tremendous conceptual problems for an area of study struggling to emerge from a highly tainted past. Second, the tendency to avoid governmental statistics has precluded the development of a respectable, empirically based literature on terrorism. Each of these areas deserves additional comment.

Conceptual Difficulties in Studying Terrorism

Unlike robbery, murder, rape, or other legally defined criminal offenses, the definition of terrorism is rather ambiguous. Officially, there is no crime called "terrorism."[1] The reasons for this are myriad, but the overwhelming reason involves conflict between traditional academic definitions of terrorism and legal definitions of terrorism. Most academic definitions of terrorism typically include "violence or the threatened use of violence to achieve political or social goals." Almost everyone would agree that "political motive" is one of the salient features of any definition of terrorism. However, including "motive" as an essential element of a criminal offense, as scholars do in defining terrorism, raises serious constitutional questions when we attempt to legislate those academic definitions into the legal codes (Smith, 1984).

Efforts to transform academic definitions of terror into legal definitions have been doomed when subjected to constitutional scrutiny. Law must go beyond the goals of empirical study, and decisions must be made regarding the social acceptability of an act, subsequently rendering empirical definitions unworkable. Only one state, California, has attempted to criminalize terrorism explicitly by including as an essential element of the offense that the crime was motivated by a desire "to achieve social or political goals."[2] That statute was subsequently challenged because of its attempt to criminalize motive. A California Supreme Court decision,

People v. *Mirmirani,* held that the phrase "to achieve social or political goals" was unconstitutionally vague.[3]

Consequently, with the exception of "terroristic threatening" statutes, which bear little relation to what most scholars would label and define as terroristic, most states and the federal government have avoided the creation of "terrorism-specific" statutes (Smith, 1988). Congress responded to this dilemma by focusing on target selection rather than motive as the defining element of terrorism as it grappled with the implementation of new federal statutes involving terrorism (Federal Criminal Code and Rules, 1995).[4] These statutes are very limited in nature, however, and have been applied sparingly. Timothy McVeigh and Terry Nichols may have been the first to be prosecuted under subsections of these statutes.

This problem of developing a legal definition of terrorism that is acceptable to academicians studying terrorism is both a cause and a consequence of the conceptual difficulties that plague the terrorism literature. The absence of an acceptable legal definition has generally precluded the use of traditional research methods among terrorism scholars. As a result, the absence of readily available government data has led some scholars to create their own empirical data sets of terrorist groups, persons, or incidents. Unfortunately, these data sets vary substantially regarding what is included as terroristic. Slight variations in the definition of terrorism become critical when practically applied. The recent proliferation of hate groups, militias, single-issue extremists, lone crusaders, and occasional violent activists further muddies the waters regarding which behaviors should be counted as acts of terrorism. To suggest that the political or ideological persuasions of the researcher do not affect the decision-making process regarding which behaviors to include as terroristic is both naive and unwise (Smith, 1994). The old cliché "one man's terrorist is another man's freedom fighter" applies to scholars of terrorism as well. Consequently, data on terrorism available for analysis may disproportionately focus, for example, on right-wing extremism, while ignoring a plethora of politically motivated violence by other groups. Other data sets specifically exclude hate crimes, crimes against abortion clinics, and bombings that cannot be attributed to a specific group. Although these definitions may be appropriate in practice, results from these studies provide little opportunity for comparative analysis on which to build a credible body of scholarly literature.

This approach is reminiscent of early uses of self-report efforts to study delinquency. Differences in questionnaires and definitions of offenses rendered comparative and trend analysis impossible. It was impossible to determine whether delinquency was increasing or decreasing from year to year because of variations in methodology and questionnaire construction. It was not until such studies became standardized (e.g., the National Youth Study) that comparisons became possible. Terrorism research currently reflects a "prestandardized" phase in our empirical endeavors.

The problem created by variations in definitions of terrorism is compounded by another problem of equal importance. The creation and utilization of nongovernmental definitions and data sources excludes an important element in our understanding of what constitutes terrorism—the government. Although Becker's (1963) description of the labeling process is, in many ways, an indictment of official statistics, it suggests that to adequately understand a phenomenon such as deviance (or in this case, terrorism), research should include all elements of the decision-making process—the rule makers and rule enforcers as well as the rule breakers. Terrorism, to paraphrase Becker, is defined by those who have the power to do so. The use of official statistics on terrorism reveals a great deal about what the polity defines as terroristic, what it believes is an appropriate method for intervening, and how severely these behaviors should be sanctioned. Like Becker (1963:155–162) suggested regarding the selective enforcement of rules, the volume of potentially defined terroristic behavior far exceeds what the polity is able to enforce and prosecute. Once defined and labeled as terroristic, investigative and prosecutorial resources are allocated in ways that far exceed those for traditional criminality. For those who are selected for prosecution, the government's response is far more concentrated and uncompromising as a result of the application of the label (Smith & Damphousse, 1996; 1998).

Patterns of governmental discretion in labeling and prosecuting terrorism are critical to understanding the lethal "cat and mouse" game that is played between the polity and terrorist groups. The way in which government defines the motives of alleged perpetrators clearly affects their strategies for investigation and intervention. We only need to recall incidents at Waco and Ruby Ridge to remind ourselves that the definitions government applies to people (correctly or incorrectly) affect the manner in which they are perceived by enforcement agents. The level of fear experienced by agents, the perceived dangerousness of the group, and its perceived potential for violence all affect the way in which governmental agencies respond to these groups. Terrorists respond in like manner—the motives they attribute to the polity frequently may be traced to an escalating set of symbolic catalysts—events that, in the eyes of the terrorists, pushed them over the threshold to violence.

This is not to suggest that harsh and uncompromising actions by the polity are inappropriate, but merely to relate that for every governmental action against terrorism, terrorists will evaluate and take what they perceive to be a rational and complementary action. Waco, Ruby Ridge, the execution of white supremacist Richard Snell on April 19, 1995—all will be forever linked to the Oklahoma City bombing. Other examples abound. Our European cousins discovered twenty years ago that virtually every major terrorist attack, hostage taking, or airline hijacking would be accompanied by demands for the release of convicted terrorists throughout Europe. Passage of the Extra-Territorial Jurisdiction Act in 1987 ensured that the United States would eventually hold its share of international terrorists in American prisons. The 1996 bombing of American airmen in Saudi Arabia was accompanied by threats of more bombings if the release of persons successfully prosecuted in the 1993 World Trade Center bombing was not forthcoming.

Symbolic catalysts, usually in the form of some governmental response, propel the interactions between terrorists and government. Frequently, the application of an official label as being a terrorist initiates this process. Studying terrorism without taking into account how government defines and responds to such behaviors trivializes a major actor in this interaction process. The only method to study this process is through the use of "officially designated" terrorists.

The Nonempirical Basis of the Terrorism Literature

The conceptual problems discussed above occur primarily because of the paucity of available official statistics from which to study terrorism. Scholars searching for ways to empirically study terrorism have been thwarted on every side. Consequently, some scholars resorted to the creation or use of terrorism statistics derived from nongovernmental definitions of terrorism. The variation in what is included or counted as terroristic in such empirical works, however, is substantial. Each published work on terrorism seems to compound the vagueness of the concept rather than provide conceptual clarity to the subject.[5] Others have turned to more limited case studies, ethnographic, or ethnomethodological approaches to the study of terrorism. Although all of these strategies clearly have their place in the criminological literature, they cannot substitute for an official measure of terroristic behavior in our country.

Why are official statistics so difficult to obtain? The answer is twofold. The first involves our previous discussion of the manner in which terrorists are prosecuted. The typical strategy employed in the prosecution of terrorists involves what Turk (1982) describes as "exceptional vagueness," a strategy Turk suggests is a governmental attempt to prevent the public from an understanding of the extent of social conflict in society. In contrast, federal prosecutors and theorists of different persuasions are less willing to impute such ulterior motives to the government. They suggest, instead, that federal prosecutorial strategies merely reflect a pragmatic method of social control. Whatever the reason, terrorists are generally tried as conventional criminals for a variety of federal offenses (Smith and Orvis, 1993).

Consequently, these criminal cases are submerged in the federal case files with no distinguishing feature that identifies them as having been part of a federal terrorism or domestic security investigation. Pulling these cases from the federal court caseloads for analysis is synonymous to the proverbial needle in the haystack. As a result, most studies of the demographic, psychological, or sociological characteristics of American terrorists have been based on samples of nonconfirmed or unofficial terrorists.

The FBI is restricted from releasing the names of persons investigated under the Counterterrorism Program. Even the number of terrorism investigations opened in the United States annually is classified. Although a study of the process of becoming a terrorist (from initial criminal behavior to investigation, indictment, and finally, sentencing) would be a fascinating study, all of us would have to acknowledge that a release of names of those investigated under the Counterterrorism Program would be an invasion of privacy. Clearly, many of those investigated are never indicted. But what of those who are indicted? Their names and federal criminal case files become part of the public record.

In the late 1980s, we were fortunate to be able to obtain a list of persons officially investigated and indicted through the FBI's Counterterrorism Program for the 1980s. Since that time, however, the FBI has been restricted from the compilation of lists of persons for purposes other than which they were originally intended (i.e., a federal criminal investigation). Despite the fact that these persons were indicted and their case files are available for perusal at federal court houses or regional archives, the compilation of such lists has been interpreted as a potential violation of the Privacy Act. Until some mechanism is created for the identification of officially designated terrorism cases in the United States, empirical analyses of American terrorism are not forthcoming. Discussants at a special planning meeting on terrorism sponsored by the National Research Council's Committee on Law and Justice concluded that the literature on terrorism is largely theoretical and nonempirical and that our understanding of the phenomenon is marginal at best. It will remain so until official records and statistics become available for analysis.

NOTES

1. Although Chapter 113B of the Federal Criminal Code and Rules is entitled "Terrorism," the offenses defined therein do not use political motive as an essential element of the offense, focusing instead on target selection as a mechanism for enhanced sentencing (Federal Rules, 1995:763).

2. California Penal Code 11.5.422.422.5 (1977).

3. *People* v. *Mirmirani,* 636-PZ-d (California, 1982).

4. See Chapter 113B, Sections 2331–2339, particularly Section 2332a, Criminal Penalties, Use of Weapons of Mass Destruction.

5. See Wardlaw, G. (1989). *Political Terrorism.* (New York: Cambridge University Press,) for a good review of the conceptual difficulties regarding the study of terrorism.

REFERENCES

Administrative Office of the United States Courts: Committee on Rules. (1995). *Federal Criminal Code and Rules: 1995.* St. Paul, MN: West.

Becker, H. (1963). *Outsiders: Studies in the sociology of deviance.* New York: Free Press.

Smith, B. L. (1984). State antiterrorism legislation in the United States: Problems and implications. *Terrorism: An International Journal, 7* (2), 213–231.

Smith, B. L. (1988). State antiterrorism legislation in the United States: A review of statutory utilization. *Conflict Quarterly, 8* (1), 29–47.

Smith, B. L. (1994). *Terrorism in America: Pipe bombs and pipe dreams.* Albany: State University of New York.

Smith, B. L., & Damphousse, K. R. (1998). Punishing political offenders: The effect of political motive on federal sentencing decisions. *Criminology, 36* (1), 67–92.

Smith, B. L., & Damphousse, K. R. (1998). Terrorism, politics, and punishment: A test of structural-contextual theory and the liberation hypothesis. *Criminology, 35* (1).

Smith, B. L., & Orvis, G. P. (1993). America's response to terrorism: An empirical analysis of federal intervention strategies during the 1980s. *Justice Quarterly, 10* (4), 663–683.

Sutherland, E. (1945). Is white collar crime crime? *American Sociological Review, 10,* 132–139.

Tappan, P. (1947). Who is the criminal? *American Sociological Review, 12,* 96–102.

Turk, A. (1982). *Political criminality: The defiance and defense of authority.* Newbury Park, CA: Sage.

Wardlaw, G. (1989). *Political terrorism.* New York: Cambridge University Press.

Rejoinder to Dr. Smith

MARK HAMM

Although Professor Smith is an articulate and respected advocate of official statistics for the quantitative study of domestic terrorism, he does more to identify the shortcomings of those numbers than to praise their utility. So we agree on that point: Official statistics are freighted with problems. But we disagree on a question of tenacity: I want to abandon them altogether in favor of case studies, but Professor Smith continues to see value in official statistics for scholastic and policy purposes. I see several flaws in his line of reasoning.

Conceptual Difficulties

The first problem relates to Professor Smith's conception of criminology's role in providing legislatures with an academically sound definition of terrorism. Problems arise "when we [criminologists] attempt to legislate...academic definitions into the legal codes." I ask you this: What other area of crime control policy has ever been influenced by academic definitions of criminality?

Here in Indiana, we have laws on the books against white collar crime—embezzlement, fraud, and so forth. Indiana was also home to the legendary criminologists Edwin Sutherland and Donald Cressey when they wrote their influential books on white collar crime. But nowhere is there any evidence to suggest that Sutherland and Cressey's academic definition was ever used to formulate white collar crime laws in Indiana or any other state. Criminologists have developed well-reasoned definitions of aggravated assault, rape, and hate crime. But again there is no evidence that those definitions have ever influenced the formulation of criminal law. So why would we expect criminologists to have a professional obligation to influence terrorism laws?

We are not surprised to learn then, as Professor Smith writes, that "Efforts to transform academic definitions of terror into legal definitions have been doomed." They will probably stay that way. Criminologists must learn to live with it and get on with their studies.

A second problem relates to a sort of hierarchy of research methods identified by Professor Smith. "The absence of an acceptable legal definition," he writes, "has precluded the use of traditional research methods among terrorism scholars." The implication here is that "traditional methods" are somehow superior to nontraditional ones. Independently created data sets (of terrorist groups, persons, and incidents), ethnographies, and case studies are all seen as "limited"—they take a backseat to traditional empirical analysis.

Professor Smith claims that "results from these [methods] provide little opportunity for comparative analysis." I disagree. Much has been learned about terroristic violence, for example, from comparative ethnographic case studies of skinhead gangs in both the United States (see Blazak, 1995; Prichard & Starr, 1994) and Europe (Hamm, 1994; Lööw, 1994). In fact, the Guggenheim Foundation recently sponsored an international symposium to share and disseminate results from these sorts of studies.

A third problem relates to what I think is a friendly disagreement on the overall goal of terrorism research. Professor Smith sees the symbolic catalysts of terrorism—"events that, in the eyes of the terrorists, pushed them over the threshold to violence"—as a byproduct of a labeling process initiated by lawmakers in the absence of sound academic thinking concerning, again, the legal definition of terrorism. The solution? Come up with a better definition of terrorism.

I am at once more pessimistic and more optimistic than Professor Smith. In my view, nothing that can be done to craft more intelligent terrorism laws. They are what they are and, once more, we should learn to live with them. Conversely, the identification of symbolic catalysts, or what I choose to call grievances, is one of the most exciting challenges now facing terrorism researchers. As Professor Smith notes, the Oklahoma City bombing will be forever linked to Waco, Ruby Ridge, and the execution of Richard Snell on April 19, 1995. Which incident, which grievance, played the greatest role in McVeigh's decision to cross the line into terrorism? And which grievance will continue to dominate the paranoid conspiracies of the radical right as we head toward the millennium? Have any new grievances been added to the mix, such as the death penalty being handed down in the McVeigh case? But perhaps most importantly, has law enforcement learned anything from past mistakes to avoid new grievances? Was the FBI's decision to wait "with endless patience" outside the Freemen compound in Jordan, Montana, the result of lessons learned at Waco? Most analysts agree that it was.

The Nonempirical Basis of Terrorism Literature

"Scholars searching for ways to empirically study terrorism," laments Professor Smith, "have been thwarted on every side." So have scholars relying on ethnographic and case study approaches. Terrorism research is not easy. It never has been and never will be. We should learn to live with it. We should learn how to turn this difficulty into a collective struggle for all manner of better information—empirical, ethnographic, and historical. But I disagree with my contemporary on how to reach that goal. Although all good quantitative and qualitative studies have their place in the criminological literature, Professor Smith argues that these studies "cannot substitute for an official measure of terroristic behavior in our country."

For the sake of argument, let us say that we did have an official measure of American terrorism that passed academic scrutiny. That still would not solve the data access problem. A better definition of terrorism would not ensure more reliable, more easily accessible information on terrorism or terrorists. It would not improve by one iota what we know about grievances. I suggest that what we truly lack is not a sound definition, or not even information on terrorism. What we lack is the intellectual resolve to make terrorism research a respected area of criminological inquiry—as respected, say, as homicide research, death penalty research, or domestic violence research. And that, in the end, is the result of a gatekeeper problem, a problem that could have profound consequences in the years ahead.

Professor Smith ends his chapter with a comment about a special planning meeting on terrorism sponsored by the National Research Council in 1996. The heavyweights at that meeting—the chairman and past chairmen—concluded that our understanding of terrorism suffered from a lack of empirical and theoretical understanding about the phenomenon. These decision makers shared two things in common: All were distinguished past presidents of the American Society of Criminology, and none had ever studied terrorism. The result of their deliberations? To recommend no future funding for terrorism research. This is logic only a politician could love. Because our knowledge of terrorism is limited, we should limit resources for terrorism research. Ronald Reagan made the same mistake about AIDS. By the time his administration recognized the enormous threat to public health of the HIV virus and began funding AIDS research, the virus had spread to 163 nations on five continents, where it would eventually infect and kill an estimated 15 million people. I think Professor Smith and I agree on this conclusion:

Erroneous doctrines perpetrated by intelligent men and women can yield greater errors in magnitude than simple ignorance.

REFERENCES

Blazak, R. (1995). *The suburbanization of hate: An ethnographic study of the skinhead subculture.* Unpublished doctoral dissertation, Emory University, Atlanta.

Hamm, M. S. (1994). Conceptualizing hate crime in a global context. In M. S. Hamm (Ed.), *Hate crime: International perspectives on causes and control.* Cincinnati: ACJS/Anderson.

Lööw, H. (1994). The cult of violence: The Swedish racist counterculture. In T. Bjorgo & R. Witte (Eds.), *Racist violence in Europe.* New York: St. Martin's.

Prichard, F., & Starr, J. M., (1994). Skinheads in New Orleans. *Humanity & Society, 18,* 19–36.

NO

MARK HAMM

Kingman, Arizona—It is the young white boys I look out for, especially the skinheads. This is why I am running in the first place. They see me coming down McVicar Avenue in my red Che Guevara t-shirt, headbanded hair blowing in the wind. I have a Walkman on, listening to a bootleg tape of a Grateful Dead show live at Madison Square Garden, really loud. I don't choose my euphoria lightly— "Sugar Magnolia" makes me strong and proud as I run down the ten extended blocks of trailer homes along McVicar. This is the kind of heartless boulevard you find in parts of cities where things are guarded and tense and it feels like there's about to be a killing. A good day for the Grateful Dead.

The skinheads have words to say and gestures to make or mean looks to look. I smile and pass by. But most of the time there's nothing happening at all. To those white guys over there leaning on a chain link fence, or those guys fixing a broken down pickup truck, I'm simply a ghost—a quick shadow passing over the sad asphalt of a late Tuesday afternoon.

It's the dogs, though, the Rottweilers, that you really have to watch for— dumb animals when suburbanized, all muscle and blood. They reinforce the sense that you are surrounded by a truly violent society.

The Rottweilers make me slow down. I ease into a walk and put out a peaceful vibe. But I don't run because of them. It's the white boys who make me run. I run for the guys drinking beer in trailer homes or garages—I want them to think I'm running for the love of running. Yes sir! I'm a runner, you see, getting my miles in. That's how I protect myself here in Kingman. I've found that it draws less suspicion than driving down the street in a rental car with out-of-state license plates, windows up, eyes fixed straight ahead, scared shitless. That is dangerous. But I run because what I'm really after is that gaggle of junked cars down at the end of McVicar, cars that double as social clubs for local teenagers. One of those cars was called the "fort" by a young drifter known around here as the "Desert Rat."

Timothy McVeigh was the Desert Rat. And this is a story about doing research on the heart of evil.

Official Statistics

American terrorism is a subject best examined through the case study approach. Even official statistics bear this out. The most recent FBI report on terrorism in the United States (the government's official publication on domestic terrorism) shows that there were a total of six acts of right-wing terrorism in the United States between 1982 and 1994 (FBI, 1996). Any student of research methods knows that six incidences do not provide enough statistical power to establish grounds for quantitative criminology. But more importantly, official statistics do not even begin to capture the full magnitude and horror of terroristic violence. No case in the nation's history demonstrates this better than the Oklahoma City bombing.

Official statistics for the year 1995 will be made public sometime during 1998. When that report appears, it will count the bombing of the Oklahoma City federal building as one incident of right-wing terrorism. And that will be it. The report will mention nothing about the three-month trial of Timothy McVeigh and the nearly five-thousand pages of transcripts that it produced. It will say nothing about the testimony of some 250 witnesses in that trial, nor will it mention the 21,000 interviews conducted by the FBI for McVeigh's grand jury hearing. It will say nothing about the five thousand photographs of the bomb site or the three hundred-page inventory of telephone calls made by McVeigh and his co-conspirators. Beyond that, it will fail to mention the fact that McVeigh's truck bomb killed 168 defenseless men, women, and children (Hamm, 1996). It will fail to mention the fact that another one thousand were grievously injured. And because of its crude quantification of the bombing (one incident), it will overlook this heartbreaking fact: Because McVeigh detonated the bomb beneath the day care center of the federal building, the blast instantly killed nineteen babies. They never had a chance. Their human remains, tiny arms and legs, were found a block away.

From what universe beyond the one that most of us inhabit does this kind of evil arise? You will not find the answer in official statistics. But you may catch a glimpse of it in the fort at the end of McVicar Avenue.

Toward an Integrated Methodology

The fact of the matter is that American terrorism is so complex in its criminality, so freighted with emotions in its social and political import, and so utterly impenetrable in terms of reliable data, that any responsible researcher must use multiple research methods. Indeed, studies show that terrorism is caused by powerful contemporary social impulses (Aho, 1990; Barkun, 1994; Kraska, 1998; Smith, 1994), and understanding those impulses demands collecting a wealth of evidence on both terrorism (a criminal behavior) and terrorists (criminals). Thus, journalistic sources, trial transcripts, official documents, original fieldwork, and narrative analysis all become legitimate research tools for re-creating the texture and situated meaning of terrorism. Traditionally, the case study is the vehicle through which this amalgam of information is presented to the academic community and the general public alike (Coates, 1987; Flynn and Gerhardt, 1989; Hamm, 1993; Kaplan, 1995). By deeply probing into one case, we are able to compare it with others. At the center of this inquiry, of course, lies the issue of causality. And causality, it bears emphasizing, is altogether ignored in official statistics.

In the case of Oklahoma City, most observers have located motive in Timothy McVeigh's outrage over the deadly use of state force against the Branch Davidians at Waco, Texas, on April 19, 1993. That is certainly true. McVeigh himself has confessed to taking "responsibility for the bombing," adding that he was motivated by his anger over Waco (Hamm, 1997, p. 121). However, the bombing was such a momentous event that it now seems barely discernable as a criminal event. In fact, professional organizations, such as the American Society of Criminology and the Academy of Criminal Justice Sciences, have not given the bombing anything near the serious attention those groups gave to the O. J. Simpson case. This is because in actuality the Oklahoma City bombing was a concatenation of hundreds of events—all of the choices and actions by federal agents at Waco, the multitude of steps taken by McVeigh on his long journey from disaffected Gulf War veteran to terrorist, law enforcement malfeasance, the rise of the American militia movement, the widespread availability of bomb-making manuals and other terrorist literature through cyberspace, and the proliferation of crystal methamphetamine along McVicar Avenue (Hamm, 1997; 1998a). For all of this, when taken together, there is simply no historical precedent. That is what sets the Oklahoma City bombing apart from any other act of American terrorism, making it a unique criminological case.

The Ethnography of Terror

Quantitative studies of domestic terrorism are wholly derivative of official versions of reality; they represent little more than secondhand observations of the criminal event—observations that are usually passed from one source to the next without the benefit of serious criminological inquiry. Howard S. Becker (1994, p. 210) has written that "the basic operation of studying society is the production and refinement of an image of the thing we are studying." No amount of secondary analysis can ever enhance the criminological image of McVeigh killing those babies.

However, we can improve that image with a healthy dose of materialistic detail derived from a methodology of attentiveness; or, from what elsewhere has been termed criminological verstehen—a method that bridges the old dualisms of researcher and research situations by using the researcher's own experiences and emotions as avenues into the meanings of the situation and the experiences of the subjects of study (Ferrell & Hamm, 1998). Not only does this method promise to improve our image of the terroristic event, it also has the potential to redirect discussion toward particularities of place and spirit (Hamm, 1998b).

***

When I reach the fort, the place is vacant. I see only the artifacts of teenage wasteland—broken beer bottles, spent shell casings, empty Krylon paint cans, a used condom. Most of the cars are marked with graffiti. The left quarter panel of an old Datsun pickup reads, "Smoke Blunts and Fuck Em."

There's no way to determine exactly which of the dozen or so abandoned cars was McVeigh's fort. But at least I've made the effort to locate it, which is more than you can say for the collectors, the disseminators, and the interpreters of official statistics on terrorism in America. At any rate, I've crawled inside one of them—a faded-blue 1975 Toyota with no tires, no doors. It sits on the desolate floor of the Mojave Desert, where the winds have blown constantly for the past 5 million years. This has invested the place with a bewitching allure of beauty and disaster. Inside the Toyota, it feels like some sort of netherworld—I'm inside a bright blue centerlight of evil. It's like virtually crawling under the skin of Timothy McVeigh.

So, it is in this way—through a criminological verstehen—that perhaps we can come to fully appreciate the situated meaning of a letter written by McVeigh, here at the fort, to Kevin Nicholas some four weeks before McVeigh committed the greatest act of terrorism in American history. As you will see, McVeigh—like so many transplanted Easterners and Midwesterners living in the Mojave—became ill at ease because of the strong winds, the constant winds. "Let me try to explain," says McVeigh:[1]

> I was in the educational/literature dissemination (desert wind is wreaking havoc on my already scratching writing) field for quite some time. I was preaching and 'passing out' before anyone had ever heard the words 'patriot' and 'militia.' Just got out of the wind.

By this time, McVeigh had left the fort and walked up McVicar to Michael Fortier's trailer. There, out of the winds, and in the comfort of Fortier's home, the mood of McVeigh's writing becomes more radical, invested with euphoria—the euphoria of crystal methamphetamine use:

> Onward and upward. I passed on that legacy about 2 years ago. I believe 'new blood' needs to start somewhere; and I have certain other 'militant' talents that are short in supply and greatly demanded.

McVeigh's "militant talents" would soon cause the slaughter in Oklahoma City. Official statistics fail to capture such lived politics. After rambling on for two more pages—about such things as a super computer in Belgium that is tracking his every move—McVeigh delivers his penultimate statement of meth-induced paranoia:

> Hell, you only live once, and I KNOW you know it's better to burn out, then...rot away in some nursing home. My philosophy is the same—in only a short 1–2 years, my body will slowly start giving away.... Might as well do some good while I can be 100 percent effective!

It is a desperate statement coming from an otherwise healthy twenty-six-year-old American white man. Sadly, like so many junkies, it signals a sudden atrophy of the mind and body. This is the end.

> My whole mindset has shifted, from intellectual to...animal (Rip the bastards heads off and shit down their necks!), and I'll show you how...

Seeya,

The Desert Rat

Note

1. *United States of America* v. *Timothy James McVeigh*. Trial transcript, May 5, 1997, pp. 42–43.

References

Aho, J. A. (1990). *The politics of righteousness: Idaho Christian patriotism.* Seattle: University of Washington Press.

Barkun, M. (1994). *Religion and the racist right: The origins of the Christian identity movement.* Chapel Hill/London: University of North Carolina Press.

Becker, H. S. (1994). Cases, causes, conjunctures, stories, and imagery. In C. C. Ragin and H. S. Becker (Eds.), *What Is a Case? Exploring the Foundations of Social Inquiry.* New York: Cambridge University Press.

Coates, J. (1987). *Armed and dangerous: The rise of the survivalist right.* New York: Noonday.

FBI. (1996). *Terrorism in the United States.* Washington, DC: U.S. Department of Justice.

Ferrell, J., & Hamm, M. S. (1998). Introduction: Crime, deviance, and field research. In J. Ferrell and M. S. Hamm (Eds.), *Ethnography at the edge: Crime, deviance, and field research.* Boston: Northeastern University Press.

Flynn, K., & Gerhardt, G. (1989). *The silent brotherhood: Inside America's racist underground.* New York: Free Press.

Hamm, M. S. (1993). *American skinheads: The criminology and control of hate crime.* Westport, CT/London: Praeger.

Hamm, M. S. (1996). *Terrorism, hate crime, and anti-government violence.* Washington, DC: National Research Council.

Hamm, M. S. (1997). *Apocalypse in Oklahoma: Waco and Ruby Ridge revenged.* Boston: Northeastern University Press.

Hamm, M. S. (1998a). Tragic irony: State malfeasance and the Oklahoma City bombing conspiracy. *The Critical Criminologist, 8* (2), 10–15.

Hamm, M. S. (1998b). The ethnography of terror: Timothy McVeigh and the blue centerlight of evil. In J. Ferrell and M. S. Hamm (Eds.), *Ethnography at the edge: Crime, deviance, and field research.* Boston: Northeastern University Press.

Kaplan, J. (1995). Right-wing violence in North America. *Terrorism and Political Violence, 7,* 44–95.

Kraska, P. B. (1998). Review Essay on Mark S. Hamm's Apocalypse in Oklahoma: Waco and Ruby Ridge Revenged. *Justice Quarterly* (forthcoming).

Smith, B. L. (1994). *Terrorism in America: Pipe bombs and pipe dreams.* Albany, NY: SUNY Press.

Rejoinder to Dr. Hamm
BRENT L. SMITH

Professor Mark Hamm's insightful description of Timothy McVeigh and the Oklahoma City bombing are of significant importance to the study of terrorism. In many ways, I suspect that Professor Hamm and I bear more marked similarities than differences in our assessment of needs for the study of terrorism. Perhaps, most importantly, I should clarify what I refer to as official statistics. Professor Hamm is correct in asserting that, because of the small number of incidents, an analysis of the number of terrorist incidents actually committed in the United States is so small that statistical inferences are meaningless. I include in the official statistics category, however, the number of persons investigated, the number of persons indicted, and all court records and official documents pertaining to these investigations or criminal cases. For example, an analysis of persons indicted as a result of FBI investigations of terrorism-related activities will render samples large enough for statistical analysis. They also provide insight into the types of groups investigated, their motivations, and group characteristics. Although one step removed from interviews with terrorists, court records contain a wealth of information gleaned from interviews with the alleged terrorists, their neighbors, friends, law enforcement agents, and attorneys.

The major issue, however, is whether official statistics should be the primary source for data collection on terrorism and terrorists. Perhaps a better way to put it is that official statistics (i.e., governmental identification of those persons officially labeled as involved in terrorism) should be the starting point for a study of American terrorism. Indeed, if we peruse the case studies of American terrorist groups in recent years, we find that most of these case studies, including Professor Hamm's, began with a person or group officially investigated or indicted for terrorism-related activities as a result of an FBI investigation under the Counterterrorism Program.

Beyond this, perhaps it is useful to put these differing methodologies in perspective. Table 4.1 provides somewhat of a polar representation, but it does delineate the major issues in the debate. The major issue (and one that has been debated for many years) involves the need for the scholar to rely on quantifiable data (which, in the past, has usually meant official statistics) to avoid the potential of biased conclusions. In addition, Professor Hamm makes the point that causality, it bears emphasizing, is altogether ignored in official statistics. Although this may be correct when considering the statistics to which Professor Hamm has reference, such is not the case when considering official statistics in general. Official statistics (i.e., statistics generated from official records) come in a variety of forms and need not be confined to merely counting the number of terrorist incidents each year. Causal issues are indeed addressed using these statistics, and quantification provides an opportunity for empirical testing of causal relationships.

Despite these differences in methodology, I think Professor Hamm and I have a great deal in common. Both of us recognize that governmental definitions of terrorism influence who is eventually officially labeled as a terrorist. Given the political nature of terrorism, we both acknowledge that a study of both the offender and the polity's response are necessary to adequately understand the phenomenon. Similarly, I think it safe to say that both of us have used official statistics as a reference point from which to orient our research. Finally, both of us recognize the need for integrative or combined methodologies to verify our findings. For example, I have found it extremely useful to refer to the case studies of other scholars, including Professor Hamm's, to verify or discount a statistical pattern that has emerged in my analyses of official court or sentencing records. Likewise, I assume that Professor Hamm has found that patterns of behavior identified in statistical studies derived from official data have been useful tools with which to formulate research hypotheses relevant to the case study method.

TABLE 4.1 **Methodological Issues in the Study of Terrorism**

Methodology	Strengths	Weaknesses
Use of Official Statistics	Provides some indication of the governmental assessment of the phenomenon	Unless closely scrutinized, the method may fail to detect subtle changes in governmental definitions of the phenomenon.
	Provides a benchmark for comparative and trend analysis	Reductionism B, a tendency to reduce a complex social problem to analysis of a few quantifiable variables.
	Allows quantification of data for the testing of macro-level propositions and hypotheses	Overreliance on purely quantitative data can result in inadequate assessments and the adoption of inappropriate public policy.
	Provides insight regarding how the polity defines the phenomenon	Is subject to drawing anecdotal conclusions.
Case studies, etc.	Provides a rich texture to criminological research that is simply not possible with official data	Unless carefully screened and quantifiably measured, scholars using case studies have a tendency to focus analyses and report conclusions based on outliers (the most outlandish or extreme) rather than on the typical responses in their sample.
	Can identify and measure variables and patterns of behavior not available through an analysis of official data	Difficult to assess trends or patterns over time.
	Can provide deeper insight into the motivation of specific offenders or terrorist groups	Definition of the problem is more subject to the researcher's ideological persuasions unless statistically verified.

I echo Professor Hamm's position on an additional point. Official statistics on American terrorism have been notoriously poor. Scholars studying the phenomenon are forced to take what little official information is available and build empirical data sets from secondary sources. What is desperately needed is a mechanism by which governmental cooperation with terrorism researchers will render data from which both statistical information can be derived and case study methodologies can be developed. Currently, such a mechanism is not in place. Consequently, research on American terrorism, of whatever methodology, is hindered.

Does Law Enforcement Need More Power to Fight the Techno-War against Computer and Credit Card Criminals?

Robert P. McNamara, Ph.D., is Assistant Professor of Sociology at Furman University. He is the author of several books, including *Crime Displacement: The Other Side of Prevention; The Times Square Hustler: Male Prostitution in New York City; Sex, Scams and Street Life: The Sociology of New York City's Times Square; Police and Policing* with Dr. Dennis Kenney; *The Urban Landscape: Selected Readings* with Dr. Kristy McNamara; and *Crossing the Line: Interracial Couples in the South,* with Maria Tempenis and Beth Walton. Dr. McNamara has also written numerous articles on a variety of topics and has been a consultant for state, federal, and private agencies on topics such as AIDS, drug abuse, urban redevelopment, homelessness, policing, and gangs.

Jerome E. Jackson, Ph.D., is Professor of Criminology at California State University in Fresno. His research interests include nonviolent gangs and white-collar crimes. He is book review editor for the *Journal of Criminal Justice Education.*

YES

JEROME E. JACKSON

The ever-changing field of computer technology is a concern that eventually will affect all criminal justice organizations, especially law enforcement agencies. Failure to prepare for anticipated future law enforcement concerns, relative to computers and computer technology, will expose consumers, retailers, and other merchants, as well as the government, to tremendous economic threats and victimization.

Advances in computer technology over the past thirty-five years have been phenomenal. The evolution of this technology from the Univac to the personal computer (PC) has been revolutionary (Pressman & Herron, 1991, p. 76). The plethora of literature concerning the ever-changing high-tech society (Budwey, 1992; Caldwell, 1990; Hanson, 1993; Naizbutt, 1982; Sanders, 1988; Toffler, 1990), continue to mount. This literature points to the wide range of advancements planned for the future. For example, forecasted technological innovations regarding the automobile include the following: (1) Radar/sonar, collision avoidance, (2) in-dash navigation system, (3) complete heads-up windshield display, (4) rear seat and door-mount air bags, and (5) in-car parking structure reservations (Fresno Bee, 1991, p. 8).

For the home of the future, a smart atmosphere consisting of high-tech toilets, automatic window controls, and motorized security cameras (San Francisco Examiner, 1992, p. E4) and automated work stations that control climate, security, and other amenities will be standard (Talarico, 1994). Personal computers will have the ability to recognize human voices in the very near future (Corcoran, 1992, p. 33). Telephones will be carried in the pocket, which will allow one to identify their callers and the nature of the call from any location (Vernaci, 1991, p. E12).

Concomitantly, an information superhighway connected by fiber-optic cable and satellite microwave will join scientists, students, educators, business people, citizens, and others. This superhighway will virtually allow us to communicate and access any number of information sources (Vizard, 1994; World Future Society, 1991).

Today, retail department stores such as Sears and Montgomery Wards are selling computer machines to households. It is estimated that during the late 1980s personal computers were in 20 percent of single-family homes. Eighty percent of American homes will have computers by the year 2000 (Hanna, 1990). Homeowners will be able to shop, bank, communicate, and develop elaborate security measures for home and personal use. Alvin Toffler's (1980) electronic cottage, which focuses on the future of work being performed from the home, is approaching reality.

The potential exists for the resident to leave an electronic message with the police beat officer regarding vacations, meetings, suspicious activity, or crime tips. It is conceivable that some reports to law enforcement could be typed and sent electronically to the police station by the resident.

In essence, technology will continue to grace our existence and provide comfort along with expeditious ways to perform tasks. Unfortunately, the dismal side of high-tech growth accompanies the good. Computer-related crimes are on the rise (Sessions, 1991). A computer or telecommunication system is linked with almost every white collar crime. The advances in computer technology have influenced the development of a number of motivating forces that are of concern to the criminal justice community and to society as a whole.

Definitions

What do we mean when we refer to an offense as a computer crime? Broadly defined, computer crimes include any illegal act involving a computer that may be prosecuted under criminal laws (Conly, 1989). Any violations of criminal law that involve a knowledge of computer technology for their perpetration, investigation, or prosecution is a computer crime.

Computer crime may be costing up to five billion dollars annually (Wilkins, 1994). Computer-related crimes include traditional law violation using a computer. These crimes also encompasses law violating against intellectual property and others that do not fall within the coverage of traditional criminal statutes (Raskin & Schaldach-Paiva, 1996). For example, opportunities for on-line pedophilia have escalated as both pedophiles and children become increasingly computer literate. More than 900,000 computer images were surveyed in a Carnegie study. This study found that 83.5 percent of all computerized photographs available on the internet are pornographic (Rimm, 1995).

Computer-Generated Crime Categories

Drawing on these broad definitions of computer crimes, several categories of computer-generated or computer-related offenses have been identified. Some categories have been developed by giving consideration to the role the computer plays as an instrument in a particular crime. Three major categories have been developed using this criteria. One category, a computer as the subject of a crime, referring to the computer being viewed as the target or object, include such offenses as (1) the theft of intellectual property, or the theft of marketing information (e.g., customer lists, pricing data, or marketing plans); (2) blackmail based on information gained from computerized files (e.g., medical information, personal history, or sexual preference); (3) sabotage of intellectual property, marketing, pricing, or personnel data or sabotage of operating systems and programs; and (4) illegally accessing government or criminal justice records (e.g., changing tax records; unlawfully accessing intelligence files; altering criminal histories, modifying warrant information; or counterfeiting driver's licenses, passports, or other documents for identification purposes. Technological trespass and technological vandalism also fall into this category of computer offending (Raskin & Schaldach-Paiva, 1996).

A second category identifies the computer as the instrument of the crime. In this category, the computer files are not used to facilitate the offense. Instead, the offense is facilitated by the processes of the computer. The offender introduces a different code of instructions into the computer's analytical processes and commits the crime. Computer criminals also use computers as instruments in law violating by converting legitimate computer processes for illegitimate purposes (Raskin & Schaldach-Paiva, 1996). Offenses in this category include fraudulent use of automated teller machine (ATM) cards and accounts; theft of money from accrual, conversion, or transfer accounts; credit card fraud; fraud from computer transactions; and telecommunications fraud. Consider for example the following scenario:

An alleged out-of-state computer hacker was arrested by San Diego Police. The hacker agreed to cooperate with the San Diego Police Department and the FBI in the investigation of an electronic network. As many as one thousand hackers between fourteen and twenty-five years of age had shared information for at least four years. The hackers accessed major computer networks such as Telnet, Signet, and Sprintnet, gaining entry into the computers of national credit card and credit-reporting agencies. One hacker learned how to break personal security codes for Automatic Teller Machines (ATMs). The ring is believed to be based in the East Coast and over time has probably been responsible for the theft of large amounts of money. Mastercard reported $381 million in credit card fraud in 1991, and Visa International lost $259 million in 1989 (Fresno Bee, 1992).

More than 90 percent of all credit card transactions are processed by and through computers. Age and economic status do not appear to be indicators of who will or will not engage in computer crimes. In 1990, a twelve-year-old boy was arrested for breaking into TRW databases, confiscating credit card numbers, and posting them on a computer bulletin board (Scuttlebutt, 1990). Media sources reported in 1993 that the FBI was "investigating Ross Perot's presidential campaign on allegations that workers accessed security codes and broke into computer systems of companies that issued credit reports" (Dallas Morning News, 1992, p. A7). This incident serves to further highlight and support the contention that computer crime potential exists at all levels of the political, social, and economic strata.

Computer crimes and the abuse and fraudulent use of credit cards seem to be directly related offenses in the criminal world. Christopher Dowdell, Assistant Vice President of the Information Technology and Operations Group Chemical Banking Corporation, estimates that instances of fraud employing computers as a tool has been increasing by almost 100 percent annually (LaPolla, 1992). It has been noted that in this country, credit card companies, banks, and retail establishments suffer losses totaling $2 billion annually as the result of credit card abuse and fraud. Total losses incurred by these enterprises amounted to more than $1.9 billion in 1990, 1991, and again in 1992. The prognosis for any reduction in losses during 1993 appears dismal (Jackson, 1993). Sixty percent of all credit card crimes in the United States occur in Los Angeles, California (Jackson, 1994).

Tamaki and Connelly (1992) reported that:

> The combination of computer knowledge and magnetic strip encoding equipment contributes to costly fraud cases committed against the credit card industry. Los Angeles is suffering widespread perpetration of computer and credit card crimes committed by offenders that include teenagers.

The U.S. Secret Service Agency in Los Angeles makes credit card encoding arrests on an almost-weekly basis. Encoding fraud accounted for $39 million in losses in 1989. Criminals obtain valid credit card numbers illegally then sell the numbers to those who in turn encode the magnetic strip on the back of their own credit cards. The solutions to this crime involves comparing the computer-generated receipt with the number on the credit card (pp. B1–42).

The Christmas season is a time when credit card usage is heaviest. "Fraud losses involving Mastercard and Visa cards rose to $92.5 million in January of 1994 from $85.6 million in November 1993. The use of lost or stolen credit cards by thieves accounts for 70 percent of all fraud charges." (Gullo, 1994, p. C2)

Electronic fund transfers are used by people as an alternative to physically taking money out of the country. This is accomplished by depositing money into a bank and then transferring the money electronically to domestic or foreign banks, financial institutions, or security accounts. Normally, money transferred by a wire to Switzerland is prewashed in a third country such as Panama, Luxembourg, or the Bahamas (Webster & McCampbell, 1992).

A third major category of computer crimes includes offenses that can occur without computer technology. That is, computer technology helps the criminal act to occur faster but is not a necessary component for the completion of the offense. This technology permits processing of greater amounts of data and information and increases the difficulty of detecting and tracing the criminal activity. This category includes money laundering and illegal banking transactions, book-making, and organized crime records. In addition, the presence of computers, especially microcomputers, helps to generate new versions of fairly traditional crimes while establishing new crime targets. Counterfeiting and piracy of software, copyright violation of computer programs, and theft of technological equipment are included in this category (Carter, 1995; Raskin & Schaldach-Paiva, 1996).

Still other computer-related crime categories have been established using the apparent motive of the offender as the standard of classification. Branscomb (1990) has identified six motives for committing computer-related crimes:

1. To highlight vulnerabilities in computer security
2. To sabotage
3. To punish or retaliate
4. To engage in computer voyeurism
5. To exhibit technical prowess
6. To assert a philosophy of open access to computer systems

In each of these categories, computers are either the subjects or the objects of law-violating.

Challenges

Select members of the criminal society are moving toward computer usage as the means to their illicit trade. Estimates suggest that computer criminals in the workplace may cost businesses up to $3 billion per year (Coutourie, 1989). Reported computer and telecommunications crime losses amount to $555 million per year, with unreported losses estimated at $5 billion annually (Watson, 1989). Law enforcement is the logical entity to address such abuse; however, its current position is tenuous at best. For example, computer crime is more esoteric and latent than crimes such as burglary or assault. Many law enforcement officers do not understand it, and because it does not place anyone in physical danger, it is likely to receive low priority when it comes to investigation and prosecution efforts.

We find a similar situation regarding the abuse and misuse of credit cards. Eighty percent of Americans use credit cards. Companies such as Visa and Mastercard handle tens of billions of credit card transactions per year. A national Electronic Money Debit Card System is now possible. Money earned can be transferred to an electronic account, and the owner is able to purchase goods and commodities with the debit card (Warwick, 1992). There is the possibility this system can be federally operated. Electronic security is now a real concern because of the potential frauds, electronic thefts, and breaches by computer hackers (Webster & McCampbell, 1992).

The potential for computer-related crimes is limitless. Consider the case in which a drug dealer buys a computer and, with an e-mail hookup, conducts his business of illicit drug marketing. The potential is here. It is more a reality than a possibility. The reason this is possible is twofold: (1) computer system hardware and software is portable and affordable, and (2) computer literacy among criminals is rapidly increasing. Criminals are moving beyond cellular phones and digital pagers to sophisticated computer systems (Zimmerman, 1991).

Silicon Valley, located in Santa Clara County, is the home of many computer-related enterprises. An interview with Mark Haynes, Supervisor for the Economic Crimes Unit, Santa Clara District Attorney's Office, was conducted in an effort to discern whether there is a pressing need to be concerned with computer crime. He reported that computer crime is a growing industry, and that the paper office will soon turn to a binary or paperless society as computers become the containers of data, which will create more opportunities for crime (Button, 1993).

Should electronic theft be a concern? The average computer theft is between $475,000 and $560,000. It is no wonder that devious minds are attracted to this type of criminal activity. Compare this figure with an average of $19,000 taken in a bank robbery (Notes and Handouts, 1990). A tremendous amount of time, effort, and publicity is spent extolling the capture of bank robbers, yet the electronic robber is being ignored. The sale of stolen goods, prostitution and pornography schemes, frauds, thefts, and vandalism (computer viruses) to our computer systems are costing the taxpayers dearly. However, offenses visible to the public generate a police response, and those not seen receive little attention.

Ferreting Out White Collar Crimes

The enforcement of laws against white-collar crime is largely the work of special fraud units in police departments and private corporate investigators. During the past few decades, many states established economic crime units to deal with white-collar crimes such as computer fraud and credit card crimes. These units, for the most part, have focused on cases that appear solvable and demand the least amount of time. Besides state and local law enforcement, there also are large numbers of computer crime investigators specifically engaged in ferreting out white-collar offenses committed against banks and corporations. Computer crimes investigations is one of the fastest growing law enforcement areas of concern in the 1990s.

Based on a 1990 survey, only 18 percent of police departments and 12 percent of sheriff's departments and prosecutors' offices had an individual unit that specialized in computer crime (Webster & McEwen, 1992). This suggests that there is a dire need for an increase in the number of computer crime units within criminal justice agencies. Unfortunately, the criminal justice system is slow to react to changes in criminal behavior. Thus, law enforcement will continue to operate behind the times. Other criminal justice agencies are lagging even further behind law enforcement. Nevertheless, the expectation is that criminal justice will eradicate computer crime, from initial detection to incarceration of the perpetrators.

Theft of Data

The number of attempts to steal data using computers and telecommunications has tripled over the last five years. More than one third of the 165 Fortune 1000 firms reported thefts or attempted thefts of corporate secrets (Datamation, 1991). Currently, the possibility of investigating the thefts rests with the local jurisdictions; if large amounts are stolen across state boundaries, the FBI or Secret Service may choose to investigate. Experience tells us that companies are reluctant to investigate such offenses because of their vulnerability to issues of public trust (Jackson, 1994).

An added dimension is the threat of terrorism and theft of national defense information, such as in the case described in the book *The Cuckoo's Egg* (Stoll, 1989). This book depicts Cliff Stoll's account of his discovering hackers from Germany who were bent on accessing secret military defense and nuclear weapons information from computer banks. There have also been reported cases of hackers breaking into police departments, hospitals, colleges, schools, and other business and government institutions. There are procedures to curtail unlawful access and each agency, business, or citizen must follow sound prevention techniques. If they do not, unwanted access will occur. May God help us if the events contained in *The Togo Virus* (Randall, 1991) become reality.

Hackers: A Powerful Counterculture

The hacker believes information is for everyone to access. Cyberpunks, who roam the techno-underground, are computer cowboys in a world of bitstreams and databases inside computer networks. With the tap of a key, they claim they can effectively cripple the economy or shut down communications systems the world over. If that is true, then Cyberpunks hold the potential for becoming the most powerful countercultural force ever (Rayl, 1992).

To compound matters, Mitch Kapor, founder of Lotus Development Corporation and Creator of Lotus 1-2-3, has founded an organization named Electronic Frontier Foundation (EFF) to defend people charged with computer-related crimes. The group is concerned with protecting constitutional rights and fostering creativity within the computer industry. They also believe penalties should be given for *unauthorized* access to computer systems. Part of EFF's intent is to ensure that ordinary people are free to access information (Caldwell, 1990).

Law Enforcement's Ability to Respond

Law enforcement is not sitting idly by while the criminal community explores the new opportunities made available in the frontier of cyberspace. Based on a 1990 survey, 18 percent of police departments, 12 percent of sheriffs' departments, and prosecutors' officers have established individual units that specialize in computer crime (Webster & McEwen, 1992).

Unfortunately, the criminal justice system is slow to act and law enforcement has trouble catching up with technology. The police are preoccupied with the more conventional and traditional types of crimes (armed robbery, rape, burglary, bank robbery). Electronic robbery, the sale of stolen goods, prostitution and pornography schemes, and thefts and vandalism using computer systems are being ignored. Thus, economic crimes, because of their low visibility, receive little attention or they do not receive a response at all.

Computer crime is serious in nature, and law enforcement is behind the times; however, the police are expected to curtail this type of activity. The electronic thief steals state-of-the-art equipment, hacking their way to riches. They have no budget process. Unfortunately, law enforcement, which has placed little emphasis on the computer criminal, must beg and purchase equipment with tight budgets.

What Can Law Enforcement Do?

The chief problem associated with law enforcement addressing computer crimes is that real-world laws apply badly, when they do at all, to cyberspace. Thus, state and federal agencies appear powerless. In fact, many states find it difficult to prosecute computer offenders on criminal charges because statutes usually do not cover electronic communications. A case in point: United States prosecutors charged an offender in 1994 with wire fraud. The federal judge hearing the case dismissed it on the ground that the laws developed and established during the telegraph era cannot possibly serve as legal remedy for the abuses of the computer information age.

A related concern is seizure of computers and records as evidence. Although law enforcement officers traditionally have seized entire computer systems to investigate white collar crimes, victims of computer manipulation cases usually cannot afford to have their businesses disrupted in this manner. Downloading of records and other data allows law enforcement to access computerized records without removing the computer itself. Still, search warrants may be required, and officers should consult their department's legal advisor or the local prosecutor for guidance.

Another legal problem arises out of concern about the admissibility of computerized records in court. In general, computerized records are subject to the hearsay rule, the best evidence rule, and the authentication requirement. Investigating officers should also seek advice from legal advisors in these areas.

Moreover, as with any piece of evidence, establishing a proper chain of custody helps to ensure the admissibility of computerized records in court cases. Officers are advised to document fully the procedures they use to obtain and store any downloaded data, including by whom, where, and under what circumstances they are able to gain access to the victim's system, and which files they downloaded. All downloaded files must be maintained on a write-protected disk, which prevents data from being altered. It is always a good practice for officers to back up all files, and to use copies of the downloaded files to sort, select, and organize the data during the investigative process.

The Government's Role in Technological Advancement

The challenge to law enforcement to adequately address computer and credit card crime problems cannot be separated from government's role in technological advancements. National, state, and local governments have come to rely on computers. Yet, economies are fiscally unsound, and demands are being placed on police administrators by politicians and citizen activists to produce more for less. Lack of resources has forced government to look for efficient and economic ways to accomplish tasks. Thus, computers are often justified and installed with the major purpose being the elimination of personnel costs, particularly because such costs consume 80 to 85 percent of general fund budgets. Consequently, entities forced to shave dollars see automation as the answer.

The acquisition of technological equipment such as computers is often delayed by several factors. Possession of information implies accountability, which often results in the phenomenon of political amnesia. Politicians forget the agreements of well-laid plans and succumb to special interest pressure. In other words, when under the gun, cut everything!

Another dilemma is the purchasing process. Computer technology changes so fast that by the time government decides to purchase an item, it is out of date. Even if the items were state-of-the-art at the time, the purchasing process of equipment is difficult and lengthy. The same problem holds true with software applications. Software vendors enhance their versions at a rapid pace, and some jurisdictions are not able to purchase an upgrade in a timely fashion.

Law enforcement and government agencies have some catching up to do. The Clinton administration proposes tightening federal copyright law to explicitly cover property transmitted on the Internet. Government agencies, as well as businesses, are now feeling their way toward a common encryption standard that would guarantee the security of commercial transactions. Regulators of every assemblage are establishing cadres to monitor their particular track on the Super Electronic Expressway.

Summary

Technology is increasing at an exponential rate. More people are becoming dependent on technology, as electronic components become more powerful and physically smaller. Increased opportunities exist for everyone to possess such components. Large amounts of information are now accessible by anyone. In three years, some 80 percent of the homes in this country will have a computer. The migration to a debit card system and the elimination of physical money motivate criminals to develop new technological talents. Historically, law enforcement and the criminal justice system have been slow to react to changes in technology. The criminal element does not seem to possess this problem. Government has not kept abreast of technological advancement, admittedly because of fiscal constraints.

The effect on the family is of grave concern, especially when parents, most of whom have not been exposed to computers, do not interact with their children because "junior is interacting with his electronic family." The children's new computer contacts and associates may lead them into law-violating behavior, and their parents will not have a clue.

In the past, hackers infiltrated computer systems for the purpose of challenge, growth, and experimentation. The hacker of today and tomorrow will not have the same kind of "ethical" understanding of hacking and will have the potential to cripple any government or private organization.

Finally, law enforcement's failure to reprioritize their efforts is indicative of their lack of foresight. This point is particularly evident when comparing the cost of a bank robbery with that of a computer crime. The law enforcement community must consider the threat of a hacker as menacing as that of the bank robber or burglar. Attention must be given to this apparently invisible crime.

What makes this issue so important is the fact that the computer criminal of the past accessed computer systems through large machines located at businesses, universities, or another remote location. In the future, however virtually everyone will possess a computer. Computers can be purchased nearly anywhere today, even at large department stores. The prices are affordable, and people can purchase computer systems via the credit card.

As society evolves into a "smart culture," in which the environment is controlled by computer technology, the computer criminal will adjust to a level of sophistication whereby future crimes will be committed through the use of a computer. Someone will have to contend with computer wizards who cover their tracks to avoid detection. Businesses may become bankrupt as computer pirates steal their assets. Will society keep pace with technological change and will governments or politicians allow law enforcement to do so? By the year 2000, law enforcement's Armageddon may very well be the collision of information, computer technology, and the computer criminal.

Yet unanswered are the questions related to whether business will cooperate with law enforcement to reduce and prevent computer-related crimes; will the right to privacy continue to be an obstacle to law enforcement efforts to manage this growing problem? Law enforcement agencies across the country must be given sufficient resources and technological support to keep the control of information in the proper hands.

REFERENCES

Branscom, A. W. (1990). Rogue computer programs and computer rogues: Tailoring the punishment to fit the crime. *Rutgers Computer & Technology L.J., 16,* 24–26.

Budwey, J. N. (1992, February). Information industry in transition. *Internet, 2,* p. 22.

Button, L. (1993). Unpublished interview conducted with Mark Haynes, Economic Crimes Unit, Santa Clara County, CA.

Caldwell, B. (1990, July). Outlaws or pioneers. *Information Week,* pp. 12–13.

Conly, C. (1989). Organizing for computer crime investigation and prosecution, National Institute of Justice, U.S. Department of Justice, *Computer Crime: Criminal Justice Resource Manual 2.*

Corcoran, C. (1992, November 11). Voice recognition moving down to PCs. *Infoworld,* p. 33.

Coutourie, L. (1989, September). The computer criminal: An investigative assessment. *FBI Law Enforcement Bulletin,* pp. 19–22.

Dallas Morning News. (1992, January 2). FBI investigates charges of computer hacking by Perot campaign. *The Fresno Bee,* p. A7.

Fresno Bee. (1991, October 17). Phones, CDs, luxury touches make cars more like home. *The Fresno Bee,* p. 8.

Fresno Bee. (1992, April 18). Hackers credit-card scam found. *The Fresno Bee,* p. A1.

Gullo, K. (1994 November 26). Holidays bring rise in theft of plastic. *The Fresno Bee,* p. C2.

Hanna, D. G. (1990). *Police Executive Leadership.* Champaign, IL: Stipes Publishing.

Hanson, W. (1993, March). Say hello to the national computer network. *Government Technology,* p. 48.

Haynes, M. (1993, Summer 1 & 2). Computer crimes and criminals. *American Criminal Justice Journal, 57,* 32–36.

Jackson, J. E. (1993). Fraud masters: Studying an illusory, non-violent, gang specializing in credit card crimes. *The Gang Journal, 1*(4), 17–36.

Jackson, J. E. (1994). Fraud masters: Professional credit card offenders and crime. *Criminal Justice Review, 19*(1), 24–55.

LaPolla, S. (1992, July). High tech's dark side: Fraud, forgery, check swindles; scanners, printers are accomplices in crime. *PC Week,* p. 23.

Naizbitt, J. (1982). *Megatrends.* New York: Warner Books.

Notes and Handouts. (1990, December 3–14). Criminal investigation in an automated environment. Glynco, VA: Federal Law Enforcement Training Center.

Pressman, R. S., & Herron, S. R. (1991). *Software Shock.* New York: Dorset House Publishing.

Randall, J. D. (1991). *The Togo Virus.* London: Randall-Kensington Publishing.

Raskin, X., & Schaldach-Paiva, J. (1996, Spring). Computer crimes. *American Criminal Law Review,* pp. 541–573.

Rayl, A. J. S. (1992, November). Secrets of the Cyberculture. *Omni,* pp. 59–67.

Rimm, M. (1995). Marketing pornography on the information superhighway: A survey of 917,410 images, descriptions, short stories, and animations downloaded 8.5 million times over 2000 cities in forty countries, provinces, and territories, 83. *Georgia Law Journal,* pp. 1849–1876.

Sanders, D. (1988). *Computers Today.* New York: McGraw Hill.

San Francisco Examiner. (1992, February 2). Gadgets ahead of their time. *San Francisco Examiner,* p. E4.

Scuttlebut. (1990, May 7). They start so young nowadays. *MIS Week,* p. 46.

Sessions, W. (1991, February). Computer crimes: An escalating crime trend. *FBI Law Enforcement Bulletin,* pp. 12–15.

Sterling, B. (1992). *The hacker crackdown.* New York: Bantam Books.

Stoll, C. (1989). *The cuckoo's egg.* New York: Doubleday.

Talarico, W. (1994, July-August). New home 2000. *Home Mechanix,* pp. 54–57.

Tamaki, J. & Connelly, M. (1992, August 23). Computer skills aid '90s credit card scam. *Los Angeles Times,* pp. B1–42.

Toffler, A. (1980). *The Third Wave.* New York: William Morrow & Company.

Toffler, A. (1990). *Powershift.* New York: Bantam Books.

Vernaci, R. L. (1991, December 29). Phones Getting Smarter. *San Francisco Examiner,* p. E12.

Vizard, F. (1994, September). Wired for the Highway. *Popular Mechanics,* pp. 36–40.

Warwick, D. R. (1992, November/December). The Cash-Free Society. *The Futurist,* pp. 19–22.

Watch your data. (1991, December 1). *Datamation,* p. 23.

Watson, N. (1989, September). Can today's hacker laws work? *Communication Week,* p. 32.

Webster, B., & McCampbell, M. S. (1992, September). International money laundering: Research and investigation join forces. *National Institute of Justice,* pp. 4–5.

Webster, B. A., & McEwen, J. T. (1992, August). Assessing Criminal Justice Needs. *National Institute of Justice,* pp. 4–5.

Wilkins, G. (1994, March 14). Wanted, in cyberspace hacker crime. *U.S. News & World Report.*

World Future Society. (1991). *Outlook '92 and Beyond: Recent Forecasts from the Futurist Magazine.* World Future Society.

Zimmerman, M. R. (1991, March 4). Drug dealers find haven in on-line services. *PC Week,* p. 43.

Rejoinder to Dr. Jackson Robert P. McNamara

In an attempt to respond to Professor Jackson's article on computer crime, I find many of his points to be valid and helpful. I think he does a solid job of describing the extent of the problem, reviewing the literature as well as accurately forecasting the future of this type of criminal activity. He is also correct in his assertion that the criminal justice system in general, and law enforcement in particular, is inadequately prepared to deal with the problems of computer-related crime.

As I mention in my corresponding article, the police lag behind in the learning curve related to computer crime. An added dilemma is that, given that the changes in technology occur so rapidly and have such a sweeping impact on our ability to gather and disseminate information, even if law enforcement officers were adequately trained, sustaining that level of sophistication would be extremely difficult. For instance, police departments sometimes have difficulty finding the funding and personnel coverage to allow K-9 officers to attend training seminars, let alone the amount of time that would be required to keep up to date on the latest forms of computer crime and how to prevent them. Thus, it is unlikely that the police or other agencies within the criminal justice system will ever be able to compete effectively with their technologically sophisticated counterparts.

In response to this situation, some of us might be tempted to lament a futile situation, and others, such as Professor Jackson, simply insist that the government provide the necessary commitment to allow law enforcement an opportunity to combat computer crime. Yet another approach might be equally as effective: limit the impact of computer crime on law enforcement. Because law enforcement has not, and probably will not, have an impact on computer crime, perhaps we should consider limiting the effect of the latter on the former. That is, instead of calling attention to the inadequacies of the system, as well as how difficult it would be to resolve the problem, it may be more productive in many cases to require private industry or individual companies to adequately protect their own databases and to educate the public about the potential risks of revealing personal information. Legislation could be passed, similar to nonsmoking statutes, that requires companies to develop, maintain, and modify security programs for their storehouses of information. If what Professor Jackson states is true, that we are headed for an increasingly paperless society, then it is incumbent on us to require companies to adequately protect their customers and clients. An added advantage is that the savings generated from having most, if not all, information stored electronically could be used to offset some of the costs of protecting the information.

I am not advocating a complete shift in enforcement to private industry, but I am suggesting that we must be progressive in our thinking about how to prevent crime, particularly this type of crime. Unfortunately, the history of policing, and of criminal justice in general, is to cling to tradition even when we realize our strategies are no longer effective. In this instance, we have the opportunity to identify a problem in its relatively early stages and to take constructive steps to parry its possible consequences. It is also fairly clear that this would be a dramatic departure from traditional practices in which more money and more officials is NOT the answer to a problem stemming from an increase in crime. Rather than adding more officers who need to be trained, we should assist companies in being more responsible for addressing computer crime. Another part of this strategy could include small, specialized law enforcement units. This would select certain types of computer crimes and focus in on them intensively. This is similar to various programs such as Tactical Narcotics Team (TNT) units or those broadly labeled as community crime prevention, in which the law enforcement agency attempts to make citizens responsible for doing something about crime in their neighborhoods, while maintaining their mandate to enforce the law.

The problems with this approach are obvious. For example, a considerable amount of research suggests the community crime prevention model is dubious in terms of its actual effectiveness. Moreover, the problem remains of attracting and retaining creative computer experts who would make up these specialized units. The answer to this, unfortunately, is not that clear, especially because many criminal justice agencies do not think computer crime should be given the attention it deserves. The reason for this, it seems, is that computer crime is relatively invisible, and its actual effects go unnoticed by most people. Consequently, it is unlikely that this activity will ever be considered so threatening that, as a matter of policy, we would view it as seriously as street crime. But blaming the police, or worse, simply adding more police to deal with the problem, is, in my view, shortsighted and counterproductive.

NO

ROBERT P. MCNAMARA

There can be little doubt that the rapid increase in technology, particularly the use of computers, has dramatically affected our lives in a variety of ways. Near the turn of the century, when another wave of technology swept the landscape in Europe and the United States, sociologists Karl Marx and Max Weber tried to describe the problems and promise of capitalism. In their individual analyses of the changes that were taking place in society, with the advent of assembly lines and mass production, both Marx and Weber described technology as a labor-saving device. This use of technology presented different problems for men such as Marx and Weber, and they pointed to it to describe a different set of situations of course, but the fact of the matter is that, even today, technology makes our lives easier and more productive. What is even more significant is that the acceleration of developments in computer technology have come at a blistering pace, and we are all feeling its effects.

One of the most interesting aspects of this growth has been the variety of ways in which people have used computers for illegal gain. As more and more Americans turn to computer technology to meet their needs, whether they be antilock brakes or navigation systems for our cars or the home shopping network, distance learning in education, automated tellers at banks, or simply e-mailing a friend or relative in another state or country, we leave ourselves vulnerable to the exploitation of others. As we construct web pages, with personal data such as resumes, hobbies, or even personal characteristics, we become increasingly susceptible to victimization. And we are not the only ones at risk. Governments, retail stores, defense contractors, banks, corporations, and universities are all at risk to computer hackers or criminals who seek economic gain from this type of personal or financial information.

While there are a litany of different types of computer crime (see for instance Carter & Katz, 1997), one can broadly define it as any crime in which an illegal act is conducted with a computer (Conly, 1989). This activity costs Americans billions of dollars per year in insurance claims, outright costs of victimization, and greater allocation of resources to arrest and prosecute offenders. Moreover, the problem appears to be getting worse. According to the National Security Institute, in a recent nationwide survey, nearly every major corporation polled said it had been a victim of computer crime—from employees browsing through confidential files to theft of trade secrets to outright embezzlement of funds. The largest reported increases were in theft of confidential client information, trade secrets, and new product plans and pricing information (National Security Institute, 1997).

Additionally, a study by the American Bar Association (1987) found that of the 300 corporations and government agencies selected, 24 percent claimed to have been the victims of a computer-related crime in the previous year. Additionally, the combined estimated loss from these crimes ranged from $145 million to $730 million.

One might think that the solution to computer crime is relatively simple: find someone smarter than the hacker or criminal and hire them to establish a security system that prevents people from gaining access to files or funds. The problem with this approach is that the technology changes quickly, and the inventiveness of offenders makes it virtually impossible to prevent all computer crime or even a significant proportion of it.

A related solution is for corporations and businesses to provide full disclosure to government agencies charged with preventing and prosecuting computer crime. This would allow prosecutors the opportunity to detect instances of computer crime more easily and make convictions more likely. However, this raises a host of other issues, most notably the intrusion of the government into the lives of its citizens.

Another issue centers around a problem related to all types of criminal victimization: reporting the incident to the police. Many companies are often reluctant to report they have been compromised or have had information stolen, largely because of the fear that customers will lose confidence and trust in the company. Thus, many companies fail to report the crime, which begins a vicious cycle in which other companies remain unaware of this particular potential for victimization, which leads to greater vulnerability. When (or if) that company is then victimized, instead of revealing this information so that others may avoid this problem (or to study the trends and patterns involved in the commission of the crime), they too fail to report it to authorities. Consequently, experts that are available to help them never learn of the problem, nor can they offer their assistance.

Law Enforcement and Computer Crime

There can be little doubt that the problems stemming from computer crime present numerous challenges for law enforcement. As Carter and Katz (1997) describe, the police are challenged not only by the phenomenon of computer crime, particularly as technology continues its rapid and exponential growth, but also in identifying it, simply because it (like a great deal of white-collar crime) is difficult to identify. To make matters worse, it is sometimes hard to convince law enforcement agencies of the significant harm and costs associated with computer crime, even though the impact from both are significant. For instance, according to one estimate, the average larceny involved a loss of between $2,000 and $5,000, whereas the average computer crime is valued around $500,000 (National Crime Security, 1997).

Because it is not considered a high priority, persuading police departments to designate precious resources toward combating it is sometimes very difficult. An added problem for law enforcement is that it has lagged behind many other industries in its use of technology. Although we are beginning to see a greater priority placed on computer technology to solve crimes and used as investigative tools, particularly in the area of fingerprint analysis (see, for instance, Anderson, 1997), policing is well behind other industries in terms of its technological sophistication. However, the problem is not simply obtaining the technology.

Lemos (1997) contends that many police officers do not have the training to secure evidence from a high-tech crime scene. As evidence of law enforcement's inability to solve computer crimes, Lemos states that in 1996 only about 1 percent of all computer crimes were reported, and of those, only about 7 percent resulted in a conviction. Yet another part of the problem for law enforcement, in addition to the lack of technological advances or training, is that some offenders commit these acts outside the United States. For instance, the FBI, perhaps the agency with the most sophisticated knowledge and expertise on computer crime, believes that more than 120 countries may be actively stealing information from U.S. corporations (Lemos, 1997). The logistical problems as well as jurisdictional issues computer-related crime presents makes it extremely difficult to successfully identify or prosecute computer criminals.

Thus, although addressing computer crime is sometimes the result of a lack of equipment and training, or perhaps a priority issue, in other cases simply locating the culprit is a nearly insurmountable task. In an effort to target this type of activity and to give law enforcement the tools it needs to have an impact on computer crime, Senator Mike DeWine has introduced a bill in Congress called the Local Law Enforcement Enhancement Act. He believes that the federal government has a responsibility to enhance law enforcement programs by providing the necessary technology and information to not only track activities, but to prosecute and convict offenders. His solution is the creation of a national electronic criminal justice identification system. He states:

> The idea is a simple one. We need to make it possible for any police officer to access a national database—a fully automated data bank including information on fingerprints, DNA analysis, ballistics and complete criminal histories. I believe this system will be an absolutely essential component of local law enforcement in the 21st century (p. 1).

Other programs designed to target computer crime include the Computer Crime Intellectual Property Section (CCIPS). This agency is responsible for implementing the Justice Department's Computer Crime Initiative, which is a comprehensive program designed to address the more global problem of computer crime. Section attorneys work with other governmental agencies such as NASA, the Department of Defense, the FBI, telecommunications companies, software vendors, as well as universities around the world to develop responses to computer crime.

In addition to collecting information and resolving many issues raised here, the attorneys for CCIPS are responsible for prosecuting cases as well as training law enforcement personnel. In sum, the law enforcement community is woefully behind in its ability to combat computer crime, whatever its form and content, and as technology continues to improve and create new opportunities for offenders, police officers will increasingly encounter problems with apprehending individuals who use the technology for illegal gain.

Do the Police Really Need More Power?

Given all that has been discussed, one might easily conclude that if the main challenge of law enforcement is to fight the techno war against computer criminals, we should, as Senator DeWine argues, equip the police with the necessary resources and expertise to win the battle. However, at the same time, the issues raise a number of fundamental questions about living in a democratic society. Are we really willing to do what is necessary to solve computer crime? Can this ever really be accomplished? More importantly, should we simply open the floodgates and pour money into the law enforcement community simply because we have discovered a need? It is important to provide the police with the necessary tools to perform their duties adequately—just about any reasonable person would agree to that. However, are there better ways to confront computer crime other than simply throwing money at the problem? In other words, we need to be very careful that our fears and concerns about computer crime do not result in rash, dangerous, and ineffective strategies to solve the problem.

In looking at these issues more carefully, perhaps the most important question is whether it is reasonable to expect that law enforcement will be able to address these problems. Here I am calling into question not whether the police should target computer crime, but whether they have the ability to deal with the problem adequately. Does law enforcement realistically have the resources to compete in the marketplace? As was mentioned, with the rapid changes taking place as well as the infinite variations of illegal activity that can be created by hackers and others, it is indeed questionable whether police departments, with their limited budgets and political obstacles, are going to be able to attract individuals with the expertise necessary to solve many of these crimes. In an attempt to lure away the best and the brightest, policing will be competing with some of the most profitable companies in the industry…a contest that a governmental agency is sure to lose. And therein lies a significant part of the problem. If we believe that it is the mission of the police to investigate and prosecute computer-related crime, how do we attract qualified personnel? This problem is exacerbated by how technologically far behind many law enforcement agencies are compared with the offender population.

The second issue is whether traditional methods of investigation/prosecution are an appropriate strategy for computer crime. That is, the first point questions whether the police have the ability to solve the problem; this point focuses on whether they should address it. Similar to our ability to regulate the Internet and pornography, a number of constitutional issues are raised here. It is true that perhaps the incidence of computer crime has begun to generate a climate of fear for many people, but we must be very cautious in terms of solving the problem. We do not want to sacrifice a number of hallowed democratic safeguards in an effort to catch up and solve the problem.

In examining this question of unchecked discretion, particularly in the area of information searches, we should be very concerned about the long-term implications this presents. Do we, for example, want the police to have access to intimate details of our lives? Moreover, do we want them to have that authority simply because they have not kept pace with a changing society? Should we as citizens be deprived of our reasonable expectations of privacy because the police are behind in the learning curve? Thus, cries of concern about the harm and cost of computer crime are balanced by screams of fear of Big Brother and the erosion of individual freedom.

Most significant is the potential for abuse on the part of the police to follow hunches and other unsubstantiated leads that invade the privacy of innocent citizens. The fact that we have an exclusionary rule, even the recently modified one, suggests that we are, as a matter of legal precedent, concerned about the potential for abuse by the police. Moreover, it can be argued that unlawful searches and seizures by the police in these instances would be more threatening than traditional investigations. In short, a person's entire life can be found on the Internet, and as such, we should be more concerned about the potential for abuse of this type of search than conventional ones. Thus, it seems reasonable that individuals as well as many corporations would be against this form of governmental intrusion.

The answer, if there is one, is found in requiring corporations and other organizations to develop a sophisticated storage system that will safeguard information from offenders. This could take many forms, given that the type of information illegally obtained is also quite varied. However, unless companies have an economic interest in protecting these data, any attempts to do so will be of limited success. Succinctly, we cannot rely on businesses' concern about the erosion of trust by consumers to motivate corporations to act responsibly. Perhaps the best approach then would be to provide the companies with the resources and allow them, rather than the police, to deal with the problem. No system is foolproof, but it seems clear that private industry is much better equipped to identify and address the problems related to computer crime, as well as to stay abreast of the changes taking place within the industry.

One final point deserves mentioning. In an effort to deal with the prosecution issues as well as concerns about individual privacy, the Electronic Frontier Foundation, a civil liberties organization, has focused its attention on the failure of law enforcement as well as the criminal justice system as a whole to address these constitutional protections in the enforcement of computer-related crime. Specifically, they call attention to warrants that may, because of the difficulties involved in investigating computer-related crime, be vague about the type of items/ information to be searched or seized. In a detailed report submitted to the American Bar Association this past year, the Foundation has proposed a number of guidelines for judges and magistrates to follow when issuing search warrants relating to computer crime.

Conclusion

The problems of computer crime are vast and will continue to be problematic for the criminal justice system for many years to come. It is incumbent on us as researchers, students, practitioners, and members of the community to discover ways in which to address and solve this problem. However, there are real questions about the ability of the police, in its present form, to deal with computer-related crime. Moreover, if we are serious about combating this type of illegal activity, we must think carefully about the intended and unintended consequences of our proposed solutions. This is not to say we should do nothing about computer crime because we live in a democracy, but rather suggests that we give our proposals considered thought and recognize our tendency to act impulsively as well as to think complex problems are easily resolved.

REFERENCES

American Bar Association. (1987). Report on white collar crime. Washington, D.C.

Anderson, M. (1997). *Electronic fingerprints: Computer evidence comes of age.* Gresham, OR: New Technologies Inc.

Bill to Aid Local Law Enforcement. (1997). *Criminal justice, America On Line.* Retrieved December 12, 1997 from the World Wide Web: http://www.acsp.uic.edu/oicj/pubs/cja/080605.htm.

Carter, D. L., & Katz, A. J. (1997). *Computer crime: An emerging challenge for law enforcement.* Retrieved December 12, 1997 from the World Wide Web: http://www.infowar.com.

Conly, C. (1989). Organizing for computer crime investigation and prosecution, National Institute of Justice, U.S. Department of Justice, *Computer Crime: Criminal Justice Resource Manual 2.*

Cybercrime on the Rise in U.S. Companies. (1997). *National Security Institute Report, 9*(3):1.

Lemos, R. (1997). *Take a bite out of net crime: cops say.* ZD net news channel. Retrieved September 11, 1997, from the World Wide Web: http://www. Zdnet.com.

Rejoinder to Dr. McNamara

JEROME E. JACKSON

The entire criminal justice system, particularly law enforcement, is drastically lagging behind the rapid increase in technology. Most Americans recognize that improved technology has contributed to our lives being made easier and more productive. At the same time we acknowledge the fact that the acceleration of techno-developments has contributed to our increased vulnerability to exploitation in society.

McNamara agrees that computer crime is costing Americans billions of dollars annually, and that the problem is getting worse. Therefore, the answer to the question of whether law enforcement needs more power to fight the growing abuse and victimization resulting from computer and credit card criminals is a resounding yes. However, the amount of power given to law enforcement and the areas in which law enforcement should focus its attention are in the estimation of McNamara's major concerns. He does not question the targeting of computer crime by the police. Instead, he diverts our attention away from the central concern to a set of alternate issues.

First, we are asked whether law enforcement has the ability to adequately deal with the problem given a marketplace with rapidly depleting human and material resources. How do we compete with the offender and profit-oriented populations for the best and the brightest?

These questions are valid. Our proper responses to them will result in the development of primary ideas and ways to address and perhaps resolve many of the contributing factors related to law enforcement's ability to better handle these new crime areas and criminals.

Second, is the issue of whether traditional methods of investigation and prosecution are appropriate. This concern points to whether law enforcement should be the agency to address this crime category. It should be apparent that it is the appropriate agency.

Notwithstanding this fact, McNamara is on point here. We must be careful in our push for increased involvement of law enforcement in the apprehension of computer and other techno-criminals that we do not grant the police the potential for abuse of power. The potential for governmental intrusion is extremely great and ever present. Law enforcement is criticized for not doing enough as often as it is for going too far.

McNamara offers a very interesting observation in lieu of an answer to our question. While this author disagrees with this position and contends, instead, that policing should be left to law enforcement agencies, the observation is one to ponder. McNamara suggests that the answer may be found in requiring corporations and other organizations to develop sophisticated storage systems that will safeguard sensitive information and data from computer criminals. He also correctly notes that unless companies and corporations have a vested economic interest in protecting these various forms of data, any attempt to police themselves will meet with limited success.

Can we imagine the latent consequences of providing private companies and corporations with the resources needed to fight the war on computer crimes, instead of providing law enforcement with these needed resources? What would we use as a means of motivating? How would we underwrite the purchase of theses resources? Moreover, where would the supplying of the resources end?

Contrary to the contention of McNamara, it is not at all clear that private industry is better equipped to either identify or address the problems currently taking place in the consumer industry as the result of the abuse of technological advancements. Future projections by experts do not indicate a closing of the gap between ill-equipped law enforcement agencies and the more sophisticated and better-equipped computer criminal. If this were the case, we would not currently be faced with the problem in such magnitude.

The very optimistic view held by McNamara is entertaining. Unfortunately, it suffers for lack of reality, practicality, and reasonable expectation—especially when we consider the harm these offenders cause in society, and the difficulty associated with identifying and prosecuting them.

Have Community "Corrections" Become Community Control?

Georgia Smith, Ph.D., received her doctorate from Florida State University in 1997. She is Assistant Professor of Criminal Justice at Jacksonville State University, where she teaches courses in corrections, theory, and research methods. Her research interests include corrections and public attitude concerning crime and punishment.

Karol Lucken is a Professor at the University of Central Florida in the department of criminal justice. She holds a Ph.D. in Criminology from Florida State University. She is currently coauthoring a text entitled *Corrections in America: Past, Present, and Future.*

YES

GEORGIA SMITH

As we approach the twenty-first century, many scholars and practitioners believe that community-based correctional programs have undergone dramatic changes during the past two decades. Typically, these transformations are characterized as involving a shift from treatment to control-oriented goals and strategies (Parent, 1993; Rhine & Humphries, 1993). Feeley and Simon (1992) argue that these changes are more profound than a mere shift in emphasis, and represent a "paradigm shift" to a "new penology" characterized by distinctive goals and practices.

This chapter considers the question of whether the goal of offender control has eclipsed that of rehabilitation to the extent that the term "corrections" is misleading. Sluder, Sapp, and Langston summarize the practical implications of this question when they note:

...organizational mission statements, philosophies, and goals imbue agencies with a source of legitimacy, provide employees with a sense of direction and a source of motivation, enable agencies to set goals and form guidelines, and provide the foundation to establish performance criteria (1994; p. 3).

An understanding of community corrections' mission, then, is necessary to evaluate the features and outcomes of these programs. For example, new control-oriented strategies such as house arrest often involve intrusions on the privacy not only of offenders sentenced to these programs but also of other individuals (i.e., offenders' family members). Can we justify such threats to the rights of third parties?

In addition, the traditional measure of program success, revocation, must be interpreted from the standpoint of the program's dominant goal. High revocation rates may be indicative of failure or success, depending on whether the primary objective is treatment or control. Finally, several writers attribute increasing parole and probation revocation rates to shifts in agency goals and employee attitudes (Parent, 1993; Rhine & Humphries, 1993). The new emphasis on control, then, may exacerbate prison overcrowding.

I begin with an overview of the historical models of community corrections. Next, a brief review of the literature is used to illustrate changes in policies, practices, and employee role perceptions. I conclude with a discussion of some implications of this new offender-control model.

Models of Community-Based Corrections

The origins of community-based corrections can be traced to the voluntary probation work of John Augustus in the early 1840s. The techniques developed by Augustus served as a blueprint for formal probation programs implemented throughout the United States during the Progressive era. The following subsections provide an overview of changes in the goals of community-based corrections since the late nineteenth century.

The Treatment Model

The correctional literature identifies treatment as the original mission of community-based sanctions. Influenced by the developing social sciences and the "medical model" of social problems, reformers envisioned probation and parole agents as trained diagnosticians capable of determining the causes of criminal behavior in each case and developing individualized treatment plans. (Rothman, 1980) Rothman argues that community-based programs bore little resemblance to those envisioned by Progressive era reformers, for several reasons.

First, reformers were overly optimistic regarding the knowledge base of corrections. This era was dominated by positivist theories that assumed that criminal behavior is caused by factors beyond the immediate control of the individual. However, there was little agreement regarding the specific causes of crime. In addition, agencies were plagued by excessive workloads and scarce resources and were unable to attract employees with the desired educational credentials. Finally, time constraints prevented the implementation of a social casework approach. (Rothman, 1980)

Simon (1993) traces the history of parole in California and concludes that despite official rhetoric suggesting a reform orientation, social casework methods were not introduced until the 1950s. At that time, increasing parole staffs allowed the development of a "clinical" model. The clinical model, which dominated the parole system until the 1970s, emphasized individualized treatment and reintegration.

To summarize, the original mission of community-based corrections was individualized diagnosis and treatment. In practice, most programs provided only superficial investigations into the backgrounds of offenders and minimal supervision until the post-World War II era. At that time, increased funding and staffing levels allowed the implementation of practices more closely resembling those envisioned by the Progressive reformers.

The "Just Deserts" Model

Several writers link the demise of the treatment model to (1) declining confidence in the efficacy of treatment, (2) concern regarding the discretion allowed decision makers, and (3) a shift toward a more conservative ideology on the part of the public (McWilliams, 1987; Simon, 1993).

MacKenzie and Souryal (1997) note that attention initially shifted to a concern with retribution. Presumably, program conditions could be tailored to provide proportionality between offense seriousness and punishment severity. The dominance of the just deserts model was short lived because this approach failed to allay public concerns over the risks posed by offenders punished in the community. As a result, an offender control model has dominated community corrections since the early 1980s.

The Offender Control Model

Feeley and Simon (1992) distinguish between the old and new models of corrections in terms of the language, goals, and techniques of each. The old model focused on individual offenders to achieve deserved punishment or diagnosis and treatment. In contrast, the new penology is concerned with risk determination aimed at managing high-risk offender groups.

New practices, such as actuarial-based prediction and electronic monitoring devices, are designed to increase the potential for risk assessment and control. Even established practices are now used for these purposes. For example, before 1980, urinalysis was used primarily to diagnose substance abuse to facilitate the development of individualized treatment plans. Currently, such tests often are used to determine risk and to provide increased control over offenders. (Simon, 1993)

The new penology involves a dual system of supervision. Offenders considered capable of self-control or subject to informal controls, such as family or work, are assigned to low-risk groups, designated for minimal supervision. High-risk groups are targeted for increased surveillance and control, and community supervision serves as a temporary, cost-effective strategy that merely delays the inevitable return to prison (Simon, 1993). Finally, the criteria for evaluating programs have changed. Under earlier models emphasizing treatment, high revocation rates were indicative of program failure. Under the current risk-management model, increased revocation rates suggest enhanced community protection and system efficiency. (MacKenzie & Souryal, 1997; Simon, 1993)

To summarize, the mission of community corrections has shifted to the identification and cost-effective management of high-risk offenders ultimately destined for reimprisonment. Both innovative and existing practices are used to accomplish these new goals, and agency policies are designed to reduce discretion and promote perceptions of system efficiency and accountability.

Empirical Evidence of an Offender Control Model

If the current mission of community-based corrections is offender control, results of empirical studies should reflect this shift. This section reviews some of the recent research in three areas: (1) the proliferation of control-oriented programs, (2) agency firearms policies, and (3) employee role preferences.

One reflection of a risk management approach is the implementation of "intermediate sanction" programs since the early 1980s. These programs are designed to provide more stringent requirements than standard probation but fewer controls than those placed on incarcerated offenders. A variety of programs are included under this term ranging from intensive supervision to "boot camp" and "shock incarceration" programs.

To illustrate the virtual explosion in these programs, Petersillia (1998, p. 69) notes that "Between 1980 and 1997 every state adopted some form of intermediate sanctions for adult and juvenile offenders." It could be argued that the widespread implementation of intermediate punishment programs reflects a renewed faith in the treatment model, because one type of intermediate sanction, intensive supervision (ISP), was introduced in the 1960s. However, current programs differ from the earlier version of ISP in terms of both goals and practices.

Most early ISP programs were distinguished from their traditional counterparts solely in terms of caseload size. It was assumed that smaller caseloads would allow agents more time to provide treatment services to facilitate rehabilitation. Petersillia (1987) describes early ISPs as "probation management systems" because decisions to assign offenders to smaller "intensive" caseloads typically were made by probation staff. In contrast, ISPs implemented since the late 1970s emphasize incapacitation, couple reduced caseloads with increased officer-offender contact requirements, and program assignment decisions generally are made by the sentencing judge.

The trend toward agency policies allowing or mandating the use of firearms by community supervision officers also is cited as a reflection of a shift toward a control model (Champion, 1998; Holt, 1998). In his discussion of changes in the goals and practices of parole, Holt (1998, p.39) notes:

> In keeping with these changes, agencies began allowing agents to carry concealed firearms in the 1980s. Firearms are now provided by thirty-three jurisdictions and represent a major investment of training resources, agent time, and administrative oversight.

A study of a state probation and parole agency illustrates the possible link between the control model and the trend of "arming" community supervision agents (Smith, 1997). In 1974, the job title of field agents was "Parole and Probation Supervisor." The employee manual described the agency's primary functions as treatment and assistance and discouraged the practice of carrying firearms while on duty. During 1978, field agents were reclassified as law enforcement officers, and the job title was changed to "Probation and Parole Officer." Officers were required to undergo firearms training and qualification and were allowed to carry firearms. The current policy manual identifies community safety as the agency's mission, and officers with caseloads are required to carry a firearm (Smith, 1997).

The diverse and potentially conflicting nature of the functions of community control agents have long been recognized. Traditionally, these tasks have been dichotomized as treatment or service versus control- or authority-oriented. For example, probation officers are expected to perform such services as counseling and job referrals. At the same time, agents are required to submit violation reports and, in some jurisdictions, arrest suspected program violators. Early studies of probation and parole agents' role preferences suggested that, although officers recognized both roles, most prioritized offender assistance functions (von Laningham et al., 1966). There are indications that this may no longer be the case.

McGraw (1983) asked field officers in a probation and parole agency to describe their role in relation to a 10-point law enforcement/treatment continuum. Respondents' role perceptions were fairly evenly distributed and slightly biased toward the law enforcement end of the scale. Similarly, a study comparing survey instruments administered to probation and parole officers in several jurisdictions during 1968–1970 and 1983 suggests a fairly dramatic shift in officers' attitudes from an emphasis on assistance functions to a concern with authority and surveillance-related tasks (Harris et al., 1989).

Conclusion

The term "community-based corrections" implies that the primary mission of these programs is the normalization of convicted offenders through deterrence, rehabilitation, reintegration, or some combination of these strategies. However, results of recent studies suggest a correctional system that has all but abandoned any expectations of "correcting" offenders in favor of providing risk assessment and incapacitation commensurate with risk profiles. These changes represent a decided shift to an offender control model. Following is a brief discussion of some implications of this new model.

Prison admissions data suggest dramatic increases in revocations since the early 1980s. A survey of all state parole and probation agencies indicated that, in several states, revoked parole and probation terms accounted for more prison admissions than did new felony sentences. (Parent, 1994) From a pragmatic standpoint, community-based sanctions under a control model may increase, rather than relieve, prison overcrowding.

In addition, punishment must be evaluated on the basis of ethical considerations. Control-oriented strategies are vulnerable to what von Hirsch describes as the "anything-but-prison theory" (1990; p. 165). This refers to the assumption that any restriction associated with a community-based sanction is acceptable because these punishments are inherently less severe than prison.

However, von Hirsch (1990) argues that, regardless of where punishment occurs, it should be no more severe nor intrusive than is necessary to achieve the stated penal intent, should not be degrading, and should not threaten the rights of third parties. Concern with the rights of third parties is particularly problematic with control-oriented strategies. Consider house arrest. Typically, curfew restrictions are monitored with unannounced home visits or random telephone contacts. Both strategies may intrude on the privacy of family members and neighbors.

One final issue involves the possible implications of a control model for community supervision agents. Proponents of policies allowing or requiring officers to carry firearms while on duty argue that more serious offenders are being punished in the community and that assaults on probation and parole officers have increased significantly over the past fifteen years. However, there has been little empirical research to determine whether agents' perceptions of increasing danger are accurate (Lindner & Bonn, 1996). It is possible that the "arming" of community supervision agents, coupled with increased contact requirements in cases classified as high-risk, escalates the danger associated with this work (see DelGrosso, 1997; Cohn, 1997; and Champion, 1998, for a discussion of this controversy).

REFERENCES

Champion, D. J. (1998). *Corrections in the United States: A Contemporary Perspective.* Upper Saddle River, NJ: Prentice-Hall.

Cohn, A. W. (1997). The arming of probation and parole officers may not be necessary. *Corrections Management Quarterly; 1*(4); 44–54.

DelGrosso, E. J. (1997). Probation officer safety and defensive weapons: A closer look. *Federal Probation, 61*(2); 45–50.

Feeley, M. M., & Simon, J. (1992). The new penology: Notes on the emerging strategy of corrections and its implications. *Criminology, 30*; 449–474.

Harris, P. M., Clear, T. R., & Baird, S. C. (1989). Have community supervision officers changed their attitudes toward their work? *Justice Quarterly, 6*; 233–246.

Holt, N. (1998). The current state of parole in America. In J. Petersillia (Ed.), *Community Corrections: Probation, Parole, and Intermediate Sanctions.* New York: Oxford University Press.

Lindner, C., & Bonn, R. L. (1996). Probation officer victimization and fieldwork practices: Results of a national study. *Federal Probation, 60*(2); 16–23.

Mackenzie, D. L., & Souryal, C. (1997). Probationer compliance with conditions of supervision. In J. W. Marquart and J. R. Sorensen (Eds.), *Correctional contexts: Contemporary and classical readings.* Los Angeles: Roxbury Publishing Company.

McGraw, B. E. (1983). *Adult probation and parole officers: Influence of their weapons, role perceptions and role conflict.* Masters Thesis, University of Alabama.

McWilliams, W. (1987). Probation, pragmatism and policy. *The Howard Journal, 26*; 97–121.

Parent, D. G. (1993). Structuring policies to address sanctions for absconders and violators. In E. E. Rhine (Ed.), *Reclaiming offender accountability: Intermediate sanctions for probation and parole violators.* Laurel, MD: American Correctional Association.

Parent, D. G. (1994). Probation and parole violations and abscondings. In D. G. Parent, D. Wentworth, P. Burke and B. Ney (Eds.), *Responding to probation and parole violations.* Washington, DC: National Institute of Justice.

Petersillia, J. (1987). *Expanding options for criminal sentencing.* Santa Monica, CA: Rand Corporation.

Petersillia, J. (1998). Experience with intermediate sanctions: Rationale and program effectiveness. In J. Petersillia (Ed.), *Community corrections: Probation, parole, and intermediate sanctions.* New York: Oxford University Press.

Rhine, E. E., & Humphries, K. (1993). Intermediate sanctions and violations policy in probation and parole: Prescriptions for the 1990s. In E. E. Rhine (Ed.), *Intermediate sanctions for probation and parole violators.* Laurel, MD: American Correctional Association.

Rothman, D. J. (1980). *Conscience and convenience: The asylum and its alternatives in progressive America.* Boston: Little, Brown.

Simon, J. (1993). *Poor discipline: Parole and the social control of the underclass, 1890–1990.* Chicago: The University of Chicago Press.

Sluder, R. D., Sapp, A. D., & Langston, D. C. (1994). Guiding philosophies for probation in the 21st century. *Federal Probation, 58*(2); 3–10.

Smith, G. B. (1997). *Contemporary parole decision making: Modern versus postmodern explanations.* Ph.D. dissertation, Florida State University.

von Hirsch, A. (1990). The ethics of community-based sanctions. *Crime & Delinquency, 36*(1); 162–173.

von Laningham, D. E., Taber, M., & Dimants, R. (1966). How adult probation officers view their responsibility. *Crime & Delinquency, 12*; 97–104.

Rejoinder to Dr. Smith
KAROL LUCKEN

Dr. Smith has argued that a "control" model has replaced the conventional "treatment" model in community sanctioning, and to demonstrate her argument she cites the development of intermediate sanctions, probation officer firearm policies, and probation officer role identification. In responding to her assertions, I would agree that the intermediate sanction movement, at least in concept, has ushered in a new wave of community-based programming. Intermediate sanctions are intended to be more punitive than their community-based program predecessors, because they have been explicitly designed for more serious offenders. These sanctions have been promoted as get-tough punishments that will reduce prison overcrowding and costs without jeopardizing public safety. The rationale underlying the goal of a reduced threat to public safety is that, with intermediate sanctions, control and monitoring will be so complete that offenders will be deterred from crime for fear of certain and rapid detection and response. In this regard, I readily agree that "control" has become a highly touted goal of community sanctioning, particularly throughout the 1980s. In fact, without the initial emphasis on control, it is unlikely that these much-needed alternatives to incarceration would have won political or public support.

Nor do I dispute the fact that the enhanced requirements of intermediate sanction programs (i.e., round-the-clock surveillance, increased field visits) have necessitated a "new" breed of officer, one that perhaps more resembles a law enforcement officer. And, as the responsibilities of probation officers have become more demanding and threatening, revised firearm policies have naturally followed. Various technological advancements, such as electronic monitoring and urinalysis testing, seem to further indicate the shift to a "control" model. However, these "signs" must be subject to greater empirical scrutiny before conclusions of structural change can be reached.

Several studies have shown that intermediate sanction programs, in practice, have not always delivered the get-tough punishment package promised (Latessa, 1987; Lemert, 1993). For example, Latessa (1987) found that the level of supervision in an Ohio program did not warrant the designation of "intensive." Lemert similarly determined that California's probation practices belied any claim of a "new" era in offender supervision. Moreover, the punitiveness of many intermediate sanction programs has been diluted because of the unintended consequences associated with the strict enforcement of multiple program conditions; enforcement contributes to increased violations, which contributes to prison overcrowding. Georgia, for instance, has outlawed returns to prison for technical violations, and, in Florida, offenders are more often referred to residential treatment after several positive drug tests than to prison (Lucken, 1998). Lurigio and Petersilia (1992) too have noted the inherent contradiction of intermediate sanctioning—to get tough is to also increase prison overcrowding—and have subsequently recommended that only the most essential conditions be imposed based on an individual offender needs or risk basis.

With regard to Dr. Smith's reference to firearms policies, permission to carry a firearm should be understood as just that, permission. Though no extensive research has been conducted on this topic in particular, in the course of interviewing probation officers throughout Florida for other purposes, the author has incidentally found that roughly 50 percent of the officers, at most, have opted to carry a firearm. It is recognized, however, that further research is needed before statements can be made about the prevalence of firearm policies and gun-toting probation officers.

A final point to be made about the community corrections/community control controversy is that, at some level, punishment and treatment have always coexisted. It is not that one objective absolutely replaces the other. Rather, one or the other objective comes into focus at different points. Recall that the punitive posture that emerged in the decade of the eighties was a response to the liberal posture of previous decades. Now that the sediments of retributive policies have settled, there is, not surprisingly, a move in the other direction and a greater sense of needing to achieve some balance (Lucken, 1998). The following statements appearing in probation officer manuals of decades past reiterate these points.

> The service that the probation or parole officer can give to the community is not merely that of exercising surveillance over the lawbreakers…but a concern with the client life… (Keve 1954, p. 83).

> Conscientious corrections workers have always asked themselves anxiously whether their duty lies more with treatment or surveillance (Keve 1967, p. 9).

> Restraint and restriction have coercive value, but force needs to be accompanied by counseling (Newman, 1958, p. 205).

This essay and these excerpts show that the rehabilitative mission is no more a relic of the past than the control mission is an invention of the present. I therefore conclude that Dr. Smith and others have exaggerated the meaning and import of certain trends and subsequently mistaken a temporary blip for a permanent pattern.

REFERENCES

Keve, P. W. (1954). *Prison, probation, or parole? A probation officer reports.* Minneapolis: University of Minnesota Press.

Keve, P. W. (1967). *Imaginative programming in probation and parole.* Minneapolis: University of Minnesota Press.

Latessa, E. J. (1987). The effectiveness of intensive supervision with high risk probationers. In Belinda R. McCarthy (Ed.), *Intermediate punishments: Intensive supervision, home confinement, and electronic surveillance,* Monsey, New York: Criminal Justice Press, pp. 99–112.

Lemert, E. M. (1993). Visions of social control: Probation considered. *Crime and Delinquency, 39,* 447–461.

Lucken, K. M. (1998). Contemporary penal trends: Modern or postmodern? *The British Journal of Criminology, 38,* p. 106–123.

Lurigio, A. J. & Petersilia, J. (1992). The emergence of intensive probation supervision programs in the U.S. In J. M. Byrne, A. J. Lurigio, and J. Petersilia (Eds.), *Smart Sentencing,* Newbury Park, CA: Sage Publications. pp. 3–17.

Newman, C. L. (1958). *Sourcebook on probation, parole and pardons.* Springfield, IL: Thomas.

NO

Karol Lucken

As the close of the twentieth century draws near, debates of old versus new, progression versus regression, or modern versus postmodern have become all too common. The essence of these debates lies in determining whether some trend or set of trends signals the end of one era and the dawning of another. Such debates are now being pursued in the realm of punishment, as scholars and practitioners alike question whether current penal trends represent a notable departure from past penal trends. (Simon & Feeley, 1992, 1995; Garland, 1995; Lemert, 1993; Lucken, 1998; McWilliams, 1987; Radzinowicz, 1991; Rhine, 1997; Rumgay, 1989; Simon, 1993). The question posed in the chapter title, "Have Community 'Corrections' Become Community Control?" reflects this controversy and what many contend is a dramatic turn of events in our approach to sanctioning.

The debate concerning the form and function of community sanctioning is indeed a timely one; it was approximately one hundred years ago that probation and parole were institutionalized as formal sanctions. At the close of the nineteenth century, Progressive reformers laid the theoretical and programmatic foundations of probation and parole (Rothman, 1980; Schlossman, 1977; Simon, 1993) that many claim have now vanished from the penal landscape (Simon & Feeley, 1992, 1995; Rhine, 1997; Simon, 1993). A distilled version of this claim is that probation and parole practices have been severed from their rehabilitative roots. For example, Feeley and Simon (1992) argue that the thrust of sanctioning is no longer the "correction," reformation, or reintegration of offenders based on their individual characteristics. Rather, they contend, it is the "control," monitoring, and maintenance of offenders based on aggregate characteristics. The most striking evidence of this presumed shift is the abundance of electronic surveillance, drug, polygraph, and other technological devices designed to track offenders' whereabouts and behaviors. On the face of it, then, perhaps community "corrections" is more justifiably termed community "control." However, on closer inspection, one finds that claims of a radically new age in sanctioning are simply overstated.

It is submitted that in the rush to ascribe new meaning to current penal practice, a highly compressed view of community sanctioning has been presented. This essay attempts to demonstrate that community "corrections" is not a misnomer and that much of what is "old" remains and what is often perceived as "new" is actually an extension of the "old." To illustrate this point, three dimensions of community sanctioning are discussed. They include the language of programs, program content, and the perceptions and roles of probation officers.

The Language of Community-Based Programs

If the nature of sanctioning has fundamentally changed, the new intentions, motivations, and ideas that underlie penal programs should be revealed in the language employed to articulate program objectives. In this section, I examine whether the language of program objectives remains grounded in notions of reform, normalization, and reintegration, or is alternatively grounded in notions of control, management, and monitoring. To address this question, the mission statements of prominent professional correctional associations and federally recognized state and local level community-based programs are presented.

Those who contend that sanctioning is no longer engaged in the work of rehabilitation or correction have apparently disregarded the "words" of those directly involved in its administration. For example, The American Probation and Parole Association (APPA) has called for a range of sanctions and services that provide safety through..."individualized sentences for offenders" (APPA, 1995). A nationally recognized Florida county corrections division has recently defined its mission as "…breaking the cycle of recidivism through treatment and success-ful reentry of inmates." New York's DTAP Program (Drug Treatment Alternative to Prison) aims to "reduce drug use and criminal recidivism and improve the vo-cational and social capabilities of program participants" and California's "Conti-nuity of Care" project seeks to prepare paroled offenders by addressing their various transitional needs. (Bureau of Justice Assistance, 1994) On a smaller scale, New Hampshire's felony pretrial diversion program acknowledges the "limited rehabilitative potential of traditional sanctions, the efficiency of rehabil-itative efforts…and the need for community involvement in the rehabilitation and reintegration of offenders" (Bureau of Justice Assistance, 1994). A Washington state program deemed by the Federal Office of Justice Programs as worthy of rep-lication provides even stronger evidence of the persistence of rehabilitative intent. Offering "a chance for change," the Pioneer Human Services program works to aid in the rehabilitation, training, care, and employment of socially handicapped individuals, including alcohol- and drug-related cases, convicts, parolees and per-sons on probation and under the jurisdiction of court (Bureau of Justice Assis-tance, 1994).

Although these mission statement examples in no way provide an exhaustive account of penal program objectives, they do show that the nation's leading profes-sional associations (i.e., APPA) and largest (e.g., New York, Florida, California) and smallest (e.g., New Hampshire) penal systems have maintained a "corrective" agenda. Nevertheless, for a more substantiated understanding of community sanc-tioning, one must go beyond the "words" of penal programs and include also the "deeds" (Blomberg, 1995). The language employed to articulate sanctioning mo-tives and ideas is indeed reminiscent of a rehabilitative era, but can the same be said of community sanctioning practices and activities?

The Contents of Community-Based Programs

The contents of community-based programs, as measured by daily practices and ac-tivities, reasonably correspond with the "corrective" language of program missions. The most glaring demonstration of this correspondence is the routine reliance on classification instruments and mandated treatment. For example, classification in-struments that help promote rational, consistent, and equitable assessments of each offender's needs and risks (Solomon & Baird, 1982) have become standard features of federal, state, and local community-based programs (Clear & Gallagh-er, 1985; Schumacher, 1985; Simon, 1993). Byrne and Pattavina (1992) note that 56 percent of all adult intermediate sanction programs in the United States con-duct offender needs assessments (this does not include the needs assessments conducted for regular probation and parole and other community-based pro-grams). Their relevance to the goal of rehabilitation and attaining knowledge on the offender's life history is illustrated by a multi-state adopted instrument known as "client management classification." This lengthy survey queries offenders on matters of family background and relationships, personal relationships, school adjustment, employment history, personality traits, mental health, and the immediate circumstances surrounding the criminal event. The survey ultimately yields a "score" that assists officers in rendering offender supervision decisions. For example, the results of individual assessments allow "officers to spend more time and energy with those offenders who need extra assistance in completing probation successfully" (Orange County Corrections, 1995) and help determine appropriate treatment and caseload placement (Bureau of Justice Assistance, 1994). For example, community-based programs rely heavily on specialized caseloads that match special needs offenders (e.g., drug, domestic violence, youthful, mental health, mentally retarded, HIV-infected, sex) with specially trained probation officers (Abadinsky, 1994; Champion, 1990). Although some would counter that classification instruments and specialized caseloads are nothing more than managerial tools for effectively allocating control and limited resources, it is equally conceivable that the coupling of offender types with officer types better serves the interests and needs of offenders.

The prevalence of treatment as a condition of community supervision lends further support to this argument. Specialized treatment has become an expected condition of supervision for drug, sex, and domestic violence offenders (Lucken, 1997) and referrals to anger management, educational, vocational, and life skills counseling for offenders in general have become equally commonplace (Blomberg & Lucken, 1994; Byrne & Pattavina, 1992; Lucken, 1997; Pearson & Harper, 1990; Petersilia & Turner, 1993). In 1996, there were approximately 2,000 known institutional and community-based sex offender program providers throughout the nation. In 1986, there were approximately 700 (Safer Society Foundation, Inc, personal communication, 1996). In the state of Washington, sex offenders must consent to participation in treatment to be considered eligible for probation. Drug intensive supervision probation programs in Washington, New Mexico, Georgia, Virginia, and Iowa stress participation in substance abuse treatment, education, and employment programs, and maintain counseling participation rates that consistently exceed 38 percent and often reach 100 percent (Petersilia, Turner, & Deschenes, 1992). MacKenzie and Parent (1992) note that, in boot camps, time spent in rehabilitative activities often outweighs time spent in physical training and work. Offenders in Alabama, Arizona, Mississippi, New York, and Louisiana boot camps spend an equal or greater amount of time in rehabilitation activities compared with nonrehabilitation activities, and Texas, Oklahoma, and Illinois have received federal funding to develop programs that specifically address offender needs (MacKenzie & Parent, 1992).

The generic counseling program known as Moral Reconation Therapy (MRT) has also been implemented in community corrections programs nationwide. Twenty-one states, including Connecticut, Oklahoma, Florida, Montana, Indiana, Ohio, California, Tennessee, and Washington, have adopted this program as a way of providing generalized treatment to offenders of all types and addictions (Bureau of Justice Assistance, 1994; Little, Robinson, & Burnette, 1994). MRT-based programs propose to "reeducate clients socially, morally, and behaviorally" (Little, Robinson, & Burnette, 1994). These programs seek to instill appropriate goals, motivations, and values by enhancing self-concept, decreasing hedonism, and developing higher stages of moral reasoning (Little et al., 1994).

The volume of offender referrals to treatment has prompted many state correctional systems to contract with private agencies for the provision of a number of mental health and substance abuse services. Florida, Texas, and Georgia have contracted for various psychological, substance abuse, and educational services, and the American Probation and Parole Association (APPA) has encouraged intensive supervision programs nationwide to do the same (APPA, 1995; Beto, 1987; Jensen, 1987). Contracts have vastly increased treatment resources and the ease with which offenders can be admitted to programs (Lucken, 1998). For example, probation officers have indicated that treatment had previously been a virtual impossibility because programs were either nonexistent or filled to capacity (Lucken, 1998). Veteran probation officers have confessed that before the advent of contracts, rehabilitative efforts were more of an assumption than a reality (Lucken, 1998). Although it may often be the case that probation and parole officers are not directly providing clinical counseling, it is being provided by the private sector at the behest of the justice system.

Again, however, the condition of treatment would be differentially interpreted by those who argue community "control" is a more apt description of current penal events. Advocates of this perspective would contend that mandated treatment constitutes a different brand of confinement, restriction, and punishment because treatment is rigorous, demanding, and coercive. In other words, when an offender with a substance abuse problem attends group counseling sessions headed by a certified therapist who elicits discussion and confrontation of each members' problems and experiences, it is unmitigated control or punishment. Yet, when a law-abiding citizen does precisely the same, it is treatment. According to this line of reasoning, then, are we to also assume that when dealing with offenders, licensed therapists abandon their professional calling and take up the cause of a wholly punitive state?

To extend this argument further, it is helpful to examine the profiles of those engaged in the supervision of offenders. After all, if those who most frequently interact with offenders identify with the social service function, then it is likely that "corrective" aims will still persist in some form or fashion.

Roles and Perceptions of Probation Officers

It is widely acknowledged that probation officers assume multiple and conflicting roles, including officer of the court, law enforcement officer, social worker, and broker of services (Abadinsky, 1994; Champion, 1990). Despite these varying roles, however, the ideal of making a positive difference is always kept in view. Gordon (1990) and others have observed (Blomberg & Lucken, 1994; Lucken, 1998) that officers still subscribe to the goal of "changing lives" so that offenders can become productive and responsible citizens. The degree to which this goal looms in the background (or in the forefront) can be illustrated in part by the educational and professional experiences of probation officers. For example, most probation officers possess degrees in social work, sociology, and psychology, and many go on to obtain such certifications as LMHCs—Licensed Mental Health Counselor, LCSWs—Licensed Clinical Social Worker, and CACs—Certified Addictions Counselor (APPA, 1995, Orange County Documents). Each of these disciplines and accreditations are firmly embedded in the study of behavior or behavioral transformation, which begs the question, "why would someone pursue career training in the helping sciences only to reject their premise and utility in the workplace?"

What's in a Name?

Observers of this debate may well be wondering to what end is this conflict over semantics being directed. Is it a sociological problem—"what is community sanctioning doing?"—or a philosophical problem—"what should community sanctioning be doing?" Clearly, it is a problem that hinges on both of these interrelated questions. Consequently, what may appear to be just a theoretical exercise does in fact have practical implications.

As already noted by Dr. Smith, it is difficult, if not impossible, for agencies to function properly without discernable goals. Moreover, it is not possible to determine a program's effectiveness in the absence of goals. Yet, the clarification of penal goals is also crucial to the task of establishing ethical and legal boundaries in community sanctioning. If goals are lacking or loosely defined, one can scarcely determine the legitimacy of conditions in terms of their degree of intrusion, coercion, and restriction (von Hirsch, 1990). For example, if "correction" is no longer a viable goal, then is it appropriate to require offenders to attend (and pay for) treatment? Conversely, if the primary goal is "correction," is it appropriate to subject offenders (and their families) to warrantless searches and home video surveillance?

These and other normative questions relating to community sanctioning have not been adequately addressed in academic, legal, or public policy forums. Community sanctioning has been the prevailing mode of punishment for more than two decades, yet it lags far behind incarcerative sanctioning in tending to issues of guidelines, individual and third-party rights, and various operational procedures. How these issues are addressed in the future will depend largely on whether community sanctioning is officially defined as a mechanism of "control" or "correction."

REFERENCES

Abadinsky, H. (1994). *Probation and parole.* Englewood Cliffs, NJ: Prentice Hall.

American Probation and Parole Association. (1995). APPA'S vision: Welcome to the land of oz: Where dreams can come true. *Perspectives 19,* 6–12.

Beto, D. R. (1987, July). Contracting for services. *Texas Probation.*

Blomberg, T., & Lucken, K. (1994). Stacking the deck by piling up sanctions: Is intermediate punishment destined to fail? *Howard Journal, 33,* 62–80.

Blomberg, T. G. (1995). Beyond metaphors: Penal reform as net-widening. In T.G. Blomberg & S. Cohen (Eds), *Punishment and social control.* New York: Aldine De Gruyter, pp. 45–61.

Bureau of Justice Assistance. (1994). *State and local programs: Focus on what works.* Vol I.

Byrne, J., & Pattavina, A. (1992), The effectiveness issue: Assessing what works in the adult community corrections system." In J. M. Byrne, A. J. Lurigio, & J. Petersilia (Eds), *Smart sentencing: The emergence of intermediate sanctions.* Sage Publications.

Champion, D. (1990). *Probation and parole in the United States.* Old Tappan, NJ: Merrill Publishing Company.

Clear, T. R., & Gallagher, K. W. (1985). Probation and parole supervision: A review of current classification practices. *Crime and Delinquency, 36,* 423–443.

Feeley, M. & Simon, J. (1992). The new penology. *Criminology, 30,* 449–474.

Garland, D. (1995). Penal modernism and post-modernism. In T. G. Blomberg & S. Cohen (Eds), *Punishment and Social Control,* New York: Aldine De Gruyter, pp. 181–209.

Gordon, D. R. (1990). *Justice juggernaut.* New Brunswick, NJ: Rutgers University Press.

Jensen, C. (1987). *Contracting for community corrections services.* Washington, DC: National Institute of Corrections.

Little, G. L., Robinson, K. D., & Burnette, K. D. (1994). Cognitive behavioral treatment review and CCI news, Memphis, Tennessee, *Correctional Counseling, Inc.,* Vol 3, No. 2 & 3.

Lucken, K. M. (1998). Contemporary penal trends: Modern or postmodern? *The British Journal of Criminology, 38.*

Lucken, K. M. (1997). Privatizing discretion: "Rehabilitating" treatment in community corrections. *Crime and Delinquency, 43,* 243–259.

MacKenzie, D. L. & Parent, D. G. (1992). Boot camp prisons for young offenders. In J. M. Byrne, A. J. Lurigio, & J. Petersilia. (Eds), *Smart sentencing: the emergence of intermediate sanctions.* Sage Publications.

McWilliams, W. (1987). Probation, pragmatism, and policy. *The Howard Journal, 26,* 97–121.

Orange County Corrections Division. (1988). *Revisioning the role of corrections.*

Orange County Corrections Division. (1995). *Classification.*

Pearson, F. S. & Harper, A. G. (1990). Contingent intermediate sentences: New Jersey's intensive supervision program. *Crime and Delinquency, 36,* 75–86.

Petersilia, J. S., Turner, S., & Deschenes, E. P. (1992). Intensive supervision programs for drug offenders. In J. M. Byrne, A. J. Lurigio, & J. Petersilia, (Eds), *Smart Sentencing: The Emergence of Intermediate Sanctions.* Sage Publications. pp. 18–37.

Petersilia, J., & Turner, S. (1993). Intensive probation and parole. In M. Tonry, (Ed), *Crime and Justice: A Review of Research,* Vol. 17. Chicago: University of Chicago Press.

Radzinowicz, Sir Leon. (1991). Penal regressions. *Cambridge Law Journal, 50,* 422–444.

Rhine, E. E. (1997). Probation and parole supervision: In need of a new narrative. *Corrections Management Quarterly, 1,* 71–75.

Rothman, D. J. (1980). *Conscience and Convenience.* Scott, Foresman, and Company.

Rumgay, J. (1989). Talking tough: Empty threats in probation practice. *Howard Journal, 28,* 177–186.

Schlossman, S. (1977). *Love and the American delinquent: The theory and practice of "progressive" juvenile justice, 1825–1920. University of Chicago Press.*

Schumacher, M. A. (1985). Implementation of a client classification and case management system: A practitioners view. *Crime and Delinquency, 31,* 445–455.

Simon, J. (1993). *Poor discipline: Parole and the social control of the underclass, 1890–1990,* University of Chicago Press.

Simon, J., & Feeley, M. M. (1995). True Crime: The new penology and public discourse on crime. In T. G. Blomberg & S. Cohen (Eds) *Punishment and Social Control,* 147–180. Aldine De Gruyter.

Solomon, L., & Baird, S. (1982). *Classification: A tool for managing today's offenders.* Laurel: American Correctional Association.

U.S. Department of Health and Human Services, Substances Abuse and Mental Health Services Administration. (1995). Overview of the National Drug and Alcoholism Treatment Unit Survey: 1992 and 1980–1992. *Advance Report Number 9.*

von Hirsch, A. (1990). The ethics of community-based corrections. *Crime & Delinquency, 36,* 162–173.

Rejoinder to Dr. Lucken
Georgia Smith

In support of her contention that treatment continues to dominate community-based corrections, Dr. Lucken examines mission statements, program content, and employee role perceptions. In this section, I will address Dr. Lucken's arguments, pointing out areas of agreement and disagreement. The chapter will conclude with a brief discussion of the utility of Feeley and Simon's (1992) concept of the new penology.

Dr. Lucken and I are in agreement on a number of points. First, she correctly notes the tension between the objectives of treatment versus punishment and control that has marked the history of community-based sanctions. Also, she identifies references to treatment, rehabilitation, and reintegration in program and agency mission statements. Finally, she notes the increase in the number and variety of treatment programs. However, we disagree regarding the conclusions to be drawn from the recent literature in this area.

First, most mission statements cited by Dr. Lucken are those of treatment programs (i.e., DTAP, "Continuity of Care," Pioneer Human Services) rather than corrections agencies. One would expect administrators of treatment programs to extol the benefits of rehabilitation. Corrections agency officials, however, must mollify a public that appears disillusioned with the rehabilitative ideal. Consequently, one would expect the more "politically correct" language of offender control in these policy statements. Recall that a study of a state probation and parole agency showed an explicit and dramatic shift in agency mission from treatment to offender control over the past twenty years (Smith, 1997).

In her discussion of program content, Dr. Lucken cites the widespread adoption of classification instruments and mandated treatment. However, classification devices of current programs differ in fundamental ways from those used during previous eras. Earlier classification instruments were based on clinical prediction methods, in which the correctional employee's training and work experiences guided classification decisions.

Current classification instruments typically use actuarial prediction methods, in which the criteria used to derive risk and needs "scores" measure offender traits that research suggests are associated with recidivism and program failure (Holt, 1998). Also, as Simon (1993) contends, several criteria that appear to be based on concern with treatment (i.e., questions regarding family and employment history) also serve to identify high-risk offenders who lack informal controls. Mandatory treatment programs may then be used to increase control over these offenders. Finally, these practices also promote perceptions of agency efficiency and accountability.

Dr. Lucken convincingly illustrates the increase in the number and variety of treatment programs. However, as she notes, many of these services are provided by the private sector or by noncriminal justice agencies. Increasingly, probation and parole agents act as "resource brokers," referring offenders to other public and private agencies for services and treatment, rather than as direct service providers (Schwartz and Travis, 1997). Again, although treatment programs have increased (particularly in the private sector), it appears that the trend among field agents is to emphasize surveillance and control functions while leaving the business or treating offenders to others.

Finally, Dr. Lucken argues that the educational and professional training of probation officers reflect a treatment orientation. A recent study of field officers and supervisors in a state probation and parole agency, however, suggests a shift away from treatment-oriented disciplines in officers' preferences for graduate study. Supervisors and veteran officers typically reported advanced degrees or graduate work in counseling or social work. Novice officers and those who began graduate study more recently, however, were more likely to report graduate work in criminal justice or public administration (Smith, 1997).

To summarize, I readily agree that treatment remains a goal of community-based sanctions and an important concern of many practitioners. However, the bulk of the recent literature in this area suggests that recent changes in ideology, goals, and practices are more basic than the periodic shifts in emphasis that have characterized the history of community corrections. Although I question Feeley and Simon's (1992) claim that these changes constitute a "paradigm shift," I believe that correctional goals and practices in most jurisdictions more closely resemble a risk-management or offender-control model than the treatment model of progressive era reformers.

Finally, I contend that the divergent conclusions drawn by Dr. Lucken and myself illustrate the utility of the new penology concept. Our respective reviews of the literature show tremendous variation in correctional goals and practices across jurisdictions, rendering sweeping generalizations about the current state of "Community-Based Corrections" suspect. Perhaps it is more useful to examine the extent to which specific programs and practices approximate "ideal" treatment or risk-management models rather than attempt to characterize the complex system of agencies, programs, and practices that comprise community-based corrections as old versus new, modern versus postmodern, or even treatment versus control-oriented.

REFERENCES

Feeley, M. M., & Simon, J. (1992). The new penology: Notes on the emerging strategy of corrections and its implications. *Criminology, 30*; 449–474.

Holt, N. (1998). The current state of parole in America. In J. Petersillia (Ed.), *Community corrections: Probation, parole, and intermediate sanctions.* New York: Oxford University Press.

Schwartz, M. D., & Travis, L. F. III. (1997). Serve or surveil? In M. D. Schwartz & L. F. Travis III (Eds.), *Corrections: An Issues Approach.* Cincinnati: Anderson Publishing Co.

Simon, J. (1993). *Poor discipline: Parole and the social control of the underclass, 1890–1990.* Chicago: The University of Chicago Press.

Smith, G. B. (1997). *Contemporary parole decision making: Modern versus postmodern explanations.* Ph.D. dissertation, Florida State University.

From a Peacemaking Perspective, Is Individual Change More Important Than Social Change?

Dr. Michael Braswell holds degrees in behavioral, humanistic, and counseling psychology as well as rehabilitation counseling. His books include *Inner Corrections* (with Bo Lozoff), *Justice, Crime, and Ethics* (with McCarthy & McCarthy), and *Human Relations and Corrections* (with Miller & Fletcher).

Wayne Gillespie holds a degree in philosophy from the College of William & Mary. He is currently completing his masters degree in criminal justice and criminology at East Tennessee State University. Primary research interests include feminist issues, particularly in areas of domestic and family violence and abuse.

M. Joan McDermott, Ph.D., is an Associate Professor in the Department of Administration of Justice and the Department of Sociology at Southern Illinois University at Carbondale. Her current interests include peacemaking and feminist criminology, girls/women and crime, and popular culture and crime.

YES

MICHAEL BRASWELL AND WAYNE GILLESPIE

If I have a feeling of anger...how would I deal with it?...I know that anger is me; and I am anger. Nonduality, not two. I have to deal with my anger with care...and nonviolence...If we annihilate anger, we annihilate ourselves... When we get angry, we have to produce awareness: I am angry. Anger is me. I am anger. (Hanh, 1987, p. 40)

Why begin an essay on peacemaking with a quote about anger? The quote by Thich Nhat Hanh not only embodies a contrasting perspective between personal and social change, it also illustrates the three themes of this essay: (1) personal awareness, (2) personal change or transformation, and (3) the power of forgiveness and compassion.

History is replete with examples of anger fueling social change. Marxist and Communist revolutions, the French Revolution, and even the civil rights violence in our own country during the sixties all offer examples of anger projected outward. When oppressed victims in a society or in a family use fear and anger to defeat the oppressor, fear and anger remain. It does not disappear, but is rather displaced. As a result, the idealistic political reformer becomes a tyrant, and the sexually abused child himself becomes a sexual predator. Subsequently, the often-heard exclamations around small-town barbershops and bars, that if we could get rid of the crooked lawyers, corrupt politicians, dangerous criminals, then we could live in decent, law-abiding neighborhoods, are more myth than reality. Why? Because we would still be there, still be a part of the social landscape.

Social change is important, but first comes personal change. As Thich Nhat Hanh (1987) states, "if we annihilate anger, we annihilate ourselves" (p. 40). When I feel angry, anger is in me and anger is more inclined to obliterate than liberate. That is why the dedication to a book on correctional peacemaking states "this book is dedicated to the keeper and the kept, the offender and the victim, the parent and the child, the teacher and the student, and the incarcerator and the liberator that is within each of us" (Lozoff & Braswell, 1989). We have to respect and take care of the fear and anger that is in us in nonviolent ways or we will express it to those we care about most as well as others, adding to their pain and our suffering. Richard Quinney (1988) writes, "rather than attempting to create a good society first, and then trying to make ourselves better human beings, we have to work on the two simultaneously" (p. 73). In truth, I cannot really control what you do. I cannot even completely control what you do to me. I can only control to some extent what I choose to do in relation to your actions: how I react to your response. If I want to change the outside world, I have to work on myself, on my inside world. Returning to the civil rights violence of the sixties, it seems clear that African Americans had every justification to feel angry about the way they were being treated. There were two basic models for them to follow. H. Rap Brown advocated meeting force with force, and Martin L. King, Jr. responded to racial violence with a form of militant nonviolence. He attempted to disarm hatred with love and compassion. M. L. King, Jr., declared peace on racial hatred and prejudice. From the one to the many, M. L. King, Jr.'s example encouraged others to join him, laws to be changed, and hearts to be transformed. He had to become personally aware that there was a better way to respond to racism, and he had to undergo personal change and transformation in his own mind and heart to become the powerful symbol of forgiveness and compassion that he remains today.

Personal Awareness

Thich Nhat Hanh's quote on anger gives an account of what can happen when we confront and engage anger, but he also reveals the first step toward personal change. Personal change is not an easy path to follow. It begins with self-awareness. The quest to *know thyself* transcends every culture and all religions. It is, perhaps, the most basic of human concerns. In Western philosophy, *know thyself* is a Socratic maxim. However, much of Western philosophy and religion seems to motivate us to objectively examine ourselves, to disassociate our mind from our body, our heart, and our emotions. Parker Palmer (1983) suggests that such an approach encourages us to live "one-eyed" lives. He believes that we should use both the heart and the head, *whole sight*, in the living of our lives.

Buddhist teachings suggest an alternative approach: self-knowledge of and in the moment. This may be a more enlightened conception of the maxim *know thyself*. As illustrated above, when we are angry, we become anger. It is a momentary condition that can be alleviated through a more holistic sense of personal awareness. The art of meditation also helps us prepare ourselves for the onset of anger, hatred, and greed by focusing on the virtues of care, love, tenderness, compassion, and nonviolence. Meditation is a means of cultivating personal awareness. By becoming more personally aware, we are not evading the problems of the world. In fact, we begin to respond to such problems more clearly and mindfully.

Richard Quinney (1988), in examining Eastern religions, writes "the higher wisdom can be attained only with the loss of the conditioned ego and the realization of the transcendental Self...life now demands an inner awakening, a spiritual development...in all of our learning and complex analysis, including our attempts at interpretation, we obscure and perhaps miss the reality of the experience that we wish to understand" (pp. 104–106). Personal or self-awareness is integral to the sense of transcendence of which Quinney writes.

We suggest that if personal awareness is cultivated throughout one's existence, we can do more than think about, believe in, financially support, and vote for peace. We can increasingly **be peace.** Peace, not anger, is the practice in which we should engage. Our contemporary society seems always to be striving toward reason. Modern society is inclined to value the term *reasonable* over the term *mindful.* Yet, mindfulness is broader than the boundaries of reason. Mindfulness interprets reality and incorporates truth in a transcendental context, simultaneously aware of the here and now—of what is probable and what is yet to come—what is possible. M. L. King, Jr.'s famous speech, "I Have a Dream," embodies the transcendental reality of mindfulness.

Modern methodology and science further obfuscate the simple wisdom that Quinney and others have advanced. In fact, Braginsky and Braginsky refer to the worship of the scientific method as *methodolatry.* The scientific method attempts to test hypotheses in an effort not to prove the truth of a precept, but rather to prove the falsity of that doctrine. Human behavior is neither true nor false; it simply is. Traditionally, as scientists, we observe phenomena of which we cannot be a part. We maintain an objective disposition, a discrete distance from that which we study. However, as Thich Nhat Hanh (1987) points out, even modern physicists are beginning to reject this notion of the uninvolved observer. For example, when physicists inquire into the nature of subatomic particles, they must use their minds to visualize the particles. Hanh (1987) suggests that the scientist and the particle become one in mind. In such a context, scientists can be considered participants, not merely observers.

There is an intimate relationship between the thoughts in our mind and the conditions of being. What we feel in our hearts and minds is extended into the world through our actions and nonactions. The concept of mindfulness involves the extension of the mind into the world. As Sri Eknath Easwaran (1995) writes, "when our mind is hostile, it sees hostility everywhere and we act on what we see." Personal awareness is essential before we begin any sort of scientific investigation, metaphysical journey, or social activism. An objective mind, as promulgated by Western philosophy, is fertile ground for the seeds of anger and violence. Easwaran (1995) suggests that we should attempt to cultivate a *disposition for benevolence*. We believe that this disposition of benevolence must be present before ideas such as Immanuel Kant's *good will* can exist. In fact, it makes little sense to speak of an *objective good will*. The good will must be preceded by a benevolent disposition. In Buddhism, personal awareness and this disposition for benevolence are both enhanced through meditation, but both also involve the realization that we are our thoughts (minds) and our feelings (heart). If we are angry, we are anger. We will perpetuate anger through actions. We will see anger in the world, which in turn may further fuel our own anger. The remedy, of course, lies in our personal awareness. Once we are aware of this condition, then what?

Personal Change and Transformation

> We cannot destroy the energy (anger); we can only convert it to a more constructive energy. Forgiveness is a constructive energy. Understanding is constructive energy. . . . So the destructive energy of anger, because of understanding, is transformed into the energy of love. (Hanh, 1987, p. 41)

The first step in the peacemaking process involves the realization and awareness that we actually are the anger that we feel in ourselves. This energy can be initially diminished by simply being aware of it. Yet, being aware of this anger is incomplete. To find or return to peace, we need to have peaceful thoughts and feelings and act in more peaceful ways. First comes awareness, then change. As stated previously, we may only possess the power to change one person: ourself. Interestingly enough, in undertaking such a task, changes in others also may occur. For instance, Mother Teresa felt her call. Twenty years later, she was given permission to start her mission. She started alone, picking up the sick and dying from the streets of Calcutta, one person at a time. The first sisters to join her were former students that she had taught at the convent school years earlier. Likewise, a janitor who is mindful and peaceful and works in a prison will change more inmate lives than all of the caseworkers and therapists with graduate degrees who do not have their own lives in order (Lozoff & Braswell, 1989).

The process of personal change is analogous to a religious or spiritual awakening. Religions differ in their respective doctrines on religious calling, yet most rely on a sense of *God's presence*. The initial experience that one undergoes when the power of God is felt in the heart is similar to the experience that one undergoes when personal awareness ignites personal change. There is an example of this type of personal change in Jerry Levin's testimonial. Jerry Levin was CNN's Bureau Chief for the Middle East. He was taken hostage in the Middle East and held against his will for a year. Ten years ago, he was released. During his confinement, Jerry was transformed from a Jewish intellectual atheist into a *man of faith*. This transformation was initiated by personal awareness, and aided by contemplation, then change. He recounts the following:

> Even more than the idea of God, I had always scorned the ideas of Jesus. His prescriptions for achieving peace on earth I had been sure were unworkable. Forgiveness in particular was an impractical act that only served to leave the forgiver dangerously vulnerable. However, the more I thought about forgiveness, and also Jesus' idea of love and reconciliation, the more I realized how exactly appropriate they have been and are for creating the only climate in which true tranquility, true peace, and true justice can universally exist…after days of intense contemplation, on April 10th, 1984, I arrived at what I call the banks of my spiritual Rubicon: a spiritual river in time, not space, that remained to be crossed, a diminishing point in time— first hour, then minute, a second, a thousandth of a second, then a millionth—on one side of which I did not believe, but on the other I simply did. (Levin, 1997)

Levin's testimony gives credence to the notion that awareness leads to change. Although this anecdote recounts one man's spiritual catharsis, it also serves as a model of how change can occur. As we have mentioned before, change such as personal awareness is not an easy process. However, as with Jerry Levin, peacemaking can only occur when lives are changed one person at a time (Bartollas & Braswell, 1993).

An existential model for personal change and transformation known as the PACTS model is one way of exploring the possibilities of peacemaking. It is a descriptive model that chronicles a sequential process of personal change: *Paradox, Absurdity, Choosing, Transcendence,* and *Significant emerging*. Although it is a personal model of change, it can be effectively shared with other persons (one at a time) to initiate change on the social level. Paradox is the first step in this process. It is a simple notion that involves an awareness of the self and world. Paradox occurs when we realize that things are not what they seem, or that which appears to be wrong may in reality be right. According to the author, "the lessons of life's paradox include: (a) pay close attention to what's going on around you and the choices you are making—things are not always what they may seem; (b) stay humble—there are no guarantees, and we don't absolutely control anyone or anything, and (c) still, if we work at being conscious of (a) and (b) and keep trying, we can still gain insight and wisdom from the bad times and become stronger" (Braswell, 1989, p. 54).

Absurdity is the second step in the PACTS model. Absurdity is the state of mind we experience as negative paradox: when our infallible plans fall apart and our world seems out of control. Absurdity shatters our preconceived notions of our reality and security. Absurdity could almost be seen as a secondary stage of self-awareness. First, when we thought that we could handle our loss, we may instead become angry. Then we may realize that we are, in fact, anger. During this stage, we may become receptive to other internal virtues or external influences. "The lessons of absurdity include: (a) life doesn't always 'add up' for anyone; (b) where my tragic and absurd experiences 'lead to' is more important than where they come from; and (c) all the experiences in our life, both good and bad, are part of the growing process; if we keep trying, even in our most absurd and despairing times can in the end work for our and others' good" (Braswell, 1989, p. 55).

Choosing is the third stage in the PACTS model. The stages of self-awareness described by paradox and absurdity create a crossroads experience. During this stage, we either choose to change (commitment) or we choose not to change (noncommitment). Relationships with others become very important during the choosing phase of the PACTS model. However, we come to learn that they cannot alleviate the anxiety and pain that is a part of process of self-awareness. We can rely on others to help us through this personal journey, but it is a journey that, in part, we must take alone. "The lessons of choosing include: (a) trying to become more responsible for who I am and who I want to be; (b) persevering in trying to put my good intentions into action; (c) making an effort to work through relationship traps of which I am a part; and (d) forgiving myself and others when we fail so that I can keep trying" (Braswell, 1989, p. 56).

Transcending is the fourth step in the PACTS model. A transcending attitude takes full responsibility for what I have done and where I am at, yet at the same time, it encompasses a leap of faith that enables me to have a vision of what I can become. Transcendence is the quality that the human spirit utilizes to transform anger into the possibility of forgiveness, hatred into the possibility of compassion, and greed into the possibility of generosity. "The lessons of transcending include: (a) accepting responsibility for where I am in my life, but being committed to a vision of hope in who I can become; (b) caring enough to struggle with whatever I am attached to—hate, power, another person, or whatever it is; (c) practicing meditation to quiet my body and mind so that I can make clearer and more meaningful choices my life" (Braswell, 1989, p. 58).

Significant emerging is the final step of the PACTS model. This phase in personal change and transformation is concerned with the costs and consequences of our choices. It requires an honest reflection on the paths that we have taken and the paths that we have ignored. It also increases our sensitivity to the connectedness that ties all of these actions together. Significant emerging involves an integration and synthesis of what we have gained and lost. The author writes, "each of us have chosen pathways that have led us to places that we did not realize we were going at emotional and physical costs we were not aware we would have to make" (Braswell, 1989, p. 58).

The PACTS model is a template for existence. It provides us with a framework by which to examine how past changes and present conditions may affect future decisions. Through such a model, personal awareness can lead to personal change. Personal awareness can be cultivated through meditation, focusing on the virtues of care, love, tenderness, and nonviolence. Such change can transform deception, fear, and anger into honesty, compassion, and inner peace.

The Power of Forgiveness and Compassion

> Speaking very generally, we may say that the criminal law institutionalizes certain feelings of anger, resentment, and even hatred that we typically direct toward wrongdoers, especially if we have been victims of those wrongdoers. In the present age, most of us do not feel comfortable talking about the criminal law in such terms, for we are inclined to think that civilized people are not given to hatred and to an anger so intense that it generates the desire for revenge.... We prefer to talk high-mindedly of our reluctancy advocating punishment of criminals perhaps because social utility or justice demands it and tend to think that it is only primitives who would actually hate criminals and want them to suffer to appease an anger or outrage that is felt toward them. Good people are above such passions, or at least they claim to be. (Murphy, 1990, pp. 2–3)

If we are to follow a peacemaking model, it seems essential that we acknowledge the personal and social problems of hypocrisy and self-deception that Murphy (1990) addresses. When we become angry, we may personally project this anger outward. When large numbers of persons in society begin to project anger, we tend to look for a morally safe target. Throughout history, we have selected groups that the "rest of us" considered untouchable. For example, consider the American slave trade, the Nazi Holocaust, and even our modern criminal justice system. In retrospect, the American slave trade and the Nazi Holocaust seem morally deplorable primarily because they were founded on the ignorance and fear of racial and ethnic prejudices. The African Americans and the European Jews are now perceived as innocent victims. However, inmates in the criminal justice system have transgressed against the "rest of us." They have not followed our rules; thus, we feel justified in our abhorrence of them. Yet, is this form of anger and hatred any different than that of the past? We have become an angry, retributive, and punitive people. We are inclined to scoff at the ideas of rehabilitation and compassion. No matter what the social mores, it always seems safe to hate criminals, never realizing the great enemy is hate rather than criminals.

Easwaran (1995) asks, "can wrong means ever lead to right ends?" How can we, as a society, expect those who make a mistake to redeem themselves when we are so angry at them? When we are angry, we become anger. We project anger and it is absorbed by others. Then we look to the world, and it is angry. In regard to anger, Levin (1997) states that it "only perpetuates resentments and hostilities and promotes vendettas, retaliations, and revenge. The absence of war is not peace." In the Hebrew language, the word for peace, *shalom,* is more holistic. Shalom concerns a fullness of meaning and purpose in one's life. Frederick Buechner (1973) writes that peace refers not to "...the absence of struggle, but the presence of love" (p. 64). Peace requires mindful diligence and a level of self-awareness that enables us to forgive. Dietrich Bonhoeffer writes, "we must learn to regard people less in the light of what they do or omit to do, and more in the light of what they suffer" (In Castle, 1988, p. 42).

The issues of suffering and service are inherent in creating personal awareness, change, and transformation in the process of peacemaking. In our culture, suffering is viewed as the great enemy rather than a teacher. Ancient wisdom and spiritual traditions are often ignored regarding their respect and reverence toward suffering. Suffering "is an intimate and enduring part of the human condition. The abused becomes the abuser, the victim, the victimizer. From Job to Ted Bundy, the innocent and guilty alike suffer" (Bartollas & Braswell, 1993, p. 50). If we become discerning enough to follow Bonhoeffer's suggestion in regarding people "in light of what they suffer," our passion for justice will become tempered by a compassionate heart. It would include the possibilities of forgiveness and serve the purpose of peace and restoration. Working examples of the power of forgiveness and compassionate service include Bo and Sita Lozoff's Human Kindness Foundation and the Restorative Justice Movement (Van Ness & Strong, 1997). Murphy and Hampton (1990) offer two additional reasons why forgiveness and compassion are worthy goals for persons who are becoming more aware and transformed in their lives:

- We should forgive to reform the wrongdoer; i.e., we should forgive, not because the wrongdoer has repented, but as a step toward bringing his or her repentance about.
- We should forgive because we ourselves need to be forgiven. (p. 30)

The power of forgiveness can also be illustrated by the response that we received from an undergraduate student during a discussion on ethics. We were discussing the personal aspects of victimology. The question was offered: "Would you choose to be the victim or the offender if great personal injury was to be suffered by the victim?" The majority of the class, as might be expected, chose to be the offender. However, one softspoken young woman answered, "I would chose to be the victim because only the victim has the power to forgive." She grasped a concept that had eluded the entire class. The power of forgiveness is inextricably tied to the power of change and compassionate service. Only those who experience this power can respect the anger and fear and respond with compassion and care.

It is much easier to talk about or even write a paper about peacemaking than to actually be peaceful and help others become at peace with themselves and their world. Mother Teresa writes, "I do not agree with the big way of doing things. To us what matters is the individual. To get to love the person we must come in close contact with him. If we wait till we get the numbers, then we will be lost in the numbers…I believe in person to person…that person is the only person in the world for me at that moment" (In de Bertodano, 1993, p. 48).

REFERENCES

Bartollas, C., & M. Braswell. (1993). Correctional treatment, peacemaking, and the new age movement. *Journal of Crime and Justice, 16*(2), 43–58.

Braginsky, B. M., & Braginsky, B. D. (1974) *Mainstream Psychology: A Critique.* New York: Holt, Rinehart & Winston.

Braswell, M. C. (1989). Correctional treatment and the human spirit: A focus on relationships. *Federal Probation, 5*(2), 49–60.

Buechner, F. (1973). *Wishful Thinking.* New York: Harper & Row.

Castle, T. (Ed.). (1988). *The New Book of Christian Quotations.* New York: Crossroads Publishing.

Easwaran, S. E. (1995). Peacemaking. *Inner Self Magazine* [On-Line]. Available from the World Wide Web: http://www.innerself.com/archives/mar95/easwaraa.htm.

Hanh, T. N. (1985). *Being Peace.* Berkeley, CA: Parallax Press.

Levin, J. (1997). One man's journey. *A Call to Peacemaking.* [On-Line]. Available from the World Wide Web: http://www.bruderhof.org/ploughs/plough43/levin.htm.

Lozoff, B., & Braswell, M. (1989). *Inner Corrections.* Cincinnati, OH: Anderson Publishing.

Murphy, J. G. (1990). In Murphy, J. G. & J. Hampton (Eds.), *Forgiveness and Mercy.* Cambridge: Cambridge University Press.

Palmer, P. (1983). *To Know as We Are Known.* San Francisco: Harper & Row.

Quinney, R. (1988). Beyond the interpretive: The way of awareness. *Sociological Inquiry, 58*(1), 101–116.

Teresa, Mother. (1993). In de Bertodano, T. (Ed.), *Daily Readings with Mother Teresa.* Glasgow, Great Britain: Harper Collins.

Van Ness, D., & Strong, K.H. (1997). *Restoring Justice.* Cincinnati: Anderson.

Rejoinder to Dr. Braswell and Mr. Gillespie

M. Joan McDermott

Because I agree with much of what Braswell and Gillespie have written, this response is brief. I think our disagreement is more in emphasis than substance. The opening paragraph of my earlier piece noted that I believe individual change and social change are interconnected, that we can't act violently in our personal lives and hope that the world around us will change. Braswell and Gillespie make this point early in their paper, as well, by quoting Quinney.

I would like to reiterate a key proposition in the perspective I offered and show how it is linked to the thinking of Braswell and Gillespie. In proposition II, I state that violence results from depersonalization and inequality. Drawing heavily on Harold Pepinsky and feminist philosophy, I suggest that conditions of inequality create the structure within which individuals are enabled to be unresponsive. I view these structural factors as cultural evils (Noddings' term). In the peacemaking literature, cultural evils are structural violence, and they inflict pain and suffering. My point is that these cultural evils may place limits on the capacity for individual change.

Toward the end of the Braswell and Gillespie piece, the authors write about suffering and forgiveness. I think that factors such as poverty, racism, sexism, heterosexualism, and other cultural evils create limits on individual change simply because they make the job of forgiveness much greater for some of us than for others. Thus, I think the task of peacemaking involves both personal change and the elimination of cultural evils.

NO

M. Joan McDermott

As the women's movement gained momentum in the early 1970s, I drew strength and understanding from consciousness-raising groups. I continue to believe that the personal is political. I also believe that individual change and social change are interconnected, that we cannot act violently in our personal lives and hope that the world around us will change.

Having said this, I still come down on the side of saying that, for peacemaking criminology, social change is just as important as individual change. Moreover, without significant elimination of inequalities in life chances, I believe that the potential for individual change is greatly limited.

There is no single peacemaking perspective. Rather, the ethic of nonviolence unites diverse peacemaking criminological perspectives (religious, humanist, critical, and feminist). Here I tie together peacemaking criminology and feminist philosophy. Ethical concerns and priorities of criminology as peacemaking are similar to those of feminist ethics, and these include (McDermott, 1994): We are tied to other human beings and also to the environment. To achieve peace and justice, we need loving and compassionate individuals. We also need equality. From love and compassion flow understanding, service, and justice. The nonviolent ethic assumes that human action is motivated by emotion as well as reason, and that knowledge is both rational and emotional.

Drawing from peacemaking criminology, primarily as developed by Harold Pepinsky,[1] and from feminist ethics, in this essay I develop six propositions about violence and use examples related to violence against women to illustrate several points. More than anything, these propositions illustrate the connections between individual change and social change in a peacemaking perspective.

I. *Violence is unresponsiveness.* Peacemaking criminologist Harold Pepinsky (1991, p. 17) defines violence as *unresponsiveness,* as involving a "willful disregard for one's effect on others." *Responsiveness* (1991, pp. 15–16) means "that what one expects to achieve by one's actions (in common law parlance, one's 'intent') is modified continually to accommodate the experience and feelings of those affected by one's actions." Violence can be physical, verbal, or even nonverbal, can occur through an action (such as an assault) or an omission (as in child neglect), and can be "direct and personal" or "indirect and structural."

The definition of violence as unresponsiveness does not separate criminal from noncriminal violence, as is the case in traditional, mainstream criminology. The distinction between criminal and noncriminal violence is not particularly useful from a feminist perspective, except in highlighting the gendered nature of the criminal law. That is, the criminal and noncriminal categories reflect power differences between men and women in a patriarchal society (for example, the point at which unwanted sex becomes forcible rape).

Numerous contemporary criminological perspectives, especially critical and postmodern views, advocate definitions of crime that are not tied to the criminal law. For example, in a recent volume on criminology, Einstadter and Henry (1995, p. 312) take the perspective that,

> In its most fundamental sense, crime is the expression and use of power to deny others their right to be human. Crime occurs when another's humanity is denied and the person is redefined as an object to be acted upon.

The peacemaking criminologist's definition of violence as unresponsiveness is consistent with such natural (non-criminal law based) definitions of crime as this.

At the interpersonal level, violence as unresponsiveness occurs when an individual acts without regard to the effect of her or his action on another or others, does not take into account the feelings or needs and denies the humanity of another or others. At the socio-structural level, unresponsiveness results from power differences that create the conditions that allow people with power to disregard those without power. In between the individual and the social structure, agencies and organizations have the potential to be unresponsive.

II. *Violence results from depersonalization and inequality.*[2]

Depersonalization, or the denial of individuality or personhood, is a necessary condition for unresponsiveness. We cannot commit violence against people we know as individuals, people whose pain we feel. This is a fundamental tenet for the peacemaking criminologist. To depersonalize is to judge another unworthy of personhood. In her feminist theory of equality, Drucilla Cornell (1995, p. 10) uses the term *degradation*, a term that is useful in this context: By 'degradation,' I mean a literal 'grading down' because of one's sexuality. By a 'grading down,' I mean that one has been 'graded' as unworthy of personhood, or at least as a lesser form of being.

The depersonalization of violence as unresponsiveness is a "grading down." To say that the feelings and wants of the individual are not taken into account is to say that she is deprived of personhood.

This degradation or depersonalization may vary in harmfulness depending on the relationship between the victim and the offender. Criminologists examine differences between violent crimes committed by strangers and those committed by nonstrangers. Unfortunately, the stranger–nonstranger distinction frequently works against an understanding of violence against women. Acts of violence are more likely to be viewed seriously and labeled crimes if they are committed by strangers. Yet some of the most brutal and degrading acts of violence against women are perpetrated by men they know. By contrast, when violence is unresponsiveness, violence by nonstrangers (friends, acquaintances, spouses, employers) is more heinous because of the intentional depersonalization of someone (presumably) known as an individual.

Unresponsiveness entails the willingness and ability to depersonalize or grade down the other. Conditions of social inequality create the structure within which individuals are enabled to be unresponsive, while the willingness to be unresponsive may derive from prior experience of unresponsiveness.[3] Categorization fosters degradation by ignoring individual differences and facilitating hierarchial arrangements. Whole categories of people are denied their worth as persons because of some characteristic. Gender hierarchies sustain the conditions that foster violence against women. Racial, ethnic, and religious inequalities set the stage for hate crimes. Heterosexism encourages gay bashing.

To elaborate on the immorality of social inequality, I draw on Nel Noddings'[4] (1989, p. 121) standpoint feminist, phenomenological analysis, which develops a sense of evil as "that which induces pain, separation, and helplessness." Evil or immorality is judged in relation to whether activities and relations are life-sustaining or life-enhancing. This feminist perspective on evil departs from prior conceptions of evil developed by the "giants" of moral philosophy (Noddings, 1989, p. 90):

> ...the traditional view of evil concentrates on evil as disobedience to the patriarch. The harm that we do to each other is not primary. Although traditionalists consider that harm, they describe it as *evil* only when it transgresses the laws of God, state, father, or chief. (Italics in original.)

By contrast, in the feminist perspective, evil is revealed in the context of relationships, and the harm that we do to each other is a primary concern. In relational ethics, "the response of another is one important criterion by which we judge the morality of our acts." (1989, p. 184)

Noddings distinguishes natural, cultural, and moral forms of evil (1989, p. 120):

> The pain of illness and death are natural evils; *poverty, racism, war, and sexism are cultural evils;* the deliberate infliction of physical or psychic pain—unless we can show convincingly that it is necessary for a desirable state in the one undergoing pain—is moral evil. (Emphasis added.)

Noddings explains *cultural evils* in greater detail (1989, p. 104):

> Human beings frequently participate in the practices of their culture without reflective evaluation. A man living in the early days of patriarchy almost certainly did not intend to inflict pain, separation, and helplessness on the female members of his family—as long as they were 'good' women. He did not consider the possibility that he was committing an evil. His evil deeds in this arena were not the deliberate acts that we must now evaluate as *cultural evils*. (Italics in original.)

Cultural evils then, are interpreted as activities and relations that—even though they inflict pain, separation, and helplessness—are accepted practices in a society (for Noddings, culture). For peacemaking criminology, then, it is because the activities and relations—the operations—of racism and sexism in society pro-duce pain, separation, and helplessness that we can view these structural inequal-ities as cultural immorality.

III. *As social beings, we have cross-currents*[5] *of violence and responsive-ness and thus we are all capable of violence.* Because we are social, we have the ability to respond with love and compassion, to modify our actions by taking into consideration their effect on others. We also have the potential to be unresponsive.

To contend that we are all capable of responsiveness is not to contend that we are all equally prone to responsiveness. Socialization, and particularly gender role socialization, may operate so that women, to a greater degree than men, are brought up to be caring, to value responsiveness, connectedness. Other factors, such as social stratification and psychobiology, probably influence tendencies to-ward responsiveness. In interaction with others and the environment, we become individuals by influencing and being influenced by society, culture, and biology.

IV. *Unresponsiveness is counternormative.* Because we are social beings, dependent on and connected to each other, unresponsiveness is counternormative, in the true sense of running counter to social norms regarding expected behaviors. However, unresponsiveness is distributed unevenly throughout society; some peo-ple more freely violate norms with which they basically agree.

For example, there is no disputing the fact that (what counts as) violent crime is related to social class, race, gender, and age. Criminologists debate the ex-istence of "subcultures of violence" whose norms and values favor the use of vio-lence in a wider array of circumstances than broader society. Research, however, suggests that no social groups unconditionally approve of crime (Agnew, 1995). More relevant to the current discussion, studies of the social correlates of violent crime are misleading to the extent that they suggest that within certain social groups violence is normative, when what they truly indicate is that individuals within specific class/race/age/gender subgroups more readily violate the norms or are more frequently apprehended.

Most recently, criminologists are engaged in analysis of masculinities and crime, especially the "manliness" of criminal violence.[6] This intriguing and growing body of research suggests, for example (Braithwaite & Daly, 1994, pp. 189–190):

> Multiple masculinities are implicated in the gendered patterning of vio-lence. Men's violence towards men involves a masculinity of status, compe-tition and bravado among peers....Men's rape and assault of women reflects a masculinity of domination, control, humiliation, and degradation of women....Other types of harmful conduct involve a shameless masculin-ity or a masculinity of unconnectedness and unconcern for others. When

called to account for exploitative conduct, men's responses may be rage rather than guilt, or an amplification of non-caring identities such as 'badass.'

It is possible to interpret this research as suggesting that, for men, or for certain masculinities, violence is normative, but this is overstating the evidence. For one thing, most men are not violent. Some men may, more easily than other men and most women, act with violence or an uncaring 'badass' orientation. This does not mean that unresponsiveness is normative for men. It may mean that social structures and processes create conditions in which men more easily violate a norm of responsiveness.

V. *Unresponsiveness is more likely to occur when there is a prior experience of unresponsiveness.* Individuals have different life chances. We become persons in interaction with social structures and processes, such as socialization, which shape alternatives and the experience of unresponsiveness. To return to proposition II above, to be unresponsive, an individual must be willing and able to depersonalize another. Social structures may *enable* depersonalization by creating conditions in which the other is degraded—for example, women, gays, people who are obese or handicapped. The *willingness* to be unresponsive—the willful choice of violence—may have more to do with social processes such as previous experience of violence. Thus, family violence researchers point to the intergenerational transmission of child abuse; the childhood experience of abuse may increase the likelihood of becoming an adult child abuser. Depersonalization by a parent—a purported caregiver—teaches lessons about parenting and caregiving, and is perhaps the ultimate interpersonal betrayal. Still, most abused children do not grow up to be child abusers (Kaufman & Zigler, 1993), and this may have something to do with their ability to form other attachments in their lives.

Because unresponsiveness occurs at the societal level, for example, in the creation of ghettoes and slums in major urban areas, the experience of unresponsiveness may be particularly profound for some individuals. Age, gender, race, and urban residence intersect and interact to limit alternatives in such a way that almost one third of young, African American men are in prison or under correctional supervision in the community.

VI. *Summary:* Violence is unresponsiveness, acting without taking into account the effect of our actions on others. Although we are all capable of unresponsiveness, unresponsiveness is counternormative. It results from social inequality, the experience of unresponsiveness, and depersonalization.

Together these propositions create a conceptual framework for understanding violence that links individual factors with broader societal and cultural level factors. From a peacemaking perspective, then, I would argue that both individual and social change are necessary. Further, if patterns of social inequality shape life chances and enable unresponsiveness, then there is a limit on the ability of individual-level change to eliminate violence.

NOTES

1. In this paper I draw on Pepinsky's (1991) *The Geometry of Violence and Democracy.* Another useful reference for readers who would like an overview of criminology as peacemaking is Pepinsky and Quinney (1991) *Criminology as Peacemaking,* an edited volume.

2. See Pepinsky's (1991) discussion. Many of the articles in Pepinsky and Quinney (1991) contain the same theme.

3. This is discussed below in proposition V.

4. Noddings' standpoint, feminist moral philosophy helps elaborate our understanding of the peacemaking concern with inequality and the destruction of relationships. However, I depart from Noddings in two ways. First, I attribute the feminist standpoint more to socialization (as opposed to biology) than she does. Second, I see the caring perspective as one of many valid voices in moral philosophy. This line of thought is developed in Charlene Haddock Seigfried's (1996) pragmatic feminism.

5. Cross-currents is Pepinsky's (1991) term.

6. See the research reported in Tim Newburn and Elizabeth Stanko's (1994) *Just Boys Doing Business?*

REFERENCES

Agnew, R. (1995). Strain and subcultural theories of criminality. In Sheley, J. H. (Ed.), *Criminology* (2nd ed., pp. 305–328). Belmont, CA: Wadsworth.

Braithwaite, J., & Daly, K. (1994). Masculinities, violence and communitarian control. In Newburn, T. and Stanko, E. A. (Eds.), *Just boys doing business?* (pp. 189–213). New York: Routledge.

Cornell, D. (1995). *The imaginary domain.* New York: Routledge.

Einstadter, W., & Henry, S. (1995). *Criminological theory.* New York: Harcourt Brace.

Kaufman, J., & Zigler E. (1993). The intergenerational transmission of abuse is overstated. In Gelles, R. J., & Loseke, D. R., *Current Controversies on Family Violence* (pp. 209–221). Newbury Park, CA: Sage Publications.

McDermott, M. J. (1994). Criminology as peacemaking, feminist ethics, and the victimization of women. *Women & Criminal Justice.* 5(2), 21–44.

Newburn, T., & Stanko, E. A. (Eds.) (1994). *Just boys doing business?* New York: Routledge.

Noddings, N. (1989). *Women and evil.* Berkeley: University of California Press.

Pepinsky, H. E. (1991). *The geometry of violence and democracy.* Bloomington: Indiana University Press.

Pepinsky, H. E., & Quinney, R. (Eds.). (1991). *Criminology as peacemaking.* Bloomington: Indiana University Press.

Seigfried, C. H. (1996). *Pragmatism and feminism.* Chicago: University of Chicago Press.

Rejoinder to Dr. McDermott Michael Braswell and Wayne Gillespie

Personal transformation and social awareness are both necessary in order to realize the goals of peacemaking within the criminal justice system. Furthermore, personal transformation, social awareness, and criminal justice boundaries are all connected. One is dependent upon the other to exist in reality. For instance, personal change will not liberate an entire class of oppressed individuals. An awareness and activism on a societal level must be present in order to have any real impact on the social reality of these individuals. Social activism cannot exist without motivated individuals who have experienced a personal transformation. Both social activism and personal change are constrained within the boundaries of the criminal justice system. A punitive and harsh criminal justice system can undoubtedly suppress social and personal change.

To some extent, we become that which we feel. Consider this analogy to the artist's palette: Imagine that we as individuals are paints, the color of which reflects the state of being (feeling) that we are experiencing. For instance, when we are angry, we become anger. This could be symbolized by red paint. When we are content, we become contentment. This could be symbolized by blue paint. When we are angry and project the anger outward, it is essential that we try not to annihilate the sensation of anger. Rather, we should focus on a disposition of benevolence and the virtues of love, compassion, and forgiveness. In reconciling our contradicting emotions and feelings, the colors mix or muddle. The red of anger and the blue of contentment may combine, restoring us to purple, the color of peace. Imagine the social sphere as the canvas on which we apply the paint. The criminal justice system could be conceptualized as the frame that encompasses the canvas. All three aspects are necessary to form a picture, or a work of art, in much the same way all three are necessary to peacemaking becoming a lasting part of our social reality.

Social Inequality and Peacemaking

Dr. McDermott initiates a treatise on peacemaking by focusing on the social inequality suffered primarily by women as well as the response of the women's movement in the 1970s. Certain feminine ethics are essential to the peacemaking movement. Three main themes of peacemaking have been identified as central to the philosophy (Braswell & Gold, 1996). These three themes include (1) care,

(2) connectedness, and (3) mindfulness. The tenet of care is particularly shaped by the feminine ethic of love and tenderness. The greatest human love is characterized by the love that a mother has for her child. Usually, a strong physical and emotional bond exists between a mother and her child. This is due in part to the very biology of the relationship. The child is temporarily a part of a woman's physical body. Regardless of the emotional or interpersonal bonds that a father may forge with his daughter or son, it may, in many cases, never compare to the closeness felt by the mother. It is this bond, this love, that we wish to aspire towards when we speak of the tenet of care. It is a bond that has the potential to unite humankind. If we attempted to emulate this type of relationship when we interact with others, it would be difficult to exhibit a *willful disregard for one's effect on others.*

The second tenet of peacemaking, connectedness, speaks to the problems associated with this willful disregard. Ultimately, everyone and everything is connected. All things are tied to the planet and to our sun. The environment plays an essential theme in peacemaking. Native American teachings contribute to our understanding of the relationship between the earth and the human race by establishing a crucial idea: we belong to the earth, the earth does not belong to us (Chief Seattle). Again, Western thought may promote a disassociation from the earth. We need to see ourselves as a part of rather than apart from the earth.

Mindfulness is the ability to think with one's heart and one's head. This is the third tenet of peacemaking. When facing social inequality, it is necessary to use global thinking. We cannot simply fight fire with fire. That is an ineffective strategy for promoting social change. In fact, if we combat inequality with force, violence will emerge. Thus, a mindful approach would focus on promoting change from nonviolence: well-planned, thoughtful, yet still passionate. Again, the women's movement may provide a good example of nonviolent means of achieving social change. Much change has occurred during the last two decades; and most, if not all, of this change has been nonviolent. While gender inequality remains an issue today, we can see the changes that have occurred as a result of a more caring, peaceful effort.

Reference

Braswell, M. C., & Gold, J. (1996). Peacemaking, justice, and ethics. In Braswell, M. C., McCarthy, B. R., & McCarthy, B. J., (Eds.), *Justice, Crime, and Ethics,* 2nd Edition. Cincinnati: Anderson (pp. 23–38).

Is Left Realism a Useful Theory for Addressing the Problems of Crime?

Martin D. Schwartz, Professor and Chair of Sociology at Ohio University, and Walter S. DeKeseredy, Professor of Sociology at Carleton University, Ottawa, have jointly or with others published dozens of articles and book chapters and more than ten books. Each has published most extensively in the field of violence against women from a pro-feminist perspective, but both have also published a number of works on left realism and critical criminology. Obviously, both reject the notion that these strands of thought are opposites or mutually exclusive. Neither has been convicted, as yet, of a felony.

Stuart Henry (Ph.D., University of Kent-Canterbury, England, 1976) is Professor of Sociology and Criminology at Eastern Michigan University. He has researched varieties of marginalized knowledge and informal institutions, including mutual aid groups, informal economies, nonstate systems of discipline and social control, and cooperatives. Most recently, he examined the relationship between social norms, private discipline, and public law. Dr. Henry has sixteen books and more than sixty articles published. His most recent works include *Criminological Theory: An Analysis of Its Underlying Assumptions* (with Werner Einstadter, 1995), *Constitutive Criminology: Beyond Postmodernism* (with Dragan Milovanovic, 1996), and *Essential Criminology* (with Mark Lanier, 1998). Dr. Henry serves on the editorial board of *Theoretical Criminology*. He has received the State of Michigan Teaching Excellence Award (1990) and Eastern Michigan University's Distinguished Faculty Scholarly–Creativity Award (1995).

YES

Martin D. Schwartz and Walter S. DeKeseredy

It is close to midnight on Saturday night in the emergency room at General Hospital, and the cases are piling up. Larry, the victim of a drive-by shooting, feels his life slowly fading away while a doctor tries to stop the flow of blood. Sally, who was raped and badly beaten by a stranger out behind the supermarket, sits weeping in a corner unattended because Larry's case is more life-threatening. Grandma Jackson, who caught a rock on the forehead when vandals in the housing project threw one through her living room window, sits dazed and bloody in a plastic chair.

"Listen up, folks," you say. "First of all you have to realize that the violence here is not all that significant compared to what major corporations do every day to their workers. Just in Bhopal, India, for example, in 1984 Union Carbide's faulty controls released enough poison gas to kill thousands and injure hundreds of thousands. It is the mass media that makes us think that lower-class, working-class, and underclass crime is more widespread than middle- and upper-class crime."

If you are lucky, you will be thrown out the door by hospital security and not held for psychological observation. Certainly these crime victims will not be comforted by your words. Nor will others. It is unlikely that many women will say, "Well, Sally got raped out behind the supermarket, but I won't worry about walking there myself tonight, given all of the men killed over the years in illegally unsafe mines in West Virginia."

Amazingly, though, that represents the arguments of a great many criminologists around the world, including altogether too many on the left. Termed "left idealists" by some, they ignore or dismiss predatory street crimes committed by economically disadvantaged and minority people by turning all of their attention to corporate crime and sensational media accounts of statistically infrequent violent acts (e.g., serial murders). Of course, it must be noted that they are right. The people of most countries, including those of North America, lose more money to the economic crimes of corporations than to all street crimes put together. The violence of illegally unsafe working conditions, and the resulting "accidents" that kill and maim workers, can be appropriately compared to street violence.

Still, people do not give up sitting on the stoop or park benches to meet with their neighbors because they are scared that General Electric will overcharge the Pentagon. They do not nail their windows shut during heat waves without air conditioning because they fear that Union Carbide will release poison gas. They do not spend large amounts of their income on security devices, taxis, and lighting because so many asbestos workers are getting cancer. All of these are true, and should be on people's minds, but generally those at the bottom of the socioeconomic ladder have another source of fear: each other.

Jock Young, at Middlesex University in England, and other people around him, first developed the argument that people politically on the left must realize that it is working-class, lower-class, and underclass men raping lower-class women. These men are the ones who commit drive-by shootings, and they also commit most of the burglaries and robberies that terrorize lower-class, working-class, and underclass inner-city neighborhoods. Economically disenfranchised men commit most of the harassment of minority groups of women, of Asians, of Hispanics. Certainly criminologists can develop dozens of reasons why this might be the case. What they have not turned their attention to adequately is that it is the case.

Like any other field of endeavor, left realists have had brilliant successes in thinking through some ideas, and they are still working hard to plug some loopholes in their theories. However, they do have some basic and important ideas. Most important is that they see themselves as "realists" rather than "idealists." The problem is that there are a lot of realists in the world, but most of them are conservative. The failure of the left to provide progressive and humane alternatives to rightwing and racist agendas on crime (e.g., radical incarceration, the death penalty, etc.) has been a total disaster. First, conservatives seized on the fear of voters generally to make a political issue out of crime. If the voters were racist, then there were always politicians available to exploit that racism by implying that criminals were African American and that to take a hard line on crime was to take a hard line on race also. By the time that liberals figured out that the voters were swayed by this line of thinking, they (such as Bill Clinton) decided that the way to win voters was to outconservative the conservatives. If they could only be anti-crime enough themselves, they could tap into a media-induced moral panic and racist backlash to win some votes themselves. Left by the wayside were progressive politics from the left that might have had some effect on crime.

Thus, for example, in the United States, Republican politicians demonized crack cocaine, knowing that their cries to get tough on crime would mainly affect young poor African American men, the main group using crack. The last decade has seen extraordinarily long prison sentences imposed on these young men, much longer than the sentences given to people using equivalent amounts of equivalent drugs, such as powder cocaine. This has had two major results: (1) U.S. prisons have become filled with young men of color, much more so than in any overtly racist period of our history, and (2) politicians discovered that ever more extravagant attacks on African American men worked to attract white votes (Tonry, 1993).

Central Principles of Left Realism

Left realism actually began in the United Kingdom with the publication of John Lea and Jock Young's (1984) *What Is To Be Done About Law and Order?* Since that time, numerous publications have described this school of thought (Lowman & MacLean, 1992; Matthews and Young, 1986, 1992; Schwartz and DeKeseredy, 1991; Young and Matthews, 1992). At this point, we can outline some major features of this school of thought, without going into some of the more complex theoretical positions.

Most important is that left realists argue that street crime is a serious problem for the lower and working classes. It is more than a media scare. Robbery, burglary, rape, assault, and property theft represent seriously antisocial behaviors that have a major effect on the material conditions of the poor and working class people. Now, as suggested above, left realism does not forget that crimes of real estate, industrial waste, unsafe working conditions, unsafe products, poor medical care, and white collar and corporate crime in general also affect working and lower-class people. In fact, some left realists, such as Frank Pearce (1992) and Walter DeKeseredy and Colin Goff (1992), have gathered survey data and published theoretical articles on these and other crimes of the powerful. Furthermore, left realists argue that suite crime may affect poor people in the same way as middle-class citizens, or it may affect them more. However, left realists explicitly assert that the more vulnerable a person is politically and economically, the more likely it is that a person will be victimized from all directions; with white collar crime, street crime, unemployment and poverty, and a host of other ills.

It is thus important to left realists that they propose short-term progressive strategies to deal with crime. They are not scientists wearing white lab coats who only have an interest in learning about why people commit crime, but no commitment at all to the communities that hire them to try to help to solve some of these problems. Rather, left realists try to develop humane and progressive policies that counter harsh right-wing policies, but which might be equally effective. Over the years, these policies have included *demarginalization,* where governments might work to avoid breeding an entire population of youth with no hopes of ever securing reasonable employment in their lives, and therefore little to gain by acting in prosocial manners. Left realists have argued for democratic control of policing, which they claim will make it more likely that police uphold the values of the community than carrying out the values of a national political and economic elite. Similarly, community participation in crime prevention is a strategy designed not only to tap the expertise of the local community, and the goals and desire of that community, but at the same time to engender a feeling of general participation so that residents "own" the form of social control they must live under. The importance of this point is underscored by numerous lower-class, underclass, and working-class people in many countries, who report to criminologists that they feel that they are being held in check by the forces of an occupying army sent in by the political elite.

Criminological Theory

Another place where left realists take issue with the most extreme criminologists is that they do not automatically reject mainstream criminological theories, such as Robert K. Merton's (1938) strain theory and Albert K. Cohen's (1955) subcultural perspective on working-class delinquent boys. Bluntly, just because someone is mainstream or right wing does not mean that their criminological analysis is automatically wrong. Several concepts that should be familiar to criminologists form an important part of left realist theory.

For one, left realists believe that relative poverty rather than absolute poverty is a key to understanding crime. There are a great many people who live around the world at a very low standard of living who do not engage in crime. However, when people come to the conclusion that they are being cheated; that other people have many more material goods than they have for no particularly good reason, this is a political situation that breeds discontent. Solutions may be broad, such as the many riots, political movements, and labor organizings that have taken place over the past century. Or, people may opt for individual solutions, which can include street crime. Of course, one of the advantages of this concept is that it does not specify a dollar or peso or ruble amount at which a person feels deprived. In the case of some of our many white collar criminals, it is the shame of being the only member of the country club who cannot afford a 700 series BMW or equivalent car that can make a person feel relatively deprived.

Subcultural and strain theories have also had a strong influence on realist theory (Matthews, 1987). In a situation in which there is no legitimate opportunity to solve this problem of relative deprivation, subcultural groups may form that give legitimacy to alternative methods of reaching goals. Thus, some people may become heroes in one community for being a very brave armed robber, whereas others will become heroes in another for embezzling millions of dollars.

Thus, left realists are unlikely to blame minority youth for being inherently or culturally criminal. Yet, they do not shy away from noting that a great deal of North American crime is intraracial minority youth victimizing other minorities. As William Julius Wilson (1996) points out, the continued deindustrialization of North American cities and the economic marginalization of whole segments of minority youth have set up a group of people with little reason to refrain from criminal activity. Relative deprivation provides subcultural aspirations and motivations to take whatever short-term measures are available to rectify this problem, and crime is often the most available measure.

Perhaps a weakness of left realism (but then again this is a weakness of most criminology) has been to continue to build on the insights of feminist theorists to understand fully why girls and women are not typically major street crime actors. After all, they suffer from relative deprivation, belong to the same subcultures, and certainly have motivation to obtain additional goods in an illegal manner. Yet, they do not do this in any manner comparable to boys. The media may be enamored with a few violent women, and the government certainly has added to the numbers of women in prison by declaring a war on drug-using women (Chesney-Lind, 1997), but overall women still do not commit the bulk of street crimes. This will be a major area for future theorizing, because explaining women as criminals and women as crime victims represents one of the most important intersections of race, gender, and class in criminological theory.

Conclusion

Crime data generated by a variety of research methods show that in the United States a substantial number of lower-class and underclass inner-city residents in this country are worse off than they were during the 1980s (Devine & Wright, 1993; Wilson, 1996). For these and other reasons described here and in other sources (e.g., DeKeseredy, MacLean, & Schwartz, 1997), it is already past the time to consider how the left realist agenda can help prevent economically and socially disenfranchised people from being victimized by predatory street crimes. After all, the A Thin Blue Line law and order model advanced by conservatives has clearly failed, and left idealism is an inadequate alternative (Young, 1997). Todd Clear (1994) has discussed our unwillingness to entertain the idea that, after thirty years of ever-increasing incarceration, this human experiment has just plain failed. Elliott Currie (1993) has complemented this analysis by showing that we will never have enough prison beds to imprison our way out of our drug crisis.

As Devine and Wright (1993, p. 185), two of the world's leading experts on the plight of the inner-city poor, point out, without some realistic sense of a better future, there is no reason to aspire to its benefits when the reality of one's existence precludes their attainment. From our standpoint, left realism has the potential to provide the truly disadvantaged with some hope, opportunities for self-empowerment, and opportunities to successfully struggle for progressive social change. The policy proposals advocated by this progressive school of criminological thought are, like decent jobs and housing, the "major bulwark" against street crime (Young, 1997).

REFERENCES

Chesney-Lind, M. (1997). *The female offender: Girls, women, and crime.* Thousand Oaks, CA: Sage.

Clear, T. (1994). *Harm in American Penology.* Albany: State University of New York Press.

Cohen, A. (1955). *Delinquent boys.* New York: Free Press.

Currie, E. (1992). Retreatism, minimalism, realism: Three styles of reasoning on crime and drugs in the United States. In J. Lowman & B. MacLean (Eds.), *Realist criminology: Crime control and policing in the 90s* (pp. 88–97). Toronto: University of Toronto Press.

Currie, E. (1993). *Reckoning: Drugs, the cities, and the American future.* New York: Hill and Wang.

DeKeseredy, W., & Goff, C. (1992). Corporate violence against Canadian women: Assessing left-realist research and policy. *The Journal of Human Justice, 4,* 55–70.

DeKeseredy, W., MacLean, B., & Schwartz, M. (1997). Thinking critically about left realism. In B. MacLean & D. Milovanovic (Eds.), *Thinking critically about crime* (pp. 19–27). Vancouver: Collective Press.

Devine, J., & Wright, J. (1993). *The greatest of evils: Urban poverty and the American underclass.* New York: Aldine de Gruyter.

Lea, J., & Young, J. (1984). *What is to be done about law and order?* New York: Penguin.

Lowman, J., & MacLean, J. (Eds.). (1992). *Realist criminology: Crime control and policing in the 1990s.* Toronto: University of Toronto Press.

Matthews, R. (1987). Taking realist criminology seriously. *Contemporary Crises 11,* 371–401.

Matthews, R., & Young, J. (Eds.). (1986). *Confronting crime.* Newbury Park, CA: Sage.

Matthews, R., & Young, J. (Eds.). (1992). *Issues in realist criminology.* Newbury Park, CA: Sage.

Merton, R. (1938). Social structure and anomie. *American Sociological Review, 3,* 672–682.

Pearce, F. (1992). The contribution of left realism to the study of commercial crime. In J. Lowman & B. MacLean (Eds.), *Realist criminology: Crime control and policing in the 1990s* (pp. 313–335). Toronto: University of Toronto Press.

Schwartz, M., & DeKeseredy, W. (1991). Left realist criminology: Strengths, weaknesses and the feminist critique. *Crime, Law and Social Change 15,* 51–72.

Tonry, M. (1993). *Malign neglect.* Chicago: University of Chicago Press.

Wilson, W. (1996). *When work disappears: The world of the new urban poor.* New York: Knopf.

Young, J. (1997). Left realism: The basics. In B. MacLean & D. Milovanovic (Eds.), *Thinking critically about crime* (pp. 28–36). Vancouver: Collective Press.

Young, J., & Matthews, R., eds. (1992). *Rethinking criminology: The realist debate.* Newbury Park, CA: Sage.

Rejoinder to Dr. Schwartz and Dr. DeKeseredy
Stuart Henry

Reading Schwartz and DeKeseredy's Introduction to Left Realism leads me to the question, What is different between their perspective and sensational journalism, or pragmatic left-wing politics? Put simply, where is the criminology in this kind of analysis? More pertinently, where is the sociology? In the opening paragraphs, we are led through a litany of graphic tabloid sensationalism about street crime. Events absent context, such as "drive-by shooting," places claiming geographical reality such as "supermarket," "housing project," and taken for granted social types such as "stranger," "doctor," "vandals," are arranged to produce self-evident sense of fear and truth to the reader. But such images fail to critically challenge the very power hierarchy that feeds on their reproduction. "Doctors," "hospital security," and "grandma" represent the natural forces of good, whereas "vandals" and "strangers" conjure the forces of evil. But where is the analysis of this socially constructed order? Might it just be that the "housing projects" are tepid liberal government sops to absorb the extremes of impoverishment wrought by capitalist inequality; whose "supermarkets" are arenas for passive consumption, one part of the division of humans into consumers and producers; whose very acts of consumption reduce their humanity to objects, not least, producing sexual objects and sexual predators; whose programmed interactive extremes are manifest as "rape"; whose "doctors" are benefactors of their professionalization of knowledge, medicalization of life, and expropriation of health care into a rationed managed-care hierarchy of power and privilege; and whose establishment is pregnant with monopolization and distillation of therapeutic drugs controlled and marketed by the major multinational pharmaceutical corporations. Might a more sociological analysis suggest that these events, types, and outcomes are interrelated, not just with each other but with the structure and power of global capitalism? Might it just be that without the fragmentation brought by these social forces communities would be so integrated that the "stranger" could not exist, the treatment of injury would be performed by friends, kin, and neighbors in the community, which as Durkheim (1893) long ago pointed out, would further serve to integrate the community and insulate it against any tendency for individuals or groups to turn on each other?

The issue is not whether corporate crime is more widespread, costly, and physically harmful than street crime, which it is, nor whether the greater victims of street crime are produced by intimates rather than strangers, which they are, but rather how the street and suite crimes are interrelated outcomes of such a nexus of power–knowledge relations. The realist claim that economically disenfranchised men commit most victimization on their own women and minority group members denies the reality of sexual exploitation, class exclusion, and institutionalized racism committed by those economically enfranchised men (the powerful) who control employment, hiring, work relations, property ownership, and the numerous other opportunities for human growth and creative possibility in social life. To give concrete examples, the crimes of racism by Denny's restaurants, Avis car rental, and Texaco against customers and employees are crimes of the powerful, not crimes of the disenfranchised. Slavery and segregation were not crimes by African Americans on each other. The point is that the problem of abusing other humans, regardless of its manifest form, is pervasive throughout hierarchical power structures, whether these be feudal, capitalist, or socialist, and to focus largely or even exclusively on its appearance in the lower classes allows us, and particularly the powerful, not to deal with the underlying causes: the production and reproduction of systems of inequality.

Furthermore, as I argued previously, because people's fears produce self-defensive actions (avoiding certain areas at night, purchasing security equipment, etc.) based on the realities that are constructed by them through popular cultural sensitivities (replayed in the media), does not mean these fears are equated with the genuine risks that they face. Indeed, that they are blind to more diffuse but deadly harms is part of the problem and one that is further entrenched as the more direct and obvious street offenses are validated.

Because some of the politically powerful right-wing seek to sustain this ideology of exploitation by building on existing media-constructed fears, demonizing those already victims of inequality through reactionary policies under the guise of pragmatic crime-control policies, is no reason for the critical left to abandon its broader and more substantive analysis. "Short-term progressive strategies" are no substitute for thoroughly thought-through analysis of the political economy, unless we are simply competing for popular votes. If that is the case, criminology has little claim to scientific or even critical analysis. It has become little more than an appendage to liberal political agendas. It has become tabloid criminology.

As I argued, and as Schwartz and DeKeseredy reiterate, the left realist position does not have its own analysis of crime; it borrows this from strain and subcultural theory. The problem is not that borrowing a theoretical analysis from the mainstream is wrong. Rather that this borrowing has not been followed through even to its own policy implications. If relative deprivation and a sense of injustice are produced by a system of inequality in the production and distribution of wealth, why do left realists endorse tinkering with the opportunity structure? Indeed, as Hofman (1996) argues, even if the left realist agenda for increased work opportunity, decent housing, and constructive leisure activities seem rational under modernity, they are impossible to implement under conditions of "postmodernity" characterized by global economic competition, pronounced stratification, and suspicion about the ultimate meaning of life. Hofman (1996) argues that under such conditions the left realist policies run the risk of perpetuating the very inequalities they strive to eradicate. Moreover, if better opportunities permanently reduced the problem of relative depravation produced by inequality, why, as they admit, do the powerful also experience this and also cheat to get even further ahead? The reason is clear. It is because the system of inequality is pervasive in creating winners and losers, and in ensuring that any winning is only a short-lived fix, that when the initial euphoria has worn off, "winning" quickly sinks us back into competitive assessments of ourselves against others, and relative deprivation emerges refreshed and pungent as we strive to feed the insatiable desires that our political economy must continue to inculcate to expand and grow. For criminologists not to address these realities is tantamount to abandoning critical analysis for piecemeal temporary relief. Sure someone's got to tend the wounded and bury the dead of competitive capitalism's relentless war, but in the end, someone has to sit down and analyze how to bring about a peace process. And that means directly confronting the social forces of global capitalism and developing long-term strategies for cooperative relations of production, genuine participatory democracy, and an appreciative sensitivity to diversity and difference. This task is beyond the tabloid criminology that left realism promulgates.

REFERENCES

Durkheim, E. (1893). *The Division of labor in society.* New York: Free Press, 1964.

Hofman, H. (1996). Critical criminology and prevention in light of a postmodern condition. *Tijdschrift voor Sociale Westenschappen, 41* (2), 192–205.

NO

STUART HENRY

Now as someone whose values come from the same socialist or communitarian liberal vision...I should be satisfied with the realist solution. And indeed I respect their political stance and their attempt to stake out a clearly radical opposition to today's grim coalition between enterprise capitalism and neutered administrative criminology. Unlike their harsh critics from the Left, I see no reason to question their continued commitment to socialist theory and practice. But why does their sociology leave me uneasy? With a sense that this is a premature closure of debate, a denial of the tension between intellectual doubt and political action? Have not some important theoretical problems, insights been forgotten in order to respond to a particular set of political contingencies? (Cohen, 1990, p. 19)

Stanley Cohen's concerns about left realism's crimped critical stance reflect the ambivalence of many toward a perspective that seems to have suspended questioning knowledge, abandoned innovating new forms of social justice, and papered over contradictions between short-term practice and long-term policy (Carlen, 1996; Pavlich, 1997). Admittedly, left realism served as a useful corrective to radical criminology's tendency to romanticize crime as the expression of revolutionary, utopian ideals, although very few actual Marxist criminological works embraced this vision and none have for fifteen years (Beirne & Messerschmidt, 1995). It also reminded us, in contrast to the cultural studies and social constructionist view, that symbolic constructions can nevertheless have harmful effects. It contributed a new understanding about the wider interrelationships in the production of crime; to get the complete picture of crime, realists argued that both crime victims and criminal offenders must be considered in relationship to each other, to the state's criminal justice agencies, and to the community. Most importantly, left realists highlighted the needs of the victim of crime and offered pragmatic solutions for minimizing victimization, as they attempted to displace the monopoly on criminal justice policy held by right-wing "administrative" or correctional criminology with pragmatic, socialist-informed, criminal justice alternatives. In doing so they claimed to save radical criminology from a tendency to talk about tomorrow's global revolution, while doing nothing about today's local suffering. In place of such "impossibilism," they proposed concrete policy solutions to simultaneously reduce the crime rate and to limit the state's victimization of offenders.

So what's to disagree with in such a perspective? Like Cohen (1990), Carlen (1996), and Pavlich (1997), my difficulty with the left realist position has to do with its foreclosing of possibilities and curtailing critical debate about the criminogenic nature of power and inequality. This retreat from critique has come through (1) an uncritical use of a narrow, commonsense concept of crime that excludes many kinds of victimization, (2) a partial analysis of crime causation that tacitly accepts the existing structure of inequality, and (3) compromise policy solutions whose implementation is more likely to further legitimize the existing order rather than to challenge its foundation. As a result, left realism contributes to, rather than detracts from, the ideological structures of oppression that constitute crime. Left realism is part of the problem rather than part of the solution. Let us look at why this is so in more detail, starting with the problem of narrowly framed concepts about crime, criminals, and victims.

Foreclosing Possibilities: The Realist Vision of Crime, Criminals, and Victims

The left realist concept of crime is founded on the idea that what is both feared and experienced by working classes as crime is the reality of crime. In other words, crime is street offenders committing conventional crimes of robbery, burglary, varieties of crimes around the drug trade, and violence against women, including rape and sexual harassment. This fear is also combined with a mistrust of the justice system's ability to protect the working classes, which is expressed through fears of police violence and court bias. The realist vision of crime is derived from the results of victimization surveys that have been read literally rather than critically. Indeed, as Jock Young, the perspective's founder has stated, left realism "starts from the problems as people experience them" (Young, 1986, p. 24), arguing that this implies an accurate victimology that acknowledges the feelings of most working class victims of crime who most fear crimes by members of their own class. Local area crime surveys were drawn on to demonstrate that "young people, working class people, racial minorities and women are the most likely to be the victims of property and personal crimes" (MacLean, 1991, p. 12).

Although such an "appreciative" understanding of working class fears about crime and victimization acknowledges their genuine concerns, ignored is any appreciation of how the nature of crime, harm, and violence is selectively shaped in the popular culture to highlight some harms and minimize, even obscure, others. Lost are the complexities of the way this fear is socially constructed, how its content is influenced by the media, and how the "fear of crime" may be a reflection of the general anxieties of one's social position and identity rather than actual experience of crime (Sparks, 1992; Williams & Dickinson, 1993). The resulting focus on working class victims of working class predatory offenders, particularly violence, has taken the spotlight off crimes of the economically powerful outside the state, especially "those forms which are normalized as accidental, or where the victimization is indirect and dispersed, as with corporate crime" (Muncie, 1996, p. 59; Downes, 1988). Similarly, a focus on crimes by the police and criminal justice system has obscured those of the wider political state, such as government policies to deregulate industry, facilitate drug trafficking while ostensibly fighting a war against it, and accede to corporate interests weakening the power of regulatory agencies to control harm-producing, profit-making practices. In short, defining crime as what is real to the working class allows what some may consider more serious crime to escape its gaze. Thus, the victimology of left realism, far from being accurate, offers a seriously flawed account of the harm of crime and is particularly deficient in its appreciation of the hidden victims of crimes of the structurally powerful.

Related to left realists' narrow concept of crime, criminals, and victims is its failure to see the all-pervasiveness of harms of inequality on society. Unlike the earlier radical perspectives whose theorists saw systems of economic and social inequality having pervasive effects throughout the class structure, and feminist-inspired criminology that highlighted gender and racial divisions as having harm-producing effects throughout the social order, left realists locate crime and victims in the working classes. Not only does this tacit acceptance of the state's definition of crime promulgated via the media, ignore the harm of crime on those who ostensibly benefit from economic inequality (the impoverishment of the humanity of those who exploit others), but it also ignores the differential effects of harm within gender divisions (Scraton, 1990) and within and between racially and ethnically diverse groups (Gilroy, 1987).

Left Realists' Limited Conception of Criminal Etiology

Although left realists affirm their concern with the etiology or causes of crime, "with the causes of criminal action and social reaction" and claim "it must learn from past theory....It must stand for theory" (Young, 1986, p. 26), examination of their theory is revealing. In broad superficial terms, their theory of crime causation seems consistent with a radical critique of capitalist society. Thus, left realists agree that offenders harm their victims as a result of the conspiring forces of capitalism, patriarchy, and racism, mediated through a state social control apparatus that not only fails to protect those most vulnerable, but exacerbates crime and produces its own victims. The powerless and exploited social categories are victims of class inequality, and of sexual and racial differentiations in power, status, and wealth. Isolated from community, rendered objects of exploitation by commercialization, and frequently abandoned by a fickle productive process, these marginal categories are available for further victimization by individual perpetrators of crime. Thus, left realists claim to see that "people in this society are victimized both from above and below, and that people at the bottom are double-victimized" (Schwartz, 1991, p. 119). Even the perpetrators recruited from the ranks of the working classes are themselves victimized by a fearful and hungry criminal justice system. It is not just the entry into crime that is shaped by these forces, it is also the state criminal justice system. Left realists show how aspects of the criminal justice system interplay with the capitalist economic structure to deliver their own casualties.

However, in addressing the specifics of crime causation, the question of exploitation from above slips into the background, escapes critical scrutiny, and even worse, escapes policy suggestions. In contrast, the foreground focus becomes the already victimized offender. Realists argue that the capitalist system promotes competitive individualism and feeds off patriarchy and racism, creating inequalities among people. Those at the bottom experience "relative deprivation" because they cannot afford the pleasures of life enjoyed by others: "These are people who watch the same TV ads as everyone else and who are hustling to obtain products and status symbols such as color TVs, fancy cars, and expensive gold jewelry—desires created almost solely by capitalism" (DeKeseredy & Schwartz, 1996, p. 250). Capitalism is the source of discontent. But because those at the bottom are politically powerless to change their situation, they become angry, particularly violent, and beat up on each other, producing violent crime incidents. Some of their number also turn to stealing the very symbols they cannot afford to buy. Rather than protect them from crime, police agencies tend to reinforce the inequalities, and the criminal justice system produces its own casualties within already impoverished neighborhoods.

This largely strain theory analysis of the cause of working class predatory crime is not extended to explain white collar crime, corporate crime, or state crime. There is no explanation of how "relative deprivation" explains why hazardous waste haulers create environmental pollution, why the Nestle corporation produced adulterated baby formulae for Third World countries, why the tobacco industry, like the asbestos industry before it, knowingly produced and sold harmful products and funded research to mystify scientific evidence of their harmful effects. In short, there is no challenge here to inequality per se, only a description of it. That the powerful escape critical scrutiny is no more clearly manifest than in the policy implications of left realism.

The Poverty of Left Realist Policy

Left realists recognize that crime, and through it the suffering in inner-city communities, is harmful and needs to be reduced (Lea & Young, 1984). They see crime as divisive of the working class and its solution one of a number of potential unifiers for recreating community. They recognize that social inequality is harmful and by implication its absence would promote community, but on how to achieve this absence, they are silent. The left realist agenda is to promote democratic socialist change by affecting relations within capitalist society toward achieving greater social justice and reduced levels of crime. They are less inclined to overthrow the existing criminal justice apparatus than to restructure it, making it more accountable and more responsive to the needs of the powerless. Left realists want to strengthen and control the criminal justice system of capitalist society, believing that the law can provide the structurally powerless with real gains, if not ideal victories. They argue that the law and criminal justice has already made real gains for the powerless over the powerful. The rule of law represents the history of victories of the powerless over the arbitrary powerful and must be expanded to deal with street crime, suite crime, and crimes of gender. Its enforcement arm, the police, should be retained but democratized. Realists claim that the powerless are not well served by radicals who side with those on the right, who want to do away with rehabilitation approaches to crime control. Left realists believe in implementing policies that reduce the pain and suffering from crime caused by the capitalist system and its agencies of social control. They argue that failure to do so is irresponsible because it allows the sole voice in the policy debate to be the right realist "law and order" lobby (Matthews, 1987). Instead of tougher sentences and more prisons as advocated by right realists, such as James Q. Wilson (Wilson & Herrnstein, 1985) and Chris Tame (1995), left realists prefer alternative practical policy interventions that they claim will deal with both the immediacy of the crime problem and people's fear of it (Lea & Young, 1984). These include preventative policies that (1) introduce problem solvers into working class neighborhoods to defuse problems and to voice and address residents' concerns through local crime surveys; (2) use alternative sanctions such as restitution and community service to "demarginalize" offenders and reintegrate them into the community; and (3) encourage community involvement and democratically accountable control of the police by community citizens. In many ways, as both Gibbons (1994) and Shoemaker (1996) point out, left realist policy proposals are similar to those that emerged from social ecology theory and strain theory and mainstream sociological criminology in general. More importantly, Carlen (1996) suggests that to sell their policies to the general public they rely on the same assumptions about criminality as used by the right, and in the process, "lose an opportunity to show how individualized problems of criminal justice are also problems of social justice in general" (1996, p. 477).

Left realists have also conceded that their policies may strengthen the power of the oppressive state (DeKeseredy & Schwartz, 1991; Schwartz & DeKeseredy, 1991). This only serves to reinforce the existing structure, not least that part that is its bureaucratic apparatus. Left realists have not reconciled the central contradictions between the call for increased powers of the state to control crime and their preferences for a minimalist state, subject to public scrutiny and accountability, a point that some advocates have acknowledged (Matthews, 1987). Moreover,

Michalowski (1991) cautions that left realists' loose concept of community could result in right wing populist and racist control of the police. He warns of the contradictions in pursuing criminal justice reform without accompanying structural changes from the capitalist system to a socialist form. Indeed, perhaps the most damning criticism of left realist policy comes from feminist scholars who have argued that, although the impact of left realism on critical criminology "has been profound...the construction of the realism/idealism debate has been diversionary, regressive and purposefully misrepresentative of the advances within critical criminology since the mid-1970s" (Scraton, 1990, p. 20). The feminist claim is that left realism, like radical criminology generally, has remained gender-blind and as such remains part of the "malestream" ignoring activism, research and theory drawn from women's experiences (Edwards, 1989; Kelly & Radford, 1987). The realist challenge lies in creating conditions that will modify or sensitize the emerging system to create the equalities needed for a less criminogenic society. How this is to be done, without strengthening the very system of inequality and oppression, along its existing class, gender, and racially segmented lines, remains its biggest challenge.

Conclusion: The Idealism of Left Realism

Left realism, originally critical of what it called left idealism, is found to contain its own idealistic strains. These include (1) the idea that strengthening the police while democratizing it will protect the working class rather than secure them in their existing exploitative relations; (2) the idea that protecting the structurally powerless from street crime will help them form socialist communities; (3) the belief that communities so protected will somehow push for changes in capitalist systems of inequality; (4) the idea that such communities will be immune from the ideology of media constructions of crime that keep them exploited and unaware; and (5) the hope that the existing power structure will not undermine any real change if that threatens their existing abilities to increase private wealth, market share, and political dominance. In short, the left realist vision is ultimately limited by its own idealism in believing that reformist policy will transform capitalist exploitative reality rather than contributing to its increased strength.

REFERENCES

Beirne, P., & Messerschmidt, J. (1995). *Criminology.* Fort Worth: Harcourt Brace.
Carlen, P. (1996). Criminal women and criminal justice: The limits to and potential of feminist and left realist perspectives. In J. Muncie, E. McLaughlin, and M. Langan (Eds.), *Criminological perspectives: A reader.* London: Sage.
Cohen, S. (1990). Intellectual scepticism and political commitment: The case of radical criminology. Bonger Memorial Lecture (May 14), University of Amsterdam.

DeKeseredy, W. S. & Schwartz, M. D. (1991). British and U.S. left realism: A critical comparison. *International Journal of Offender Therapy and Comparative Criminology, 35,* 248–262.

DeKeseredy, W. S. & Schwartz, M. D. (1996). *Contemporary criminology.* Belmont, CA: Wadsworth.

Downes, D. (1988). Crime and social control in Britain. *British Journal of Criminology, 28,* 45–57.

Edwards, S. (1989). Sex/gender, sexism and criminal justices, some theoretical considerations. *International Journal of the Sociology of Law, 17,* 165–184.

Gibbons, D. C. (1994). *Talking about crime and criminals: Problems and issues in theory development in criminology.* Englewood Cliffs, NJ: Prentice Hall.

Gilroy, P. (1987). *There ain't no black in the Union Jack.* London: Hutchinson.

Kelly, L., & Radford, J. (1987). The problem of men: Feminist perspectives on sexual violence. In P. Scraton (Ed.), *Law, order and the authoritarian state: Readings in critical criminology.* Philadelphia: Open University Press.

Lea, J., & Young, J. (1984). *What is to be done about law and order?* Harmondsworth: Penguin.

MacLean, B. D. (1991). The origins of left realism. In B. MacLean and D. Milovanovic (Eds.), *New directions in critical criminology.* Vancouver: The Collective Press.

Matthews, R. (1987). Taking realist criminology seriously. *Contemporary Crisis, 11,* 371–401.

Michalowski, R. (1991). 'Niggers, welfare scum and homeless assholes:' The problems of idealism, consciousness and context in left realism. In B. MacLean and D. Milovanovic (Eds.), *New directions in critical criminology.* Vancouver: Collective Press.

Muncie, J. (1996). The construction and deconstruction of crime. In J. Muncie and E. McLaughlin (Eds.), *The Problem of Crime.* London: Sage.

Pavlich, G. (1997). Criticism in criminology: The forgotten concept. *The Critical Criminologist, 8:* 1, 6.

Schwartz, M. D. (1991). The future of criminology. In B. MacLean and D. Milovanovic. *New directions in critical criminology.* Vancouver: The Collective Press.

Schwartz, M. D., & DeKeseredy, W. S. 1991. Left realist criminology: Strengths, weaknesses and feminist critique. *Crime, Law and Social Change, 15,* 51–72.

Scraton, P. (1990). Scientific knowledge or masculine discourses? Challenging patriarchy in criminology. In L. Gelsthorpe and A. Morris (Eds.), *Feminist perspectives in criminology.* Milton Keynes: Open University Press.

Shoemaker, D. J. (1996). *Theories of delinquency: An examination of explanations of delinquent behavior.* (3rd ed.). New York: Oxford University Press.

Sparks, R. (1992). *Television and the drama of crime.* Buckingham: Open University Press.

Tame, C. R. (1995). Freedom, responsibility and justice: The criminology of the "New Right." In K. Stenson and D. Cowell (Eds.), *The politics of crime control.* Thousand Oaks, CA: Sage.

Williams, P., & Dickinson, J. (1993). "Fear of crime: Read all about it? *British Journal of Criminology, 33*, 33–56.

Wilson, J. Q., & Herrnstein, R. (1985). *Crime and human nature.* New York: Simon and Schuster.

Young, J. (1986). The failure of criminology: The need for a radical realism. In R. Matthews and J. Young (Eds.), *Confronting crime.* London: Sage.

Rejoinder to
Dr. Stuart Henry
Martin D. Schwartz and Walter S. DeKeseredy

Like any theoretical, empirical, or political perspective on crime and its control, left realism has several limitations, and Stuart Henry's attempt to point some of them out is a constructive way of encouraging the development of a more adequate critical criminological understanding of how the criminal justice system and crimes committed from all directions (e.g., on the street, in corporate boardrooms and government offices, etc.) are influenced and shaped by structured social and economic inequality. However, Henry's critique of left realism is not new and is, in some ways, incorrect, for reasons described here and in other sources (e.g., Young, 1991). As we shall see, and as an examination of his original document makes clear, the problem is that Henry is not critiquing left realism so much as the work of Jock Young and his colleagues in the mid-1980s. He does not investigate the value of the approach for explaining crime, but rather critiques what Young and others actually did ten to fifteen years ago.

Let us look at Henry's specific complaints.

Left Realism Takes Crimes
of the Powerful Seriously

Henry contends that left realists advance "an uncritical use of a narrow, common-sense concept of crime that excludes many kinds of victimization," especially the pain and suffering caused by political and economic elites. This is a common criticism of left realism; however, nothing can be further from the truth. In fact, it is somewhat disingenuous. Left realism, which, as Henry notes, claims that working class people are victimized from above and below, is attacked for paying attention to crime from below. For the most part, these attacks come from people who do exactly the opposite: only look at crimes of the powerful but not at crimes of the working classes.

In fact, left realists take crimes of the powerful very seriously. Consider the second sweep of the Islington Crime Survey (ICSII) (Crawford, Jones, Wood-house, and Young, 1990), a British left realist study that provides rich, reliable, and valid quantitative data on three variants of "commercial crime": workplace hazards, unlawful trading practices, and the victimization of housing tenants. These data provide a much more reliable account of workplace health and safety problems caused by corporations than do official British statistics. For example, the ICSII uncovered an accident rate that was thirty times the British national average (Pearce, 1992).

Henry also overlooks other recent left realist work on "hidden victims of the structurally powerful." To pick just one other example, one might look at Basran et al.'s (1995) Canadian study of corporate violence against Punjabi farmworkers and their children. This local survey influenced both Kwantlen University College and the British Columbia government to provide suitable and affordable child care for Punjabi farmworkers. So much for the assertion that left realists ignore the "differential effects of harm within and between racially and ethnically diverse groups."

Left Realism Has a Broad Conception of Etiology

Henry argues that left realists have a "limited conception of etiology." Although it is true that Jock Young, John Lea, and some other left realists are heavily informed by strain theory, others, like ourselves and Dawn Currie (Currie, 1991, 1992; Schwartz and DeKeseredy, 1991, 1997), are guided primarily by feminist perspectives on crime and a large body of international theoretical work on masculinities (e.g., Messerschmidt, 1993; Newburn & Stanko, 1994). Some left realist research is also heavily informed by Marxist perspectives on corporate violence and racial oppression (Basran et al., 1995). In sum, Henry incorrectly paints all left realists with the same brush and neglects to identify variations in left realist theoretical perspectives on crime and its control. He equates "left realism" with "Jock Young," and Young's writings of the 1980s at that.

Left Realism Proposes a Broad Range of Progressive Policies

If left realists offer a diverse range of critical theories, the same can be said about their policy proposals, another point overlooked by Henry. For example, some left realists focus primarily on street crime and view democratizing the police and various types of community involvement in crime control as solutions (Lea & Young, 1984; Kinsey, Lea, & Young, 1986), whereas others concentrate on male-to-female victimization and call for short-term profeminist men's strategies that "chip away" at the patriarchal forces that perpetuate and legitimate rape, wife-beating, sexual harassment, and so on (DeKeseredy, 1996a, 1996b, DeKeseredy & Schwartz, 1998; Messerschmidt, 1986; Schwartz & DeKeseredy, 1997). Some realists also propose progressive ways of curbing corporate crime (Basran, Charan, & MacLean, 1995; DeKeseredy & Goff, 1992; Pearce & Tombs, 1992).

Space limitations preclude a detailed review of all left realist policies, and even if we did describe them here, Henry would probably view these short-term, progressive strategies as doing little more than strengthening the power of political and economic elites. What, then, are his alternatives? Can he provide socially and economically disenfranchised people with some hope, a blueprint for progressive social change, and what Devine and Wright (1993) refer to as "some realistic sense of a better future?" We know he can; however, his response to our chapter does not offer more effective alternative solutions.

The biggest problem within the left over the past thirty years is implicit in Henry's response: that we believe in the "rule of law," and that we seem "less inclined to overthrow the existing criminal justice apparatus." "Less inclined" than whom? Under what world conditions and historical moments have leftist scholars successfully conducted this overthrow? Certainly he cannot be asking for the state socialist or Communist systems, or even the officially socialist systems of Israel and the United Kingdom? What then? Do we give up all progressive struggle while awaiting that glorious day of the revolution when magically all crime will disappear because it will not be allowed under Marxist theory?

Of course, doing something is not necessarily better than doing nothing at all, especially if doing something means reinforcing the oppressive status quo. However, some left realist policies and studies are currently making a difference. Recall the positive consequences of Basran et al.'s (1995) study of Punjabi farmworkers and their children. Should we view affordable child care as simply a means of strengthening inequality, so that people can go on working under Capitalism, or is it a progressive step toward improving oppressed people's quality of life?

Conclusion

Left realism is far from being a "cosmetic criminology of an establishment sort." Rather, it is a diverse school of progressive criminological thought, one that is antiestablishment, radical in its analysis of various types of crime, and realist in its policy (Young, 1997). Of course, this new direction in critical criminology has several pitfalls, but what is Henry's alternative? How does he propose to help prevent gang-related violence, wife-beating, corporate crime, and other serious threats to the "truly disadvantaged's" economic, social, physical, and psychological well-being (Wilson, 1987)? In fairness to Henry, he was not specifically asked to address these questions in his critique of left realism. Nevertheless, useful alternatives to left realism should be provided because critical commentaries divorced from concrete, alternative blueprints for change do little, if anything, to minimize or overcome crimes committed by and against those at the bottom of the socio-economic ladder. What these people need are "realistic solutions to distorted social conditions" (Devine & Wright, 1993), and if there was ever a need for such solutions, it is clearly now.

REFERENCES

Basran, G. S., Charan, G., & MacLean, B. D. (1995). *Farmworkers and their children.* Vancouver: Collective Press.

Crawford, A., Jones, T., Woodhouse, T., & Young, J. (1990). *Second Islington crime survey.* Middlesex: Centre for Criminology, Middlesex Polytechnic.

Currie, D. (1991). Realist criminology, women, and social transformation in Canada. In B. D. MacLean and D. Milovanovic (Eds.), *New directions in critical criminology.* Vancouver: Collective Press.

Currie, D. (1992). Feminism and realism in the Canadian context. In J. Lowman and B. D. MacLean (Eds.), *Realist criminology: Crime control and policing in the 1990s.* Toronto: University of Toronto Press.

DeKeseredy, W. S. (1996a). Left realism and woman abuse in dating. In B. D. MacLean (Ed.), *Crime and society: Readings in critical criminology.* Toronto: Copp Clark.

DeKeseredy, W. S. (1996b). Making an unsafe learning environment safer: Some progressive policy proposals to curb woman abuse in university/college dating relationships. In C. Stark-Adamec (Ed.), *Violence: A collective responsibility.* Ottawa: Social Science Federation of Canada.

DeKeseredy, W. S., & Goff, C. (1992). Corporate violence against Canadian women: Assessing left realist research and policy. *The Journal of Human Justice, 4,* 55–70.

DeKeseredy, W. S., & Schwartz, M. D. (1998). *Woman abuse on campus: Results from the Canadian National Survey.* Thousand Oaks, CA: Sage.

Devine, J. A., & Wright, J. D. (1993). *The greatest of evils: Urban poverty and the American underclass.* New York: Aldine de Gruyter.

Lea, J., & Young, J. (1984). *What is to be done about law and order?* London: Penguin.

Kinsey, R., Lea, J., & Young, J. (1986). *Losing the fight against crime.* London: Blackwell.

Messerschmidt, J. W. (1986). *Capitalism, Patriarchy, and Crime.* Totowa, NJ: Roman and Littlefield.

Messerschmidt, J. W. (1993). *Masculinities and crime: Critique and reconceptualization of theory.* Lanham, MD: Roman and Littlefield.

Newburn, T., & Stanko, E. A. (Eds.). (1994). *Just boys doing business: Men, masculinities and crime.* New York: Routledge.

Pearce, F. (1992). The contribution of 'left realism' to the study of commercial crime. In J. Lowman and B. D. MacLean (Eds.), *Realist criminology: Crime control and policing in the 1990s.* Toronto: University of Toronto Press.

Pearce, F., & Tombs, S. (1992). Realism and corporate crime. In R. Matthews and J. Young (Eds.), *Issues in realist criminology.* London: Sage.

Schwartz, M. D., & DeKeseredy, W. S. (1991). Left realist criminology: Strengths, weaknesses and the feminist critique. *Crime, Law and Social Change, 15,* 51–72.

Schwartz, M. D., & DeKeseredy, W. S. (1997). *Sexual assault on the college campus: The role of male peer support.* Thousand Oaks, CA: Sage.

Wilson, W. J. (1987). *The truly disadvantaged: The inner city, the underclass, and public policy.* Chicago: University of Chicago Press.

Young, J. (1991). Asking questions of left realism. In B. D. MacLean and D. Milovanovic (Eds.), *New directions in critical criminology.* Vancouver: Collective Press.

Young, J. (1997). Left realist criminology: Radical in its analysis, realist in its policy. In P. Walton and J. Young (Eds.) *The new criminology revisited.* London: Macmillan.

Can Students Benefit from an Intensive Engagement with Postmodern Criminology?

Bruce A. Arrigo, Ph.D., is Professor of Criminology and Forensic Psychology and is the Director of the Institute of Psychology Law and Public Policy at the California School of Professional Psychology. He has published widely in the areas of critical criminology, mental health and criminal justice, and the sociology of law. His recent books include *The Contours of Psychiatric Justice* (Garland, 1996) and *Social Justice/Criminal Justice: The Maturation of Critical Theory in Law, Crime, and Deviance* (Wadsworth, 1998). Professor Arrigo is also the editor of the peer review social science quarterly, *Humanity and Society.*

David O. Friedrichs is Professor of Sociology and Criminal Justice at the University of Scranton (PA). He is the author of *Trusted Criminals: White Collar Crime in Contemporary Society* (ITP/Wadsworth, 1996) and some sixty articles, book chapters, and essays on legitimation of legal order, violence, victimology, narrative jurisprudence, radical/critical criminology, and various other topics.

YES

BRUCE A. ARRIGO

Postmodern Overview

There is no single entity called *postmodernism*. Postmodernism represents an array of theoretical and methodological frames of reference that are incomplete, fragmented, and evolving. Postmodernism is simultaneously historical period; a reaction against established Euro-Western beliefs about progress, science, and culture, and an intellectual discipline; a kaleidoscopic prism through which truth, knowledge, power, agency, being, etc., are radically reconceptualized.

One of the core features of postmodernism is the role of language. Postmodernists believe that the written and spoken word represent texts or stories that when read or heard always convey implicit messages and hidden assumptions about the world in which we live. When decoded or studied more closely, these implicit messages and hidden assumptions embody values about people, places, and events. Moreover, these values structure and inform our thinking. When in the postmodern attitude, the question to ask is what values (and whose interests) are reflected in the written or spoken words that we use to communicate? In other words, precise meaning and clear intent are not contained *within* what we say or write. There is also meaning/intent behind, under, around, and over the discourse we employ. Thus, the stories we tell are never finished; they always explode and scatter, represent a departure from absolute sense, and resist total comprehension.

For example, when purchasing an automobile and discussing a potential purchase with a sales representative, many things happen at the same time. That is, many "conversations" occur simultaneously. I am keenly aware of some of these conversations, and others I experience unconsciously. Imagine a person walks into a dealership and says, "I'm looking for a new car." Initially, this statement sounds harmless and straightforward. On closer inspection, however, other stories are or may be folded into this expression about which the individual may or may not be immediately aware. Some of these additional meanings include: (1) I *desperately* need a car, (2) I don't want to *appear overly interested* in any one car, (3) I want something that's *attractive and sleek,* (4) I need something that's *affordable,* (5) I want to feel as if I *got a deal,* (6) I don't want to feel as if I'm being *tricked, cajoled, or otherwise "taken for a ride."*

Each of the above italicized words or expressions is part of a larger subtext or constellation of meanings/intents that remain concealed during mere surface level analysis. They imply something more or something other about the phrase "I'm looking for a new car." In short, they are values (anchoring points) that the author of the initial phrase may, knowingly or not, cling to throughout his or her negotiation for an automobile. Precisely because they are unconscious, hidden, repressed, or dormant, postmodernists argue that it is important to unpack these values (identify them and examine them) if more nuanced communication is to be transmitted and more complete meaning is to be grasped.

Although the subtext (points 1 through 6) in this example is ostensibly unproblemmatic, and although no one is visibly harmed given the values behind, under, over, around, etc., the statement "I'm looking for a new car," there are occasions when what we say or write is of profound consequence. There are occasions when the unspoken values that structure our thinking cause harm. Postmodern criminology is one field of inquiry that demonstrates this. Postmodern criminology is one subdiscipline that draws attention to the violence perpetrated through the activity of speech production (text making), whether written or verbal.

Postmodern Criminology

Similar to postmodernism, there is no single perspective on postmodern criminology. Postmodern criminology encompasses many different conceptual strains, methodological orientations, and political dimensions (Arrigo, 1995). A principal distinction often debated by its architects is the impact of postmodern analysis in yielding a more pessimistic, negative, fatalistic reality (Arrigo, 1996a; Schwartz & Friedrichs, 1994) versus a more optimistic, affirmative, potentialistic world (Arrigo & Bernard, 1997; Henry & Milovanovic, 1991). In short, this tension questions whether, following the wisdom of postmodernism, we can ever arrive at definitive truth, categorical knowledge, or absolute understanding.

For the postmodern skeptic, the problem is that (criminological) discourse is saturated with multiple (and contradictory) values. Thus, it is never possible to unveil exhaustively all embedded meaning (Borgman, 1992; Derrida, 1978). For some critics of postmodernism, this position is wholly inadequate because it privileges multiple perspectives without ever anchoring any one of them (Handler, 1992). At best, there are only approximations of truth, knowledge, and understanding.

For the postmodern proponent, the multiple and contradictory values contained within (criminological) discourse represent moments of uncertainty, ambiguity, contradiction, absurdity, multiplicity, incompleteness, etc. But these are the necessary ingredients for fostering new and different truths, knowledges, and understandings about the changing world in which we live (Henry & Milovanovic, 1996). The hidden messages and implicit assumptions struggling to be heard in what we say or write, then, represent the untapped and unspoken voices of an evolving script. In criminological discourse, this may be the narrative of a rape survivor giving courtroom testimony (Arrigo, 1993a), of a police officer making an arrest (Manning, 1988), of a criminally confined mental patient petitioning for release (Arrigo, 1993b, 1996b), of a jailhouse lawyer presenting his or her case before a judge (Milovanovic, 1988), or of a juvenile offender participating in a victim offender mediation program (Arrigo & Schehr, 1997). Thus, the approximations of truth, knowledge, and understanding that critics dismiss epitomize positional, relational, and provisional justice (Arrigo, 1995), which advocates applaud. According to postmodern proponents, these forms of justice more authentically personify the process of human social interaction (Arrigo, 1998).

Although the negative/affirmative chasm in postmodern circles is deep and of consequence, it does not directly address the issue of violence as conveyed through words. The notion that there is or may be violence communicated through language (speech) may seem ludicrous at first. After all, how can words harm people? But on closer inspection, the words that we use to convey the thoughts that we think can harm others. It is in this context that affirmative postmodern criminology both explains this process and offers some solutions by which to confront the problem.

Application of Postmodern Criminology

To illustrate the power of language to harm, I will use three different examples. These include the jailhouse lawyer who litigates his or her own case, the in-court testimony of rape survivors, and the confinement of the mental patient petitioning for release. After presenting these scenarios, I will then draw on selected affirmative postmodern criminological principles to explain what happens, through language, such that violence occurs. It is in this context that we can begin to appreciate how harm is reenacted, relegitimized, and reinforced in the justice system.

Examples in Law and Criminology

Jailhouse Lawyers. When an inmate chooses to represent himself or another prisoner in a court of law, the person is functioning as a jailhouse lawyer. Jailhouse lawyers confront a dilemma when presenting a legal case before a judge. Often, although not always, jailhouse lawyers are minimally trained in the particulars of the law. They learn about these details by sitting in courtrooms, filing motions, reading legal briefs, interacting with other prisoners, and talking with lawyers. However, the narrative of law is not the same as the narrative of the inmate subculture. In other words, the jargon and speech of many prisoners, as they describe the circumstances involved in their legal cases (i.e., the "what happened"), is not consistent with how a jailhouse lawyer would *re-present* the facts of the case in a courtroom.

Jailhouse lawyers must rely on a language consistent with what is taken to be "good" lawyering. We refer to this grammar as *legalese.* Without legalese, jailhouse lawyers risk objection by opposing counsel. This could result in a judge declaring their case non-justiciable (Milovanovic, 1988). In this process, though, there is much that is missing from the original inmate story. All the subtleties of meaning, all the nuances of intent, all the shadings of value are silenced and cleansed. They are made compatible with the language of the law. Through discourse, the jailhouse lawyer sacrifices his or her own unique understanding of what happened in the criminal case for an understanding that endorses the perspective of the legal apparatus. This is the manifestation of harm perpetrated through language.

Courtroom Testimony of Rape Survivors. Rape survivors testifying in a court of law confront a similar problem (Arrigo, 1993a). Often victims are coached by attorneys on what to say and on how to speak. The intent on the litigator's part is to ensure that the victim *appears believable and credible.* The concern is that the rape survivor not sound hysterical, out of control, too hostile, vindictive, and the like.

But in this staged process of witness preparation, what is lost in the courtroom exchange is the opportunity for the rape survivor to speak freely without the constraints of the legal system imposing (linguistic) control. Much of the pain, anguish, guilt, shame, fear, and rage constituting the rape experience is quieted or muffled in courtroom dialogue. Similar to the jailhouse lawyer, however, this unarticulated speech potentially embodies the survivor's interiorized sense of identity. Nonetheless, it remains concealed and shut off from the rest of the world. Even though the outcome of the case may produce a victory for the victim, the process silences certain speech, certain communications. This is not a triumph for the rape survivor. Again, we have the presence of violence as fostered through language.

Petition for Release from Involuntary Psychiatric Confinement. People can be involuntarily hospitalized for psychiatric care and treatment. When such individuals petition to be released, they must present their case to an administrative tribunal consisting of attorneys, psychiatrists, mental health clinicians, and other interested parties. The "petitioner" (the person requesting release from psychiatric custody) is represented by counsel.

Throughout the hearing, the petitioner is confronted with a forced choice (Arrigo, 1994, 1996c, 1996d). To be released, petitioners must adopt speech-thought-behavior patterns that are indicative of psychological wellness. Otherwise, extended involuntary hospitalization will be ordered. By adopting such mannerisms, however, the mentally disordered person may be endorsing a way of speaking, thinking, and being that is not entirely consistent with how the person truly expresses him or herself. Thus, a significant piece of one's identity is lost in the process. Conversely, if petitioners opt not to embrace, through speech, the established commonsense approach to psychological wellness, and if, instead, individuals remain faithful to their own nonconventional, idiosyncratic spoken orientations to life, then such persons may be subjected to extended institutional confinement. I would venture to argue that this *double bind* in discourse contributes to the transcarceration of individuals; that is, the back-and-forth funneling of persons from the criminal justice to the mental health system (Arrigo, 1997). Here too, then, we have the presence of harm enacted through language.

Postmodern Criminological Theory

Dialectics of Linguistic Struggle and Control. The problem that reappears in each of the cited examples is dialectical (Henry & Milovanovic, 1996). In other words, there is, simultaneously, a *push* from the existing parameters of sense making (underscored by values) to maintain an established code of speech, and a *pull* from alternative boundaries of meaning (underscored by replacement values) to communicate differently. Regardless of the choice, there is violence through language. Using conventional speech is tantamount to surrendering a portion of one's Self. Embracing different methods of communicating may result in misunderstanding and, eventually, in criminal confinement (jailhouse lawyer), an acquittal (rape case), and transcarceration (mental patient). Again, these experiences represent the double bind in discourse. The dialectical experience through speech produces in practice profound struggle and violence. It is a struggle over how to speak about people, places, and events. It is a war waged over how to convey the thoughts that we think. What is additionally disturbing in the examples above is that during those moments when jailhouse lawyers, rape survivors, and mental patients give themselves over to the prevailing system of communication (i.e., legalese, criminal courtroom discourse, medicolegal jargon), they contribute, knowingly or not, to the very self-harm they seek to renounce. This is how, in part, linguistic control is reenacted, relegitimized, and, thus, reinforced in society's justice system.

Transpraxis. Affirmative postmodern criminology argues that there is a way out of the dialectical struggle experienced in language. Transpraxis is a response to language systems and values that dominate what we say/write and how we say/write it. For example, transpraxis is not concerned with validating the voice of the jailhouse lawyer, the rape survivor, and the mental patient *over* the confinement system, the criminal law, or the clinical community. This would simply reverse hierarchies. Rather, transpraxis is about affirming the ways of knowing and the voices of various individuals and citizen groups. What is resisted in transpraxis is any *single* form of authority, privilege, truth, meaning, being, and, thus, any particular vision of justice. In every act of resistance, while asserting our point of view, we must make sure to affirm (not negate) the place for other articulated perspectives.

Recovering the Subject. For transpraxis to occur, people must articulate, without the imposition of control mechanisms, the way in which they experience life. As a society, we are routinely told how to express our thoughts and, by extension, how to conduct ourselves. This is substantially the problem with quashing prospects for new and different ways of understanding.

One relatively recent example in which an attempt was made to recover the subject comes to mind. A young African American man who was a former California police officer wanted to assess whether the police force of which he was previously a member practiced and condoned institutionalized racism. He chose to drive late at night in an area known to be populated by high levels of crime perpetrated by black males. He was trained in the use of undercover surveillance operations and so equipped his automobile so that one could observe and listen to the events that unfolded.

The former officer eventually found himself being followed by a police patrol car. Although one could plainly see the speedometer and how the car was moving (i.e., within the speed limit and not breaking any moving violations), the patrol car signaled for the man to pull over. The man complied, exited the car, and proceeded to ask, politely and repeatedly, for an explanation from the officer for this stop. The officer, who was white, did not wish to discuss the matter with the individual. This exchange went on for a while. After some time, the officer insisted that the man return to his car and put his hands on his head. The officer pulled out his night stick to ensure complete compliance. The citizen, calmly but firmly, agreed to return to his car, provided some explanation was given. The next thing we see from the video footage is the citizen, with hands behind his head, being pushed through a nearby plate glass window by the officer.

This exchange, this text, as it transpired, is indicative of the type of problem that confronts the criminal justice system. The citizen, despite expressions of politeness and deference to the officer, was not interpreted as a good and docile citizen-suspect by the law enforcement agent. The citizen endeavored to communicate from outside the established and recognized parameters of officer–suspect interaction. Not only did physical harm result from the exchange, but this very violence stemmed from the person's efforts to reclaim, *through words,* his sense of self, and his sense of how to convey this uniquely to the officer.

Conclusions

Students can benefit from an intensive engagement with postmodern criminology. It is not simply enough to identify what values are embedded in the thoughts that we think when we speak (or write), it is essential to assess how we can transcend these anchoring points, particularly if they victimize others. Moving beyond the double bind in discourse requires, in our resistance to words and expressions that marginalize and harm us, an affirmation of all speech. Recovering the subject in language is an effort to surpass what is expected and acceptable. Although it may come with a price, as it did for the former California police officer, speaking in our own voice offers us the greatest prospects for cultivating new and different ways by which to make peace with crime and to restore justice in society.

References

Arrigo, B. (1993a). An experientially-informed feminist jurisprudence: Rape and the move toward praxis. *Humanity and Society, 17*(1), 28–47.

Arrigo, B. (1993b). *Madness, language and the law.* Albany, NY: Harrow and Heston.

Arrigo, B. (1994). Legal discourse and the disordered criminal defendant: Contributions from psychoanalytic semiotics and chaos theory. *Legal Studies Forum, 18*(1), 93–112.

Arrigo, B. (1995). The peripheral core of law and criminology: On postmodern social theory and conceptual integration. *Justice Quarterly, 12*(3), 447–472.

Arrigo, B. (1996a). Media madness as a crime in the making: On O.J. Simpson, cultural icons, and hyper-reality. In G. Barak (ed.), *Representing OJ: Murder, criminal justice & mass culture* (pp. 123–136). New York: Harrow & Heston.

Arrigo, B. (1996b). *The contours of psychiatric justice: A postmodern critique of mental illness, criminal insanity, and the law.* New York: Garland.

Arrigo, B. (1996c). Desire in the psychiatric courtroom: On Lacan and the dialectics of linguistic oppression. *Current Perspectives in Social Theory, 16,* 159–187.

Arrigo, B. (1996d). Toward a theory of punishment in the psychiatric courtroom: On language, law and Lacan. *Journal of Crime and Justice, 19*(1), 15–32.

Arrigo, B. (1997). Transcarceration: Notes on a psychoanalytically-informed theory of social practice in the criminal justice and mental health systems. *Crime, Law, and Social Change: An International Journal, 27*(1), 31–48.

Arrigo, B. (1998). In search of social justice: Toward an integrative and critical criminological theory. In B. Arrigo (Ed.), *Social justice/criminal justice: The maturation of critical theory in law, crime, and deviance.* Belmont, CA: Wadsworth.

Arrigo, B., & Bernard, T. (1997). Postmodern criminology in relation to radical and conflict theory: A preliminary explication. *Critical Criminology: An International Journal, 9*(1).

Arrigo, B., Schehr, R. (1997). *Restoring justice for juveniles: Toward a critical analysis of victim offender mediation.* Available at the Institute of Psychology, Law, and Public Policy, Fresno, CA.

Borgmann, A. (1992). *Crossing the postmodern divide.* Chicago: University of Chicago Press.

Derrida, J. (1978). *Writing and difference.* London: Routledge and Kegan Paul.

Handler, J. (1992). Postmodernism, protest, and the new social movement. *Law and Society Review, 26*(4), 697–731.

Henry, S., & Milovanovic, D. (1991). Constitutive criminology: Maturation of critical theory. *Criminology: An Interdisciplinary Journal, 29*(2), 293–315.

Henry, S., & Milovanovic, D. (1996). *Constitutive criminology: Beyond postmodernism.* London: Sage.

Manning, P. K. (1988). *Symbolic communication: Signifying calls and the police response.* Cambridge: MIT Press.

Milovanovic, D. (1988). Jailhouse lawyers and jailhouse lawyering. *International Journal of the Sociology of Law, 16*, 455–475.

Schwartz, M. D. and Friedrichs, D. O. (1994). Postmodern thought and criminological discontent: New metaphors for understanding violence. *Criminology: An Interdisciplinary Journal, 32*, 221–246.

Rejoinder to Dr. Arrigo

DAVID O. FRIEDRICHS

Postmodern thought has quite a number of distinctive strains. Bruce Arrigo and I are surely agreed on this point. In his essay on behalf of the claim that students can benefit from an intense engagement with postmodern criminology, Arrigo chooses to highlight a strain of postmodern thought—focusing on language—that I deemphasized in my corresponding essay on the negative side of the question. I will here attempt to respond as directly as possible to the themes of his essay.

At the outset of this response, a paradox pertaining to postmodern thought (at least implicitly acknowledged by Arrigo) should be identified: If meaning and "truth" are fundamentally unstable, and if various latent meanings underlie surface meaning, then there are no firm grounds to accept as valid, informative, or whatever, the meanings and readings offered up by the postmodernist critic. This caveat should be borne in mind as we attend to a postmodern interpretation of crime and criminal justice.

We are told that jailhouse lawyers must adapt to the language of the official legal system to function effectively and are accordingly harmed by the need to suppress (or repress) their own voice. This proposition generates two questions. First, is it not the case that any and all communication requires some compromises of this type? Second, are these insights available only through postmodern criminology, or are they equally available through the application of an existing theoretical or empirical perspective? On the first point, for example, a student may experience a teacher as dull, pedantic, and pompous (and the teacher may likewise experience the student as dumb, unmotivated, and hostile). But such perceptions and "meanings" are likely to be suppressed, at least to some degree, in formal interaction between student and teacher. And similarly, some thoughts or observations are typically suppressed in boss/employee, parent/child, and wife/husband interaction. We are told—and surely this is true—that a rape victim may be coached to be a more "effective" witness by suppressing emotion. But at least some rape victims who then testify as witnesses—and primary and secondary victims of crime generally—opt to vent their rage in highly emotional terms. The empirically interesting question to my mind is this: What informs the choices victims and witnesses make in these circumstances? Parallel issues arise in connection with the psychiatric patient who is appearing before a tribunal while seeking release from involuntary psychiatric commitment.

On the second question raised about this form of postmodern criminological analysis, how does it differ in substance from the dramaturgic analysis of Erving Goffman? His famously familiar thesis is that human beings quite routinely attempt to present themselves to others in ways that manage the impression others have of them, to emphasize what might be perceived as positive and to conceal what might be perceived as discreditable. It is surely implicit (if not explicit) in dramaturgic analysis that we routinely suppress certain of our perceptions or feelings to enhance our chances of realizing some instrumental goal.

Does real harm in the circumstances Arrigo presents us with come from the uses of language, and does this constitute "violence" in a meaningful sense? Surely no one would deny that words can provoke physical violence and can be experienced as a very real form of psychic violence (i.e., what you said wounded me terribly, and cut through me like a knife). But it is somewhat less clear that the inevitable compromises we make in our interactions with others merit the characterization of violence. Furthermore, does an actual "loss" of identity occur in such situations, or is it simply the case that a dimension of one's identity is suppressed or concealed in a particular set of circumstances? In fact, it is surely the norm in virtually any circumstance that only some aspects of our identity are manifested.

Then Arrigo presents us with a situation in which an African American man (and former police officer) puts the matter of racial bias in law enforcement to test. This situation has two dimensions. First, there is the misfortune of belonging demographically to a segment of the population that has a proportionally higher involvement with conventional criminal activity, and accordingly makes all those in the segment appear more suspicious. Drug courier profiles used by border police are premised on these demographic realities. And in everyday life, who would deny that teenage males of any race are more likely to be pulled over by the police than are middle-aged women? Whether this is good policing or biased policing continues to be debated. Second, in the situation described by Arrigo, we have manifestly abusive conduct by the police officer. Questioning or challenging authority figures (e.g., parents, teachers, coaches, and so on) in any context runs the risks of eliciting an angry response, although the response in the described situation was certainly extreme by any measure.

Finally, Arrigo concludes with a call for transpraxis, or allowing for diverse voices and perceptions. This is surely a noble ideal in a complex, heterogeneous society; whether it is ever realistically possible in the context of unequal distribution of power is open to question.

Have we entered into a postmodern era, representing a fundamental break with the modern era? In my view, the single most promising contribution of a postmodern criminology to the discipline is to engage with emerging attributes of a postmodern social environment. Although attention to the postmodern world has been an important focus of some of the postmodern literature, it has not been a central preoccupation of self-identified postmodernist criminologists. It does seem self-evident to me that some of the defining attributes of modernity—for example, industrialization, bureaucratization and mass communication—are giving way to newly emerging institutional forms. Of course we live—and will continue to live—in a world characterized by premodern and modern as well as postmodern attributes. The real challenge is to accurately gauge how these attributes coexist and interact, rather than somewhat arbitrarily declaring that we have passed over into a postmodern world. But surely the institutional transformations are impacting, and will continue to impact, on many dimensions of crime and crime control.

Some questions that, to my mind, remain to be resolved include the following: Can a postmodern criminology be "defined," or is this an inherently contradictory enterprise? Does the postmodern repudiation of "foundationalism" and claims regarding objective truth ultimately lead to epistemological incoherence? Should one separate a criminological concern with understanding an emerging postmodern society from a distinctly postmodern criminology? How does one reconcile the inherent elitism of "postmodernist discourse" (i.e., its inaccessibility to all but a relatively small group of intellectually sophisticated people) with its denial of privileged truth and status? Can the themes and insights of postmodernist analysis be communicated in a far more accessible language and form, or is the difficulty of postmodernist discourse intrinsic to its value? Is a selective cooptation of some of its metaphors and insights by mainstream criminology the most likely fate of a postmodern criminology, or does it require an "all or nothing" commitment? When all is said and done, does postmodern criminology provide us with a fundamentally new, more profound, and ultimately useful way of understanding criminological phenomena, or is it simply old ideas provided with pretentious new labels, simplistic or misguided, and ultimately not applicable in any useful way?

NO

DAVID O. FRIEDRICHS

Postmodernism, Postmodernity, and Postmodern Criminology

The term *postmodern* has been quite widely invoked in recent times, although it has no settled meaning. One wit has observed that postmodernism is "whatever you want it to be, if you want it bad enough" (Handy, 1988; p. 102). More seriously, the postmodern has referred to certain aesthetic styles or approaches within architecture and the arts, to the collective (if somewhat haphazardly linked) ideas of several late twentieth century French philosophers and intellectuals (especially Baudrillard, Lyotard, Derrida, DeLeuze, Foucault, Barthes, Lacan, Bataille, and Kristeva), and to a new period in human history (emerging in the latter part of the 20th century) representing a fundamental break with modernity. The distinguished social theorist Anthony Giddens (1990) has emphasized that we should not confuse postmodernism—an intellectual movement—with postmodernity—a description of a changing society.

The association of postmodernism with architectural and fine arts styles need not concern us here. Some of the themes of the French "postmodernist" thinkers include the following: a challenge to exclusive truth claims, and to the notion of stable, fixed meaning in the world; a celebration of difference; a rejection of totalizing concepts (such as the state); an emphasis on local action, and a profound skepticism regarding the potential of collective action to transform society; and a repudiation of positivism (or the scientific method) as an appropriate methodology for understanding human existence (Rosenau, 1992). Postmodernist thought in at least some of its manifestations challenges conventional conceptions of the individual or human subject, denying the existence of any such entity (which is regarded as a creation of language). This claim in particular is difficult for many of us to accept, or even fully comprehend. Postmodernism contends that modernity is no longer liberating, but has become rather a force of subjugation, oppression, and repression. For postmodernism, language plays a central role in the human experience of reality.

However, it should be noted that the so-called postmodernist philosophers and writers have adopted highly individualistic (or idiosyncratic) perspectives and concepts, hardly share a single, coherent outlook or mode of analysis, and in one or more cases have specifically disavowed the "postmodernist" label. A basic distinction has been made between skeptical postmodernists—who engage in deconstruction of conventional thought and doctrine—and affirmative postmodernists—who promote a constitutive approach to making sense of and re-creating our world (Henry & Milovanovic, 1996; Rosenau, 1992).

Why Is There a Postmodern Criminology?

Overall, I take the current interest in postmodern thought to reflect the following: First, it is one response to disillusionment with positivism and mainstream forms of analysis. It comes out of a recognition of some limitations of "linear" logic. Some adherents seem to regard it as a humanistic equivalent of the challenge to the Newtonian model in physics. It challenges the privileging of mainstream science, and in at least some versions (e.g., semiotics) offers a specific technical alternative to such science.

Second, it is a response to the collapse of what some have called the master "metanarratives" of the twentieth century: for example, that Marxism offers a comprehensive vision for both understanding the world and organizing social existence. More broadly, it reflects a certain level of disenchantment with the conditions of modernity. We experience growing globalism; conversely, localism becomes more pronounced. We experience increasing challenges to state socialism, eurocentric culture, and male dominance. Postmodern thought is viewed by some as offering an approach to why this is happening and what it means.

Third, it can be understood as a form of intellectual faddism or trendiness (e.g., Lamont, 1987). It appeals to those who like to be associated with the avant garde or "cutting edge," who are attracted to provocative new ideas and lines of thought. In the early stages of the emergence of a new theory or intellectual "movement," it is rarely if ever obvious what its long-term fate will be. Some who believe that postmodern thought has already peaked; others seem to believe its influence will expand greatly as we move into the future. It remains to be seen, then, whether it will in time be regarded as a passing—ultimately discredited—intellectual fad or an enduring contribution to social thought.

One can admire much about the endeavors of postmodern criminologists. They include Stephen Pfohl, Dragan Milovanovic, Peter Manning, Stuart Henry, T. R. Young, and Bruce Arrigo, among others. They are risk-takers, academic high-wire walkers: that is, they have staked their careers and reputations on exploring largely uncharted terrain (It is unsurprising that the single most energetic and prolific promoter of postmodern criminology, Dragan Milovanovic, likes to spend his spare time jumping out of planes with a parachute). Postmodern criminologists have expended an enormous amount of intellectual energy grappling with a large and exceptionally difficult literature, cutting across many disciplines (from literature to physics), and in many cases transcending recognizable disciplinary boundaries. Some of this work conforms to the basic style of conventional criminological scholarship, but other work (e.g., that of Pfohl, 1993) calls for new, multimedia modes of communication and for the juxtaposition of direct observation, literary allusions, textual analysis, epiphanies, parenthetical observations, visual images, transcriptions of dialogue, and so forth. The use of schematic diagrams based on theories developed by mathematicians and physicists is also a novel dimension of some postmodern criminology (e.g., Milovanovic, 1997a; 1997b). Like oil wildcatters going out into the field hoping to strike it rich, postmodern criminologists have "drilled" many holes in search of profound criminological insights; whether they have indeed mined valuable intellectual "oil," or simply produced "dry holes," is a matter of some controversy (See Schwartz & Friedrichs, 1994).

Postmodern Criminology and the Undergraduate Curriculum

I do think it is useful to undergraduate students of criminology to be conscious of the fact that the criminological mainstream has been subjected to a "postmodern" challenge. I have serious reservations, however, about the value of an intense engagement with postmodern criminology on the part of the typical undergraduate student.

First, the principal mission of an undergraduate education in criminology must be the acquisition of "criminological literacy" and a thorough familiarity with the criminological canon. As a practical matter, this is necessary if students are to master a sequence of courses most likely to adopt some version of a mainstream criminological perspective, to qualify for postgraduate study in criminology and related fields, and to function successfully as professionals in some capacity within criminal justice. From my own perspective, it is certainly essential as well that students are exposed to the critique of the criminological mainstream, especially through the various strains of contemporary critical criminology. In my view, however, an intense engagement with postmodern criminology on the undergraduate level is likely to frustrate and baffle most students. The occasional undergraduate student with a powerful appetite for intellectual challenges may indeed be sufficiently intrigued by references to postmodern criminology to want to pursue it further (Allison Forker's [1997] "Chaos and Modeling Crime: Quinney's *Class, State and Crime*" is an extraordinary illustrative case of an undergraduate criminology student contending with and contributing to the postmodern criminological literature).

Second, I question whether postmodern thought can really be comprehended without a rich familiarity with the enlightenment and modernist tradition to which it is reacting. Indeed, a broadly based undergraduate education in philosophy, history, and science is a necessary precondition for grappling in a meaningful way with the claims of postmodern criminology.

The Critique of Postmodernism and Postmodern Criminology

The language and terminology of postmodernist thought generally, and of postmodern criminology specifically, is indisputably dense, diffuse, and difficult. For example, in recent work within postmodern criminology (e.g., Henry & Milovanovic, 1996; Milovanovic, 1997a; Milovanovic, 1997b) one encounters constitutive interrelational (COREL) sets, phase maps, attractors, fractals, torus, striated space, bifurcation diagrams, Mandelbrot sets, Mobius bands, and Borromean knots, among other phenomena. One encounters, as well, invocation of Lacanian psychoanalytical semiotics, signifiers and juridico-linguistic communicative markets, as well as French terms such as jouissance, parletre, and an ecriture feminine. There is an ongoing debate on the issue of such complex formulations and unfamiliar terminology. Is it willfully obscure jargon and perverse obfuscation? On the one side, postmodern criminologists explicitly or implicitly make the argument that complex, profound modes of analysis cannot be reduced to or translated into simple, easily accessible terminology. In the case of physics and mathematics, for example, it is not a matter of controversy that important work is expressed in terms only understandable to a small core of specialists. On the other side, there is the position that postmodern work is too often pitched in language that is pretentiously and unnecessarily difficult or incoherent, and that bad writing simply shields an absence of substantive content. Reading and studying scholarly work has been characterized as a zero-sum game. If it takes several times as long to read and make sense of an article or book of postmodern criminology than another article or book of comparable length, then it might be argued that the payoff should be roughly equivalent to this investment. It is far from clear, at this point, that this is the case. In other words, there is some burden on postmodern criminologists to demonstrate, in some convincing way, the necessity for abstruseness.

One emergent strain of postmodern criminology has adopted some propositions and concepts from twentieth century physics and mathematics and has applied them to an understanding of criminological phenomena. Dragan Milovanovic (1997a; 1997b) and T. R. Young (1997) in particular draw on quantum mechanics, catastrophe theory, chaos theory, Godel's theorem, and topology. This enterprise raises several questions. First, are those without special training in physics and mathematics capable of fully understanding highly sophisticated principles and concepts developed within these fields? Second, are these principles and concepts properly applicable to literary, social, or criminological phenomena? And third, if they are, do they really provide us with a deeper, more profound (and ultimately more useful) understanding than can be obtained through existing concepts or principles, or without resorting to such a complex, difficult framework? On the first two points, in particular, some of those from the hard sciences, including Nobel Prize–winning physicist Steven Weinberg (1996), have insisted that postmodernist thinkers such as Derrida in his invocation of the Einsteinian constant, Latour (special relativity), Lacan (algebra), and Irigaray (fluid mechanics), both get the science itself wrong and apply the scientific concepts incoherently (and pretentiously). NYU Physicist Alan Sokal (1996), whose satirical parody of postmodernist studies of natural sciences was accepted as a serious contribution by the editors of the postmodernist journal *Social Text* (generating a good deal of discussion and debate in the media), identifies objectionable themes of this literature:

> …appeals to authority in lieu of logic, speculative theories passed off as established science, strained and even absurd analogies, rhetoric that sounds good but whose meaning is ambiguous, and confusion between the technical and everyday senses of English words.

I am certainly not qualified to evaluate the accuracy of renditions of various scientific concepts in postmodern criminology, and wonder whether many (or any) criminologists are. But even assuming correct understanding, the appropriateness and fruitfulness of applying these ideas to criminological phenomena is still far from self-evident.

Conclusion

The argument put forth here is that postmodern criminology at present is a highly speculative enterprise and one that makes exceptional demands on those who would contend with it. Although it is certainly appropriate for undergraduate criminology students to be made aware of the basic contours of this heretical challenge to mainstream criminology, it does not follow that systematic incorporation of postmodern criminology into the undergraduate curriculum makes sense. **Advanced** students of criminological theory—academics and graduate students—are likely to be provoked at a minimum, and possibly enlightened, if they attend to the emerging postmodern criminology literature.

References

Forker, A. (1997). Chaos and modeling crime: Quinney's class, state and crime. In D. Milovanovic (Ed.), *Chaos, Criminology, and Social Justice* (pp. 55–76). Westport, CT: Praeger.

Giddens, A. (1990). *The consequences of modernity.* Cambridge, UK: Polity Press.

Handy, B. (1988, April). A Spy guide to postmodern everything. *Spy*, 100–108.

Henry, S., & Milovanovic, D. (1996). *Constitutive criminology: Beyond postmodernism*. London: Sage.

Lamont, M. (1987). How to become a dominant French philosopher: The case of Jacques Derrida. *American Journal of Sociology, 93*, 584–622.

Milovanovic, D. (Ed.). (1997a). *Chaos, criminology, and social justice: The new orderly (dis)order*. Westport, CT: Praeger.

Milovanovic, D. (1997b) *Postmodern criminology*. New York: Garland.

Pfohl, S. (1993). Twilight of the parasites: Ultramodern capital and the new world order. *Social Problems, 40*, 125–151.

Rosenau, P. M. (1992). *Post-modernism and the social sciences*. Princeton, NJ: Princeton University Press.

Schwartz, M. D., & Friedrichs, D. O. (1994). Postmodern thought and criminological discontent: New metaphors for understanding violence. *Criminology, 32*, 281–295.

Sokal, A. D. (1996, Fall). Transgressing the boundaries: An afterword. *Dissent*, 93–99.

Weinberg, S. (1996, August 8). Sokal's hoax. *The New York Review of Books*, 11–15.

Young, T. R. (1997). The ABCs of crime: Attractors, bifurcations, and chaotic dynamics. In D. Milovanovic, (Ed.), *Chaos, Criminology, and Social Justice* (pp. 77–96). Westport, CT: Praeger.

Rejoinder to Dr. Friedrichs   Bruce A. Arrigo

David O. Friedrichs offers a compelling critique of postmodern criminology and its utility for undergraduates and their university instruction. In the pages that follow, rather than responding to his general critique, my rejoinder will address four questions Friedrichs identifies at the conclusion of his reply to my substantive arguments. The intention here is to offer the reader some additional commentary with which to decide on the merits of postmodern social theory and its value for criminological practice.

Friedrichs ponders whether it is possible to "define" postmodern criminology or whether this is an inherently contradictory endeavor. The problem with the question is that it already assumes a certain (modernist) understanding of the knowledge process itself. Some opponents of postmodernism believe that knowledge must unfold in a certain way; that is, that meaning must be grasped instantaneously and immediately. Reading a sentence from beginning to end—including the punctuation point—must produce full and complete understanding. Digressions from this perspective foster incoherence, "fuzzy logic," and questionable thinking. Thus, all expressions of inconsistency, contradiction, incompleteness, or other so-called anomalies must be cleansed or purged from what we say or what we write. Some postmodernist (especially several with feminist leanings) claim that occasions such as these may be crucial moments of knowing, crucial moments of sense making in which new vistas of understanding are born. In other words, defining postmodernism as if it is essentially retrievable, reducible, knowable and, therefore, controllable and predictable, misses the direction of the theory. There are many postmodernisms and they are all fluid. Their fluidity is related to the positional, provisional, and relational meanings (hidden assumptions and implicit values) they seek to uncover as conveyed through language. Postmodern criminology, then, is an effort to announce contingent universalisms or conditional truths about how crime, law, social control, punishment, and deviance are embodied in speech and regulate our lives.

Friedrichs questions whether postmodernism's resistance to foundationalism results in "epistemological incoherence." This concern is an outgrowth of the first issue he raises. Again, the assumption that there is such a thing as "objective truth" belies the view held by many postmodernists. Reality is subject to the meanings we accent or assign to it; that is, the values we privilege, knowingly or not, in speech when describing events such as the arrest of a fleeing suspect, the execution of a death row inmate, the waiver of a juvenile to the adult system, or the psychological treatment of a convicted sex offender. Thus, truth has meaning through the words that we select to convey the thoughts that we think when describing experiences we interpret. Given the postmodern attitude of repudiating ultimate truths or fixed truths, it follows that what meanings are discerned and announced must be relational, positional, and provisional. Truth is not an arrival at incontrovertible meaning but always a departure from it. Epistemologically what is produced is not incoherence but a position on the knowledge process that recognizes the contingent nature of our own existences.

Friedrichs wonders whether postmodernism produces elitist language in its attempt to resist privileging any one voice or manner of conversing. The result is a form of dialogue that renders understanding unintelligible to all but a small cadre of fellow travelers who walk along the postmodern trail. This leads Friedrichs to question whether the complex language of postmodernism is an essential function of its overall value. The language of postmodernism is, at times, difficult to decipher, but there are reasons for this. These justifications are at the core of what postmodernism and postmodern criminologists value.

To break away from the conventional modes of speech and methods of communicating (practices that, according to postmodern advocates, reproduce hierarchical arrangements, status quo convictions, and established forms of domination), it is important to transcend the imposed parameters of sense making by constructing alternative vistas for conveying knowledge about self, others, and society. An aspect of this interactive and dynamic triadic relationship is the knowledge we have regarding crime. Affirmative postmodernists embrace methods of discourse analysis that seek to reveal (not conceal) those voices or points of view silenced in the "texts" we listen to or read. Thus, many of the dependent clauses, free-floating images, literary allusions, algebraic formulations, and so on, are designed to loosen up the text so that the subject (the person) may be retrieved. Liberating discourse from entrenched meaning is necessary if we are to understand what values are or are not folded into it. As a result, there is a "shattering" of speech or a "de-centering" of language. The aim is to foster greater and divergent expressions of being and becoming; perspectives that more fully embody the manifold ways by which reality as we know and live it uniquely may be understood.

Friedrichs concludes by raising an important and basic matter. He considers whether postmodern criminology provides society in general and the student in particular with a fundamentally original way by which to grasp the problem of crime. Unlike the dramaturgical analysis of Erving Goffman, postmodernists are not so much interested in how human beings present themselves to others such that they "manage the impressions" others have of them through either "front" or "back" stage social engineering maneuvers. Unearthing how such efforts find expression, reproduction, and legitimacy in certain contexts (and others not) in ways that convey, consciously or otherwise, meanings that advance circumscribed interests, is central to the postmodern agenda. This is the direction that postmodern criminology charts for itself. It is simultaneously a call to resist established norms (including its own) while, all the while, insisting on better, more complete demonstrations of justice. It is a movement away from what is—and all that this implies, to what could be—and all that this leaves undecided. Not only is postmodern criminology a useful way of understanding the complexities of our fragile, fast-paced, media-induced, simulated society, it may be one of the few remaining and honest points of access by which we can meaningfully dialogue with our uncertain, problematic future.

Are Restorative Justice Processes Too Lenient toward Offenders?

Arthur V. N. Wint, J.D., is Associate Professor of Criminology at California State University, Fresno. His current interests include victimology and victim rights, juvenile delinquency; and community policing. He previously served as vice chair of the Fresno County Juvenile Justice Commission and is currently a mediator with the Fresno Victim Offender Reconciliation Program. He served as the Fresno Site Coordinator for the National Victim Assistance Academy Summer 1997 Academy. He has written articles on various subjects, including police liability for use of deadly force and victims' attitudes toward the criminal justice system. He is currently doing research on the role of community-based organizations in assessing the merits of alternative detention approaches in juvenile justice and preparing a book on child molestation and abuse.

Duane Ruth-Heffelbower, M.Div., J.D., is Associate Director and a member of the graduate faculty of the Center for Peacemaking and Conflict Studies of Fresno Pacific University. As chair of the founding board of Victim Offender Reconciliation Program of the Central Valley, Inc. (VORP), he helped bring restorative justice to California in the early 1980s. He now serves on the advisory committee of the Restorative Justice Project and continues to work with VORP and the national Victim Offender Mediation Association. An attorney and ordained Mennonite Minister trained in family therapy, he has worked with the criminal justice system, victims and offenders on many levels for over twenty years.

YES

Arthur V. N. Wint

It might be useful at the outset for purpose of this exercise to state the adage, "the perception is the reality." Indeed, for a significant majority of society, the reality is that juvenile crime is "out of control," particularly violent crime committed by juveniles. A further assertion is that juveniles are seen as being "coddled," "slapped on the wrist," or simply not being "punished" enough.

Unfortunately, practitioners involved in restorative justice programs may be feeding into this perception. For example, a juvenile steals a van, and with his "homies" goes on a joy ride in which the van is vandalized inside and out then abandoned in a vacant lot. The reaction of the victim's five-year-old daughter to the crime is to ask her father whether the "bad guys will be coming back to cut up the family the way they cut up the seats in the van." She suffers for a time from nightmares in which she dreams that the "bad guys" have returned for her. On his adjudication, the juvenile offender is offered the opportunity to participate in a VORP reconciliation process, which he accepts. The end result is that the offender signs a contract to participate in an early morning school program and to perform community service. The victim agrees to this consequence but still wonders whether that is "enough." Has the offender been punished enough?

Punishment: Controlling Behavior

The principal idea behind punishment is to control behavior. That is, the focus of punishment is to control deviant behavior. Various authors have expressed the view that punishment works. Among them are James Q. Wilson and Ernest van den Haag. These authors assert that the more certain and severe the punishment, the less likely it will be that delinquency will occur (van den Haag, 1975; Wilson, 1975). Four justifications are made for the use of punishment: (1) General deterrence: Punishment causes other would-be criminals to become fearful of the consequences of criminal behavior, thus making it less likely that they will engage in that behavior; (2) Specific deterrence: Punishment strikes fear in the offender, making it less likely that he or she will re-offend; (3) Incapacitation: Removing offenders from society, thus taking away their capacity to commit crime; (4) Retribution: Punishment is the consequence that flows from the offending behavior. Punishment is morally right and just in light of the harm to society (Regoli & Hewitt, 1994).

Researchers in the field of psychology have concluded that when punishment is applied swiftly, consistently, and explained, it may be effective in deterring unwanted behavior (Church, 1963; Parke 1970; Baumrind, 1971). Economists have also concluded that punishment works. According to the economic model, people commit crime because of the economic utility of engaging in the behavior

(Becker, 1968). Among criminologists, however, there has been a mixed review. Many believe that because there is a significant time lag between the commission of the crime, arrest, conviction, and sentencing, the effectiveness of punishment may very well be diminished, if not totally neutralized. Punishment is neither swift nor certain (Regoli & Hewitt, 1994; Tittle & Rowe, 1974).

Ethical Construct: Restoration Versus Retribution

Punishment serves to "satisfy" society's need for assuring that offenders get their "just deserts." In this regard, there may very well be a clash, or conflict of values as far as the foundation on which our penal system/expectations are built, and the foundation on which restorative justice is built. This may be even more pronounced when dealing with juvenile offenders. We espouse a "treatment" model for juvenile offenders, yet we decry the amount of "punishment" meted out to offending juveniles. We aspire to the level of moral development in which we no longer react punitively; however, we have yet to attain that lofty state. The penal system is based in significant measure on the concept of retribution. Part and parcel of that is the expectation that an offender will receive a penalty proportionate to his or her offense.

Classical theorists in the sixteenth and seventeenth centuries grappled with the whole idea of punishment and deterrence. Among them was an Italian, Cesare Beccaria, who believed that people made decisions based on free will. As rational beings, offenders committed crimes based on an assessment of the benefits as opposed to the costs of committing crime. Punishment was therefore justified because offenders purposefully set out to harm others. He was, however concerned that punishment be "rational and sane," rather than excessive or cruel (Regoli & Hewitt, 1994). Another classical theorist was Jeremy Bentham, an Englishman, who developed the utilitarian theory of criminality, asserting that people made choices based on the pleasure–pain principle; therefore, it was imperative to set punishments that were specific and applicable to all, regardless of status or wealth (Regoli & Hewitt, 1994). Other theoretical models have included the neoclassical model, which focuses on mitigating circumstances that might affect the nature of criminality, and consequently the type/extent of punishment; the Marxist model, which focuses on crime as an outgrowth of social and economic forces; and various psychological models, which look at the characteristics of the offender and the impact of the environment on criminality.

Regardless of the model one prefers, any comparison of the two models makes it clear that the restorative justice approach stands in stark contrast to the retributive model. Restorationists look at the relationship between the offender, the victim, and society as having been broken, and they attempt to "fix" this relationship, whereas retributionists are concerned with the offender "paying" for his or her crime.

Restoration

The restorative justice paradigm is one in which an attempt is made to restore the inequities between the victim and offender and to bring about a state of "shalom"—peace between the parties and the community in which they live. Restorative justice approaches crime from the vantage point of a violation of one person by another, rather than as a violation against the state (Umbreit & Carey, 1995). This approach has some similarity to earlier pioneer, or clan, justice, in which the offense was seen as a violation of the individual wronged, and "swift justice" was meted out to the offender—from the end of either a gun or a rope. In contrast, restorative justice approach focuses on establishing dialogue to address problem-solving as it relates to understanding crime, understanding accountability, and understanding justice, as well as to negotiate change, rather than to punish and fix blame—to key in on the following principles identified by Howard Zehr (1990) as being of paramount importance to the restorative justice process:

Regarding Understanding of Crime. Victims' needs/rights are central; the offense must be understood in its full moral, social, economic, political context; people *and* relationships are the victims, not the state; crime is therefore harm to people and relationships, not just a violation of rules.

Regarding Understanding of Accountability. Wrongs create liabilities and obligations, not just "guilt;" debts are paid by making "right," not just by exacting punishment; and accountability means taking responsibility, not just taking ones "medicine."

Regarding Understanding of Justice. Victims' needs and problem-solving are central, rather than fixing blame and focusing on the rights of the offender; justice is seen as right relationships; dialogue is normative as opposed to the adversarial, battle mode; and restitution is a normal outcome of the process. Under this model, the goal is to gain closure for victims (to impress on offenders the impact that their behavior has had on their victims), and to facilitate restitution to the victims (Zehr, 1990).

The restorative justice model allows the victim and offender both to have the opportunity to interact in a problem-solving mode to resolve the conflict created by the offender's action. Rather than passively awaiting the State's action against the offender, the victim is placed in an active participant role in addressing his or her victimization (Umbreit & Carey, 1995). Victim–offender restorative programs use a process whereby victims and offenders review and discuss the incident, develop mutual understanding, negotiate restitution where appropriate, and express their future intentions (Bakker, 1994).

In summary, the basis on which restorative justice operates is an attempt to attain a win–win solution for the victim and for the offender. It aspires to a moral position that seeks "shalom"—true peace between the parties, in which the need for punitive action becomes unnecessary. However, as seen in the example taken from an actual situation, sometimes the victim walks away from a mediation agreement with the question of adequate punishment for the offender still unanswered. Even in the restorative justice model, the "need" for retribution still abounds.

Retribution

The focus of retribution is that people deserve punishment for their wrongful acts. Like restorative justice, retributive justice tries to establish an essential link between punishment and "moral wrongdoing." Punishment serves as a public condemnation of crime. Among the principles that retributionists offer to justify the use of punishment are the following:

Just Desert. Viewed as central to the retribution model. Offenders must pay for their voluntary conduct that violates society's rules.

Wrongdoers Deserve to Suffer. This is based on comparative justice. The offender should share a comparative level of suffering as did the victim and society.

Fairness to Law-Abiding Citizens. This keys on the idea of restoring a "just equilibrium" between the offender and the victim, and society.

Satisfaction. This rests on what some retributive theorists refer to as the "intuitive perceptions of justice." That is, they assert that in our culture it is expected that offenders be required to pay what is owed—to pay a debt owed to society as a result of the offending conduct (Ten, 1987; Walker, 1991).

I submit that almost every leisure activity in our culture reinforces the idea of just deserts: we root for the "good guys" to overcome the "bad guys" in our movies, and, indeed, we participate vicariously in innumerable acts of violence and mayhem toward achieving that goal, applauding at the end when the "star" emerges from the inferno with just a few scratches; we send unruly hockey players to the "penalty box;" grid iron warriors face losing yardage and other penalties for their infractions; basketball players can "foul out;" and, of course, baseball players and errant boyfriends are all aware of "three strikes and you are out." In the face of all this cultural predisposition, restorationists propose a counterintuitive approach that leaves many with the feeling that the restorative justice process is just too lenient toward offenders.

Retribution and Community Expectations

The role of community expectations cannot be discounted. Sometimes community expectations get translated over in ways that are deemed inappropriate, or unconstitutional, as in the landmark case of *Solem* v. *Helm* (1983). There the United States Supreme Court overturned the conviction of the defendant, Helm, on the basis that the punishment imposed was disproportionate to the offense for which he was convicted. The Court outlined the three-pronged approach to be used in determining whether the proposed punishment will meet the standard imposed by the Eighth Amendment to the United States Constitution: (1) the gravity of the of-

fense and the harshness of the penalty; (2) the sentences imposed on other criminals in the same jurisdiction; and (3) the sentences imposed for the commission of
the same crime in other jurisdictions. The underlying principle driving the South
Dakota legislature, however, was not addressed. Indeed, it was not even an issue
presented to the Court. That is, the perception that crime control was a serious
problem in that state needed attention, and strong, punitive measures had to be
taken to stem the tide of crime. The community expectations were that retribution
was what was needed to address their crime problem. The court found that in that
particular instance that the measures imposed went too far. The issue of community expectations, however, still remains.

Clearly there has been a growing trend toward retribution. Indeed, one
could assert that we have come "full circle," with states using recidivist statutes.
The "three strikes, you're out" analogy has been translated over into the penal
system, with a growing number of states enacting more punitive incarceration
statutes such as the "Three Strikes" measure signed into law by the Governor of
California in March of 1994 (Turner, Sundt, Applegate, & Cullen, 1995). The
trend appears to be toward highly retributive laws evidencing a "low tolerance,"
or "zero tolerance" toward criminal offenders. One author has suggested that in
times of rapid social and economic change such as our recent experience in this
country, in which traditional values are perceived to be challenged or to be losing
authority, many communities revert to a model that reinforces the sense of the old
revered values (McCorkle, 1995). Criminologists and politicians alike have called
for swift sure punishment—just deserts—for deviant behavior. Many appear to
agree with philosophers such as Herbert Morris, who, three decades ago, asserted
that justice demands that a person be punished if he or she is guilty. Indeed, Morris offers the following four propositions: we have a right to punishment; this
right derives from the fundamental human right to be treated as a person; this
right is a natural, inalienable and absolute right; and denial of this right implies a
denial of all moral rights and duties. He goes on to explain,

> [I]t is just to punish those who have violated the rules and caused the unfair
> distribution of benefits and burdens. A person who violates the rules has
> something others have—the benefits of the system—but by renouncing what
> others have assumed, the burdens of self-restraint, he has acquired an unfair
> advantage. Matters are not even until this advantage is in some way erased.
> Another way of putting it is that he owes something to others, for he has
> something that does not rightfully belong to him. Justice—that is, punishing
> such individuals—restores the equilibrium of benefits and burdens by taking
> from the individual what he owes, that is, exacting the debt (1968)

As Richard Quinney has stated, criminologists are engaged in a moral enterprise
(1997). Thirty years after Morris' pronouncement, above, the country is still guided
by the conservative moral philosophy that lay behind the quote. The "moral im-

perative" calls for punishment—retribution. The community demands that offenders be "rewarded" for their offenses against society.

Conclusion

The idea of justice is one that has occupied the attention of philosophers and prophets for millennia. The moral underpinnings of both restorative justice and retributive justice rest in the Judeo-Christian ethic. Restorative justice derives from concepts of redemption. If the mediation process can result in redeeming the inequities that exist between the parties, then the state of "shalom" will have been met and equity restored. The focus is on the ideal, and it is claimed to have been met if the parties involved—victim, offender, and mediator—agree that it has been met. The reality, however, does not match the ideal. Notwithstanding the ideal of redemption, there still pervades in our society the compelling ethic of retribution—also flowing from the same ethical construct. Wrongs must be righted, and offenders must pay back to society. "Justice" has not been met if the offender does not "suffer the consequences of his/her behavior." Society "needs" the satisfaction of "just deserts" being meted out to the offender. The restorative justice model does not address this need. Indeed, it is seen as part of giving offenders a "slap on the wrist," whereas society and the victims of crime suffer the consequences—ongoing inequities—of criminal conduct.

REFERENCES

Bakker, M. W. (1994). Repairing the breach and reconciling the discordant: Mediation in the criminal justice system. *North Carolina Law Review, 72,* 1478.

Baumrind, D. (1971). Harmonious parents and their preschool children. *Developmental Psychology, 41,* 92–102.

Becker, G. (1968). *The economic approach to human behavior.* Chicago: University of Chicago Press.

Church, R. (1963) The varied effects of punishment on behavior. *Psychological Review 70*; 369–402.

McCorkle, R. C. (1995). Correctional boot camps and attitude change: Is all this shouting necessary? *Justice Quarterly, 12,* 365–75.

Morris, H. (1968). Persons and prisons. In Murphy, J. G. (1973). *Punishment and rehabilitation.* Belmont, CA: Wadsworth.

Parke, R. (1970). The role of punishment in the socialization process. In R. Hoope, G. Milton, & E. Simmel (Eds.), *Early experiences and the process of socialization.* New York: Academic Press.

Quinney, R. (1997). *Criminology as moral philosophy, criminologists as witnesses.* Paper presented at the annual meeting of the American Society of Criminology, November 20, 1997, San Diego, CA.

Regoli, R. M., & Hewitt, J. D. (1994). *Delinquency in society; A child-centered approach.* (2nd ed.). New York: McGraw-Hill.

Ten, C. L. (1987). *Crime, guilt and punishment.* Oxford: Clarendon Press.

Tittle, C., & Rowe, A. (1974). Certainty of arrest and crime rates. *Social Forces, 52*, 455–462.

Turner, M. G., Sundt, J. L., Applegate, B. K., & Cullen, F. T. (1995) 'Three strikes and you're out' legislation: A national assessment. *Federal Probation, 59*, 16–35.

Umbreit, M. S., & Carey, M. (1995). Restorative justice: Implications for Organized change. *Federal Probation, 59,* 47–54.

van den Haag, (1975). *Punishing criminals; concerning a very old and painful question.* New York: Basi Books.

Walker, N. (1991). *Why punish?* New York: Oxford University Press.

Wilson, J. Q. (1975). *Thinking about crime.* New York: Basic Books.

Zehr, H. (1990). *Changing lenses: A new focus for crime and justice.* Scottsdale, PA: Herald Press.

Case Cited

Solem v. *Helm,* 463 U.S. 277, 103 S. Ct. 3001, 77 L.Ed.2d 627 (1983).

Rejoinder to Mr. Wint

DUANE RUTH-HEFFELBOWER

Arthur Wint has done a good job of pulling together the usual arguments against Restorative Justice processes. Let me suggest some alternate ways of viewing the same material.

The van theft victim described as an example did not leave the VORP session sure that enough had been done. Were this to happen in real life, it would be the result of the victim not fully participating in the process. No one dictates to the victim what enough is. There needs to be a solid consensus among the participants that the agreements reached do what needs to be done. Proper preparation of both victims and offenders to participate fully in VORP processes is crucial to their success. Although second thoughts at the conclusion of a process are natural, those in the Restorative Justice movement need to do their best to ensure victim satisfaction with the outcome.

The idea of applying just the right amount of pain to prevent recurrence of bad behavior, or to deter it in the first place, is one of those logical ideas that flies in the face of illogical criminal behavior, particularly on the part of juveniles. It assumes that offenders make a logical, rational choice to offend, in light of the potential cost of the behavior. I believe it is well accepted that drives other than cost-benefit analysis tend to produce most criminal behavior, and that juveniles have a difficult time in correctly applying cost-benefit analysis in any event.

The concept of "paying for your crime" is an interesting one. Who gets paid? Your spending six months in jail does not help me get my television back. Not only do I have to buy a new set, my taxes support you for six months. I will still be double-locking the door, paying the alarm company, and wondering when you will be back. The retributive system addresses none of my problems. At best I will know that you won't rob me for six months.

The "need for retribution" is another well-known wrong idea. When you are harmed by an unknown evil, it is natural to want revenge. It is part of the revenge fantasy that all victims have. That need evaporates when the unknown evil is a person who is sitting with you trying to make things right. In the retributive system, this never happens, and the revenge fantasy is allowed to blossom and flourish. The argument for revenge is circular. People who have little or no information about their offender have fantasies of revenge. The retributive system keeps that knowledge from you, then gloats that people need revenge.

When some offenders are handled through a retributive system and some through a restorative system, there will be inequities. Two burglars will have very different outcomes. This is not the fault of restorative justice, but of a retributive system that has to maintain its hold on the populace by force and fear. Restorative justice is better for victims and communities, but it probably will not keep the jails full. Those with vested interests in the dominant system will need to use every argument they can muster, which does not, by the way, include effectiveness, to survive.

Fairness is a popular concept, but no one knows what it means. If two men each burglarize two houses and take identical television sets, should they each receive the same sentence? Most people would want to know about the two men before answering. If one is a drug addict living on the street and another is an assembly line worker who has been out of a job for six months and cannot feed his family, most people would probably have different sentences in mind. That is what Restorative Justice is all about.

Zero tolerance statutes sound great until you analyze their effects. In a school, for instance, a zero tolerance policy toward possession of tobacco really means that the decision maker in a particular case is pushed further down the hierarchy. Rather than the principal deciding how to treat the offender, it is the teacher or the janitor who discovers the violation who gets to decide whether the behavior will be punished. It does not take much imagination to see that the further down the hierarchy a decision is pushed, the greater the chances for dissimilar results in similar cases. In a three-strikes felony case, it is now the arresting officer or the Deputy District Attorney who decides what will happen, not the judge. What to call the violation and whether to charge priors become more important than the trial for many offenders.

Short delays between offense and consequence are generally thought to be important to preventing new offenses. Restorative justice processes offer the opportunity to create truly appropriate consequences much more quickly than retributive systems. The delays inherent in an adversarial system, and the uncertain results they produce, tend to make their consequences seem remote to offenders. One of the important benefits of Restorative Justice processes is their ability to respond quickly. There is no benefit to the offender in delaying a restorative process.

What is justice? That the person harmed by injustice be made as whole as possible as soon as possible, and that offenders be restored to the community as useful citizens, thereby eliminating new offenses and discouraging others from offending. I would submit that calls for anything less are more political demagoguery than criminology. For those unable to participate in restorative processes because of willfulness, or mental or physical conditions, protecting society by separating them from it may be required. Restorative processes are available to them when they are ready.

NO

DUANE RUTH-HEFFELBOWER

Restorative Justice is a big tent. Many different processes can be included (Presbyterian Church, 1997). To make sense out of the possibilities, we have developed the Principles of Restorative Justice.[1] Any process can be more or less restorative, and it is probably more helpful to think of a continuum with "most restorative" on one end and "least restorative" on the other. By testing a particular process against the Principles, its place on the continuum can be ascertained (Claassen, 1996b).

Restorative Justice processes generally have in common the inclusion of all those affected directly by a crime in the creation of the solution. This means that the victim, offender, and community all have a say in crafting the response to the offense. If that is so, it would seem presumptuous for someone outside the process to complain that the process has been too lenient. The critical questions are whether the right people have been involved in the process, and whether the process has been fairly run.

There has been a movement away from the traditional understandings of humankind about criminal justice (Van Ness, 1986). What we know of criminal justice in clans and villages before the advent of the nation-state, or in areas outside central control, tells us that people understand crime to be an offense against victims that damages the fabric of the community. The interest of the community is to make victims whole while finding a way to re-integrate the offender into a constructive role within the community. In these close communities, it is shameful to violate another, and this healthy type of shame does much to prevent criminal acts.

With the breakdown of village and clan authority structures in the rise of centralized authority, there is a movement toward seeing crime as a violation of the sovereign's peace, rather than of another individual. It makes sense in this new way of understanding criminality to have the offended sovereign be the victim, and for restitution to take the form of fines to the sovereign. This new way of seeing crime and justice has resulted in our current western criminal justice systems, with victims forgotten and offenders punished by measured doses of pain, but with offenders never having to accept responsibility for their acts (Zehr, 1990).

The movement from clan and village identity, by which a person only existed within a web of relationships (commonly referred to as high context or corporate personality cultures) to the modern understanding of individuals being independent actors (low context cultures) (Augsburger, 1992), has created a modern Western culture of shamelessness (Braithwaite, 1989). I can be accused of crime, tried, convicted, and serve my prison sentence without ever acknowledging my guilt. In fact, the current system assumes no acknowledgment of guilt. There is no effort made to re-integrate offenders into the community. Because I do not acknowledge guilt, I do not feel shame. My family and I are victims of "the system," not shamed offenders.

Restorative Justice seeks to return to the days when crimes were understood to be committed against individual victims, and family structures existed to take responsibility for the work of re-integrating offenders into the community and making victims whole. The assumption of Restorative Justice is that the offender takes personal responsibility for the harm done and does what can be done to make things as right as possible with the victim. RJ assumes that the offender will be supported in this effort by his or her family and other significant community persons, and that they will continue to hold the offender accountable for following through.

So what does a typical Restorative Justice process look like? Here in Fresno, California we are using two permutations of victim–offender mediation through the Victim Offender Reconciliation Program (VORP). The traditional VORP case, developed in 1978 in Elkhart, Indiana and Waterloo, Ontario (Zehr, 1990), brings together the victim, offender, and a trained mediator to do three things: (1) acknowledge injustices; (2) restore equity; and (3) make future intentions clear (Claassen, 1991; 1996). The offender takes responsibility for his or her actions, including hearing from the victim about the impact of the crime and answering the victim's questions, a restitution agreement is created, and the offender and victim are clear with each other about their future intentions (Umbreit, 1994).

In recent years, this traditional style of doing VORP has added more participants, and now goes by various names, including family group conference, community justice conference, and others. The usual group in these cases includes the victim and his or her advocate(s), the offender and his or her extended family, criminal justice system representatives and other community representatives. It is common for these groups to number twelve to twenty persons. The process is similar to the traditional VORP case, except that everyone must come to consensus on a plan for making things right. These plans tend to be more complete than the traditional VORP agreement, including everything the offender needs to become a productive member of society and to empower his or her family, supported by community resources, to assist in that project.

Three basic models of these larger group gatherings have been developed and are in use all over the world: (1) the New Zealand model, where the meeting is facilitated by a social worker; (2) the Australian or Wagga Wagga model, in which a police officer leads the meeting; and (3) the Fresno model, in which a trained community volunteer serves as facilitator (Ruth-Heffelbower, 1998).

Key to the success of these victim–offender meetings is the offender taking personal responsibility for his or her actions. After introductions, the meetings usually begin with the offender describing the offense, answering the victims' questions for clarification, then hearing from the victims as to how the event affected them. This is radically different from the typical criminal justice process. In a court setting, the defendant is forced to plead "not guilty," even when that really means "prove it if you can." The victim in a court case is seldom involved unless a witness is needed, and many victims were not witnesses to the offense.

The adversarial system of criminal justice requires the defendant to either deny that he or she committed the acts complained of or to remain silent throughout the proceedings. Even after a conviction, the defendant must maintain innocence as appeals proceed. There is no incentive to admit the crime at any stage unless a plea bargain is offered, and then the admission is to the agreed facts supporting the plea bargain, not a description of what really happened.

Victims are greatly frustrated by this charade of innocence, if they even know it is happening (Zehr, 1990). It is not uncommon for a victim to first learn that arrest, trial, and conviction have taken place when the probation officer contacts them for a statement of loss for purposes of a restitution order.

The current criminal justice system in North America is a retributive system. If you commit a crime, and are caught and convicted, you will receive a measured dose of pain, usually in the form of incarceration, as punishment or retribution for your action. When you are released from prison, you will be placed on parole, but unless you are arrested for another crime, it is unlikely that your parole officer will spend significant time with you. The idea of prisons rehabilitating inmates has disappeared with funding shortfalls and the failure of studies to demonstrate the effectiveness of rehabilitation strategies. The role of prison is to punish. The hope, of course, is that people will fear this potential punishment and avoid it by avoiding criminal behavior. The fact that the United States incarcerates more persons per capita than any other country suggests that the deterrence strategy may not be working.

Forgotten in all of this is the victim who was directly injured by the crime. There are victim–witness programs and funds for victims of crime these days, but they tend to be inadequate to the need in most cases. Victims demonstrate the same posttraumatic stress disorder symptoms that soldiers in combat face. Yet their needs are largely overlooked. Victims have a deep need to know why this happened to them, to know that they are not being stalked, and that the chances of them being revictimized by the same person are remote. They need to have the unknown "they" that injured them be a real person with understandable motives. They need to be made as whole as possible again, healing the sense of violation that persists (Zehr, 1990).

The current western criminal justice systems do not attempt in any meaningful way to meet the needs of victims. They are offender-driven, focusing on processing offenders as expeditiously and cheaply as possible. Neither do these systems attempt in any significant way to meet the needs of the community beyond the desire for expeditious and inexpensive processing of those criminals who are caught.

Restorative justice recognizes that "Crime is a violation of people and relationships. It creates obligations to make things right. Justice involves the victim, the offender, and the community in a search for solutions which promote repair, reconciliation, and reassurance" (Zehr, 1990, p. 181). Restorative Justice sees victims, offenders, and communities as inextricably interwoven components of any effective approach to crime. The needs of victims must be paramount. Victimology is a science in itself, and I will not try to cover the field here. Suffice it to say that victims need at least to regain a sense of control in their lives, to tell and hear the truth about their situation, to be made as whole as possible financially, and to have questions answered that help them re-integrate their lives and their place in society. Communities need to restore the order and predictability they lose when crime occurs, and to reweave the broken social contract (McCold, 1996). Offenders, to change, need to accept personal responsibility for their actions and make amends to those harmed. The current criminal justice system does not do these things in a meaningful way.

Restorative Justice works to meet these needs through direct involvement of the affected parties, including appropriate community representatives. Responses to crime that require less are, in my view, too lenient. A sentence that calls for an offender to be supported by the community for a time, without more, is lenient in the extreme. The offender leaves the victim with all the bad effects, yet is able to say, "I've paid my debt to society." That is lenient.

We have found that victims move rapidly toward healing when they meet with their offender in a safe setting and hear the offender take responsibility for the crime, including paying restitution, which the victim helps to define. Victim fantasies of revenge against an unknown assailant evaporate when they hear a real person accept responsibility for the crime and absolve the victim of fault. Victims are relieved to learn that they were a target of opportunity rather than a carefully researched and stalked target. As the offender keeps the agreements made, the victim is able to begin restoring the orderliness of their world (Zehr, 1990).

It takes dedicated people to bring victims and offenders together and to monitor compliance with agreements. A meeting that is ineptly run between unprepared victims and offenders can revictimize the victim. Victim Offender programs train their staff and volunteers, and screen offenders and victims, preparing them for a productive time together. The program then follows up to make sure agreements are kept, providing encouragement. In the case of Community Justice Conferences, the agreement can be quite extensive, calling for a variety of social services for both victim and offender. Offenders who want to pay restitution but have no income need to be assisted with job referrals or training. Some victim–offender programs have work programs that enable unemployed offenders to earn their restitution money.

Offenders need to understand that what they did is shameful, and that the community requires more of them (Leibrich, 1996). They also need resources to enable them to change. This type of assistance only works when it is voluntary. Restorative Justice offers offenders the opportunity to take responsibility and also offers assistance in helping the offender live up to the community standard. It is holistic in its treatment of the effects of crime. Offenders who have participated in Restorative Justice programs agree that it is tougher than the traditional response to their actions (Enns, 1996). It is not tough to deny your responsibility and spend time in jail compared with having to look your victim in the eye and take responsibility for your actions.

Particularly in the field of juvenile justice, neither the treatment nor the retributive models have been effective. Both, among other faults, disempower the family when it is that institution that is generally recognized as having the best hope of turning a juvenile offender around. Restorative Justice instead seeks to empower and resource the family (Bazemore, 1996).

The idea that punishment for crime can be too lenient assumes that punishment is useful and that there is some correct degree of punishment that will achieve the desired effect of extinguishing criminal behavior. Indeterminate sentencing was tried when fixed terms did not work, and now we are swinging the pendulum back to fixed sentences because indeterminate ones did not work. Neither method has been able to successfully ascertain the correct dose of punishment necessary to get the desired effect. Restorative Justice programs, however, have been very successful in identifying what was needed in an individual case to extinguish the negative behavior, or to at least lower the level of offense (Umbreit, 1994).

I would propose that the retributive system by which one trails, nails, and jails an offender is the one that is too lenient. Offenders in that system receive no meaningful sanction demonstrated to change their behavior.

When an offender is prepared to cooperate with restorative processes, those should be the preferred method. For those uncooperative offenders, which we will always have with us, providing suitable housing for them for the protection of the community is certainly appropriate (Claassen, 1996e). It is time that we stopped using prison, proven ineffective in a large number of cases, as our only approach to sanction for crime. Holding offenders accountable while assisting victims and communities with their healing processes should instead be our criminal justice goals (Claassen, 1996d).

Notes

1. *Restorative Justice—Fundamental Principles,* by Ron Claassen, Co-Director, Center for Peacemaking and Conflict Studies of Fresno Pacific University. Presented May 1995 at NCPCR; revised May 1996 at UN Alliance of NGOs Working Party on Restorative Justice © 1996 Ron Claassen. These principles may be reproduced so long as they are not edited for content, the source is listed, and the legend "Printed by permission" is included.

1. Crime is primarily an offense against human relationships, and secondarily a violation of a law (because laws are written to protect safety and fairness in human relationships).

2. Restorative Justice recognizes that crime (violation of persons and relationships) is wrong and should not occur and also recognizes that after it does there are dangers and opportunities. The danger is that the community, victim(s), or offender emerge from the response further alienated, more damaged, disrespected, disempowered, and feeling less safe and less cooperative with society. The opportunity is that injustice is recognized, the equity is restored (restitution and grace), and the future is clarified so that participants are safer, more respectful, and more empowered and cooperative with each other and society.

3. Restorative Justice is a process to "make things as right as possible," which includes attending to needs created by the offense, such as safety and repair of injuries to relationships and physical damage resulting from the offense; and attending to needs related to the cause of the offense (addictions, lack of social or employment skills or resources, lack of moral or ethical base, etc.).

4. The primary victim(s) of a crime is/are the one(s) most impacted by the offense. The secondary victims are others impacted by the crime and might include family members, friends, witnesses, criminal justice officials, community, etc.

5. As soon as immediate victim, community, and offender safety concerns are satisfied, Restorative Justice views the situation as a teachable moment for the offender; an opportunity to encourage the offender to learn new ways of acting and being in community.

6. Restorative Justice prefers responding to the crime at the earliest point possible and with the maximum amount of voluntary cooperation

and minimum coercion, because healing in relationships and new learning are voluntary and cooperative processes.

7. Restorative Justice prefers that most crimes are handled using a cooperative structure, including those impacted by the offense as a community to provide support and accountability. This might include primary and secondary victims and family (or substitutes if they choose not to participate), the offender and family, community representatives, government representatives, faith community representatives, school representatives and so on.

8. Restorative Justice recognizes that not all offenders will choose to be cooperative. Therefore, there is a need for outside authority to make decisions for the offender who is not cooperative. The actions of the authorities and the consequences imposed should be tested by whether they are reasonable, restorative, and respectful (for victim(s), offender, and community).

9. Restorative Justice prefers that offenders who pose significant safety risks and are not yet cooperative be placed in settings where the emphasis is on safety, values, ethics, responsibility, accountability, and civility. They should be exposed to the impact of their crime(s) on victims, invited to learn empathy, and offered learning opportunities to become better equipped with skills to be a productive member of society. They should continually be invited (not coerced) to become cooperative with the community and be given the opportunity to demonstrate this in appropriate settings as soon as possible.

10. Restorative Justice requires follow-up and accountability structures utilizing the natural community as much as possible, since keeping agreements is the key to building a trusting community.

11. Restorative Justice recognizes and encourages the role of community institutions, including the religious/faith community, in teaching and establishing the moral and ethical standards that build up the community.

For more information contact: Center for Peacemaking and Conflict Studies, Fresno Pacific University, 1717 South Chestnut Avenue, Fresno, CA 93702. ph (209) 455–5840 FAX (209) 252-4800; rjpvorp.org; http://www.fresno.edu/dept/pacs.

References

Augsburger, D. (1992). *Conflict mediation across cultures.* Louisville: Westminster/John Knox Press.

Bazemore, G. (1996). Three paradigms for juvenile justice." In *Restorative Justice: International Perspectives.* Monsey, NY: Criminal Justice Press, pp. 37–67.

Braithwaite, J. (1989). *Crime, shame and reintegration.* Cambridge: Cambridge University Press.

Claassen, R. (1991). *VORP mediation: A peacemaking model* [Videotape]. Akron, PA: Mennonite Central Committee.

Claassen, R. (1996a). "What is forgiveness." Retrieved January 7, 1998 from the World Wide Web: http://www.fresno.edu/dept/pacs/docs/restj2.html.

Claassen, R. (1996b, July). Measuring restorative justice. *VORP News.* Retrieved January 7, 1998 from the World Wide Web: http://vorp.org/vorpnews/9607.pdf and http://www.fresno.edu/dept/pacs/docs/jscale.html.

Claassen, R. (1996d, October). Accountability and restorative justice. *VORP News.* Retrieved January 7, 1998 from the World Wide Web: http://vorp.org/vorpnews/9610.pdf or http://www.fresno.edu/dept/pacs/docs/account.html

Claassen, R. (1996e). Restorative justice 1. Retrieved January 7, 1998 from the World Wide Web: http://www.fresno.edu/dept/pacs/docs/restj1.html

Enns, E. (1996, April). Offender calls VORP toughest (and best) response to crime. *VORP News.* Retrieved January 7, 1998 from the World Wide Web. http://vorp.org/vorpnews/9604.pdf.

Leibrich, J. (1996). The role of shame in going straight: A study of former Offenders. In *Restorative justice: International perspectives.* Monsey, NY: Criminal Justice Press, pp. 283–302.

McCold, P. (1996). Restorative justice and the role of community." In *Restorative justice: International perspectives.* Monsey, NY: Criminal Justice Press, pp. 85–101.

Presbyterian Church (U.S.A.). (1997). *Restoring justice* [Videotape]. Louisville: Presbyterian Church (U.S.A.).

Ruth-Heffelbower, D. (1998). Restorative justice current best practices in California. *The Correctional Psychologist.*

Umbreit, M. (1994). *Victim meets offender: The impact of restorative justice and mediation.* Monsey, NY: Criminal Justice Press.

Van Ness, D. W. (1986). *Crime and its victims.* Downers Grove: InterVarsity Press.

Zehr, H. (1990). *Changing lenses.* Scottdale: Herald Press.

Rejoinder to Mr. Ruth-Heffelbower ARTHUR V. N. WINT

In her study of the nostalgic ways in which society tends to view the family, Stephanie Coontz challenged her readers to be aware of the ways in which their assessment of the family was based on ideas about how things "ought" to be, as opposed to how historically things really were in family life (1992). Similarly, my colleague Duane Ruth-Heffelbower in his overview of the role of restorative justice in our society focuses on what "ought" to be as opposed to what "is." I have no quarrel with the moral position—the core value behind the position that he takes is one to which many of us aspire. My concern, though, is to respond to the question presented, which deals with what is clearly the public's perception: restorative justice processes are too lenient toward offenders.

By whatever measure we use, it is apparent that the attitude of the pubic toward crime as we approach the end of the twentieth century is one of getting tough, and seeking to punish offenders, rather than to seek mediation between the victim, offender, and the community. Whether we look at attitudes toward the death penalty, or perceived need for shock incarceration of adults and juveniles, or the role of religion in retribution, the constant is the public's attitude toward a more punitive approach toward offenders. For example, since their beginning in 1983, boot camps, or "shock incarceration" facilities have become quite widespread. By 1993, more than forty-five programs were operating in twenty-nine state jurisdictions, representing over 7500 beds (MacKenzie & Souryal, 1995). According to McCorkle (1995), the popularity of boot camps is an outgrowth of a growing punitiveness on the part of the public, as well as a perception that boot camps represent a return to the principles of order, stability, and prosperity. The public likes the "utility" of more punitive measures. Restorative justice procedures do not measure up to that standard of "utility."

Another example is the nexus between religion and retribution. Researchers cite the fact that there has been a corresponding growth in evangelical fundamentalist Protestants along with the growth in more punitive attitude toward crime (Grasmick, Cochran, Bursik & Kimpel, 1993). This is significant because historically religion has had a major influence on the society's reaction to offenders (Garland, 1990). As Grasmick et al. discovered in their research, individuals affiliated with evangelical and fundamentalist Protestant denominations are more punitive than others in their criminal justice policy preferences. It is important to note that this group constitutes a significant number of the membership of what has been called the New Christian Right, which has had a significant influence on public policy issues over the past decade. Indeed, Grasmick et al. found that, among their research subjects, significantly, those claiming no religious affiliation were least likely to be punitive, while those favoring a more punitive policy came from the evangelical fundamentalist Protestant groups. Criminality is equated with sinfulness, and sin must be punished.

Finally, Ruth-Heffelbower asserts that it is the retributive justice process that is lenient. In his view, offenders get off too easily if they are not required to go through the experience of having to meet their victims face-to-face and talk about the offending event. As a mediator, I can understand the basis for Duane's assertion. However, he proposes a definition of *lenient* that is both counterintuitive and the opposite of the public's perception of leniency. As demonstrated in the examples cited in this rejoinder, we are in the middle of a retributive cycle in which the public expectation is to see offenders receive their just deserts. Restorative justice processes just do not provide the perceived level of punishment to satisfy this expectation. In other words, restorative justice processes are too lenient toward offenders.

REFERENCES

Coontz, S. (1992). *The way we never were.* New York: Basic Books.

Garland, D. (1990). *Punishment and modern society.* Chicago: University of Chicago Press.

Grasmick, H. G., Cochran, J. K., Bursik, R. J., & Kimpel, M. (1993). Religion, punitive justice, and support for the death penalty." *Justice Quarterly, 10,* 289–314.

McCorkle, R. C. (1995). Correctional boot camps and attitude change: Is all this shouting necessary?" *Justice Quarterly, 12,* 365–375.

MacKenzie, D. L., & Souryal, C. (1995). "Inmates' attitude change during incarceration: A comparison of boot camp and traditional prison." *Justice Quarterly, 12,* 325–353.

Is the "Broken Windows" Theory an Effective Way to Reduce Crime?

Craig Fraser's undergraduate degree is from Duke University and his doctorate is from Purdue University. He has been an administrator in four police departments and has held appointments at five universities, including Chair of the Criminology and Criminal Justice Department at Virginia Union University. Dr. Fraser is currently Director of Management Services at the Police Executive Research Forum, a Washington, D.C.–based nonprofit police research and consulting organization. He oversees PERF's management studies, strategic planning assistance, automated systems planning, and performance audits of state, county, and city police departments.

William Norton, J. D., Ph.D., is Professor and Chairman of the Department of Criminal Justice at the University of New Haven. His research focuses on economic factors and crime, the relationship between drugs and crime, and issues of civil rights and criminal procedure. Before joining the faculty of the university, he was engaged in the private practice of law in Hartford, Connecticut.

YES

CRAIG FRASER

New York City's successes in reducing crime in the mid-1990s attracted attention throughout the country. What works on New York crime, went the thinking, surely would work in other communities. Although the drop in crime rates in New York is due to a number of factors, some portion of it is attributable to the NYPD's application of the "broken windows" (Wilson & Kelling, 1989) approach to crime prevention. The theory is that the failure to fix the first broken window leads to a second broken window and so on. Small-scale disorder, unchecked, will lead to serious crime. This theory is based on several understandings about the nature of crime, the nature of communities, and how the police operate.

Because most crime is local, it is all around us. A geographic barrier, such as a major thoroughfare or expressway, a river or lake, or a park will slow the spread of crime from one area into another, but such physical barriers ultimately fail. The key to neighborhood decline seems to be physical and social disorder (Skogan, 1990). It is disorder that seems to be the harbinger of crime. Bring order back to a neighborhood, fix the broken windows, and crime will decrease. Any neighborhood can be subject to crime. Criminal acts occur in certain places because it is a convenient location for the criminal. A littered, abandoned, dark neighborhood gives street muggers much more camouflage than a well-lit suburban street.

We are all to some extent defined by our surroundings. If we live in a community that places a strong emphasis on self-reliance, education, and the value of work, then these are the values most of us internalize. If, however, we live in communities where the common courtesies are no longer practiced or valued, we tend not to value them either. If we live where power and force are the predominant cultural values, we will judge ourselves by how much control we can wield over our social milieu. If our community looks bombed out, abandoned, and forgotten, then we will assume that we too have been abandoned, forgotten, and devalued.

Perception becomes reality. If we believe that our neighborhood is safe, despite what high crime statistics the police may have, we are less likely to abandon the public areas to the criminals, thereby reducing their opportunity for unnoticed or unchallenged criminal behavior. As any parent can tell you, the child under supervision gets into less trouble than the child left to his own devices. If we believe, however, despite low crime rates in police statistics, that our neighborhood is unsafe, we will avoid those public places and deprive the community of our eyes, our standards, and our censure. Perception will affect the incidence of crime either way. The more a community fears itself, the less it will invest in its children and institutions. It will cede the community to the elements it fears.

But this social infrastructure is an important component in the continuation of criminal activity in a neighborhood. If the neighborhood denies safe havens for offenders, they cannot operate long in that neighborhood. This means that driving criminal activity from a neighborhood will not automatically cause a new set of problems for some other neighborhood. As with any business, the conditions that help crime take hold take time to cultivate and develop.

These factors form the essence of the broken windows hypothesis. If the conditions that make a person or neighborhood a more likely victim, or more likely cover for a perpetrator, are unchecked, crime will start small, as perpetrators test the limits to see what they can get away with. As they find that they can get away with more and more, they effectively take over and act with virtual impunity. Small, unchecked antisocial acts prompt larger and more serious behaviors until a neighborhood becomes perceived of as out of control, crime flourishes, and even the police fear going in to the neighborhood.

Broken windows is essentially about cause and effect. If the police can understand what conditions seem to trigger the downhill slide of a neighborhood and reverse those conditions, the neighborhood may make a comeback. In neighborhoods just beginning to fray around the edges, prompt attention to key factors may avert decline.

The difficulty for the police is understanding what the triggers are and recognizing that they will differ from place to place. In one neighborhood, the decline may start with one problem family whose bullying and obnoxious behavior seems of little importance, at first, to the police. In another neighborhood, it may be abandoned cars—dangerous places for children to play and good cover for drug dealers and buyers, prostitutes and their clients, and gangs. In another area, litter, abandoned buildings, and broken street lights may signal no one cares, anything goes.

Defining the problem for a given place requires careful thought and attention to a variety of social, demographic, and economic factors that police are now learning how to identify and analyze. These factors then become the focal points for intervention or remediations with the police acting as a catalyst to prod a seemingly indifferent bureaucracy into action or in getting a neighborhood willing to act.

New lighting, litter removal, and repaired infrastructure all may help create a perception that an area is cared for and is under control. Physical fixes, although sometimes costly, are not all that difficult to accomplish. What is more problematic is broken window behavior that puts the police into new and different roles, requiring them to become arbiters of proper social conduct. Broken windows is about social and behavioral decay as much as it is about physical decay. In some neighborhoods, problems are created by youth hanging out in the streets, open air drug dealing, and street prostitution. The broken window may be broken behavioral standards rather than physical deterioration.

In this world, status becomes thoroughly connected to behavior. Any unchallenged behavior quickly becomes the norm. Those intent on challenging society or testing boundaries must indulge in rising levels of unacceptable behaviors to be noticed. To set yourself apart on mean streets requires an increasing willingness to speak of violence, then to greater willingness to use violence for trivial reasons. This escalation parallels those in other parts of American society. In the early days of rock and roll, the music was attractive to teens in that it rebelled from the expected norms of music. Today, to shock and get attention, it is not enough that the music be different. There must also be the use of expletives, and increasingly these expletives must be used in ever viler descriptions of aberrant behaviors. Long hair, once the emblem of counterculture, now is often merely a style choice. Today's countercultures must shave their heads and pierce multiple body parts to announce their disdain for conventional values.

In many neighborhoods, group behavior, the mob mentality, gets added to this mix. There is safety in numbers, as the old saying goes, but once a crowd gathers, it is easier to flow with it than try moving against the prevailing will. This is what makes youth gangs both safe and dangerous. A gang provides a sense of security for the youth awash in this sea of unchallenged behaviors and open crime, while simultaneously being desensitized to the types and amount of crime he's willing to commit.

A group will always feel more powerful than will the lone individual. How much easier to rob an old woman in broad daylight when you've got a band of friends to back you up. Who is going to challenge you? Who will challenge you when you sell drugs on the corner? Who will challenge you when you shoot someone for wearing the wrong color? Unchallenged behavior will beget worse behavior. Which behaviors should be the ones that start the criminal justice process: spitting, littering, graffiti? Or do we begin with vandalism, shoplifting, purse snatching? Or should we wait until we have robbery or murder? What should be the official starting point?

In these circumstances, the law offers powerful tools for the police. Criminal laws are passed with the intent that they be enforced. The police are invested with a tremendous level of discretion as to what laws they enforce, when they enforce them, and on whom they are enforced. This discretion is a vital piece of the puzzle that makes the job of a police officer possible. However, the more infractions of laws that the police, for whatever operational or management motive, do not enforce, the greater the public's perception of corruption, indifference, or plain incompetence. Inaction can have as much impact as action.

Yet in a number of cities, well before the New York City efforts, new ways of addressing these issues began to be attempted. Houston and Newark conducted experiments to reduce fear and fix neighborhood broken windows (Pate, Wycoff, Skogan, & Sherman, 1986). A variety of strategies were used, and multiple measures showed that paying attention to neighborhood decay and disorder can "reduce levels of perceived crime and disorder, reduce fear and concern about crime, improve evaluations of police service, increase satisfaction with neighborhoods and, in some cases, reduce crime itself" (Pate et al., p. 3).

Broken window repair can offer great opportunities for the police. But, they must begin by gaining citizen trust. In the "broken windows" school, emphasis is also placed on a citizen–police partnership. The idea is that by aiding the citizen with what impacts most on his daily life, for instance, abandoned cars in vacant lots, the police officer generates good will, which in turn leads to citizen aid in the things that most impact on the liveability of the community…crime.

Public expectations of the police do not always match the precise descriptions of the police mission statement, nor the police officer's own perception of his duties and responsibilities. But public expectations place as important a part in community safety as do perceptions of crime and safety. And here dilemmas for the police exist.

Is the police officer a part of the community or an outside occupying force? How the public and the police themselves perceive the answer to this question determines how well the police do their job in that community. Do the police have support for using the law to establish more stringent norms for public behavior and enforcing even very minor infractions? When do we roust the homeless from public parks, sidewalks, and doorways, and where do they go? When do we arrest spitters, search litterers for weapons, and cite them for violations? How much strong exercise of power are we willing to accept to maintain order? How much liberty do we cede for security?

The process of fixing broken windows should not be for the police alone to become arbiters of acceptable public behavior and to use nuisance laws to compel conformity. The goal is to search for alternatives through which the community and the police act together. At times, the police and citizens will work as partners in cleaning up health hazards and code violations. At times, with community acceptance, the police will enforce little-used ordinances to help stabilize a neighborhood until the community can reassert social control. Broken windows is about more than the aggressive exercise of power. Saturation and zero tolerance for any law violations can be sustained only for short periods.

Traditional incident-oriented policing has been focused on solving the symptoms (i.e., burglary) of problems (crime). This focus made the police a foe as often as it did a friend in the struggle for the community's support. By chasing after the symptoms only, the police failed to ease the community's problem, resulting in an ever-renewing supply of "symptoms" for them to respond to. Focus on a neighborhood, paying attention to all of the problems, systematically going about a clean-up, will effect changes not only on the lives of the community but on the crime rate itself.

Creating new relationships between the police and neighborhoods concerns some who believe that too close a relationship between the community and officers leads inevitably to corruption. We will effectively end corruption in police forces when we have ended crime in society. Just as society is composed of human beings of many types, so are police agencies composed of human beings with a multitude of human failings and virtues. We should focus on the culture of corruption that flourishes in police departments, and the best way to do so is to remove the mentality of occupying army that is persistent in so many police agencies because the officers who police do not live in nor care about the places they police. Abuse of power breeds contempt if a police culture is already sickened with corruption and indifference. Unless the police have an investment in the community, then they are an occupying army. Unless the police can understand the realities of life in these communities and have some level of empathy for the people who must live here, then they will never be more than an occupying force.

"Broken windows" is about fixing the small transgressions so that the big ones die, choked off at the root. It is also about reinvesting police departments in the communities they serve, committing them to be more than an occupying force. It is about giving the citizens power over their environment, making their lives better, and setting limits on what behaviors society will accept from its citizens. "Broken windows" is not a tool of control, but a multifaceted approach to turning large impersonal urban areas back into the communities we remember from our earlier history. As with all human endeavors, the potential for abuse is there, but the potential to make a difference in our society is there also.

References

Pate, A., Wycoff, M. A., Skogan, W. G., & Sherman, L. W. (1986). *Reducing fear of crime in Houston and Newark: A summary report.* Washington, D.C.: The Police Foundation, 1986.

Skogan, W. G. (1990). *Disorder and decline: Crime and the spiral of decay in American neighborhoods,* 1990. New York: Free Press.

Wilson, J. Q., & Kelling, G. L. (1982, March). Broken windows. *Atlantic Monthly,* 29–38.

Rejoinder to Dr. Fraser
William Norton

The "Progressive Policing" efforts described by Dr. Fraser in his "Fixing Broken Windows" article are excellent examples of the innovative and thoughtful efforts currently being developed in American policing. These efforts may make some contribution to the general declines in crime that are reported in many urban areas. These trends, however, continue a general decline in crime as reported in national victimization data over the last decade, and they also follow unusually strong economic expansion, record declines in unemployment, unusually low population cohorts of youth, record levels of incarceration, and incapacitation of high-risk/high-rate offenders and a general maturation of many urban drug markets. Based on the available data and prior research, each of these factors seems highly likely to make a significant contribution to the welcome declines in crime. Unfortunately, however, the careful evaluation studies of the effectiveness of the forms of community-based policing most closely linked to the tradition of the Wilson and Kellings original "Broken Windows" thesis do not clearly support the argument that such programs are effective in reducing crime (Bayley, 1998; Cordner, 1997).

Furthermore, even if we accept the thesis that fixing broken windows accounts for a majority of the reduction in crime, we also must ask whether this end justifies the means employed. Dr. Fraser cites the success of the New York Police Department in using aggressive order maintenance tactics, but fails to effectively deal with the issues of August 9, 1997 when a Haitian immigrant, Abner Louima, was savagely beaten and had a stick shoved into his rectum in the bathroom of the 70th Precinct Station. George Kelling has recently recognized the dangers and risks in such aggressive police behavior:

> Much more significant…are the worries of civil libertarians, advocates for the homeless or minorities, police leaders, scholars, and even proponents of aggressive order maintenance themselves, over whether police can be trusted to maintain order equitably, justly, and in ways that preserve public peace. For while it does not have to, order-maintenance policing can enforce a tyranny of the majority, a repression of minority or marginal elements within the community. Critics to the contrary, most police leaders are themselves worried about police abuse of citizens, especially minorities. (Kelling & Coles, 1996, p. 164)

Modern policing needs to continue to experiment with and evaluate new strategies and tactics. Dr. Fraser's suggestion that defining problems requires careful thought and attention to a variety of factors is drawn directly from Herman Goldstein's problem-oriented policing (1990). Problem-oriented policing and the Wilson-Kelling (W-K) argument for community-oriented policing are frequently confused and treated as one in popular discussions. The two approaches are quite different in several important ways, however. First, Goldstein has not suggested that the use of aggressive extra-legal "kick-ass" tactics should be condoned or allowed. Second, Goldstein has suggested a mechanism by which police accountability can actually be increased and excessive use of force minimized. Third, Goldstein argues that the police should not attempt to become involved in ambitious, comprehensive, yet amorphous efforts to become coproducers of police service. Such efforts tend to fall back on the notion that community-based policing is a philosophy and tend to give little direction to officers on the front lines. Such efforts also begin to raise fundamental questions about police use of force and power to enforce group norms that are not codified by law. Clearly, Wilson and Kelling have made an enormous contribution to the development of problem-oriented policing, but in the end the stronger analysis and more promising approach appears to be found in Goldstein's problem-oriented policing.

REFERENCES

Bayley, D. H. (1998). *What works in policing.* New York: Oxford University Press.

Cordner, G. W. (1997). Community policing: Elements and effects. In R. G. Dunham and G. P. Alpert (Eds.), *Critical Issues In Policing: Contemporary Readings (3rd ed.)*. Prospect Heights, Illinois: Waveland Press.

Goldstein, H. (1990). *Problem-oriented policing*. New York: McGraw-Hill.

Kelling, G. L., & Coles, C. M. (1996). *Fixing broken windows: Restoring order and reducing crime in our communities*. New York: Touchstone.

NO

WILLIAM NORTON

In research on the effectiveness of policing, the concept of "broken windows" refers to an article written by James Q. Wilson and George L. Kelling (1982), in which they argued that crime was the direct byproduct of decay in communities. They argued that communities are similar to abandoned buildings, in which a broken window that went unrepaired would send a signal that breaking windows in this building was acceptable and thereby invite more broken windows and a spiral of further decay. In this concept, the community is said to be in endangered when individuals within the community openly violate the norms and customs of the community to create disorder. Like the broken window in the abandoned building, these violations of social norms act as invitations to more serious forms of deviance. Following this theory, police are encouraged to aggressively attack disorder to promote order and send a message that disorder and rule violation will not be tolerated.

Conceptually, this approach to policing has won many admirers over the last decade. Although it is a valuable idea that offers promise, it also raises several subtle but important issues for policing and society. First, how much order do we desire? American society has historically held freedom of expression and independence as cornerstone values in our law and society. As we become a more diverse nation, are we now going to abandoned these virtues of freedom and independence? Wilson and Kelling emphasize enforcement of social norms of behavior, but whose definition of acceptable normal behavior will the police enforce? Placing the American police officer in this role of determining what is normal and what is abnormal is a risky endeavor for both the police and the society the police are sworn to serve. Wilson and Kelling hint at the one of the fundamental critiques of policing based on their article when they approvingly comment on the virtues of a patrol officer fictitiously named Kelly:

> Sometimes what Kelly did could be described as enforcing the law, but just as often it involved taking informal or extralegal steps to help protect what the neighborhood had decided was the appropriate level of public order. Some of the things he did probably would not withstand a legal challenge.

American police officers are held in high esteem when they are understood as neutral professionals enforcing the criminal law. If the police become oppressive agents of order, they run the risk of being drawn into social conflicts that are not best described as criminal matters. For example, during the turmoil of the 1960s and early 1970s, many police departments came to be seen as the agents of order rather than law, acting to oppress minority groups in some areas, attacking peaceful demonstrators seeking social change in other areas. Police and the profession of policing always suffer when they become too closely entwined with issues of order as opposed to issues of crime. The most pressing issue for police today is a growing distrust of police by segments of society. This distrust is too frequently fueled by extralegal actions by individual police officers. The suggestion that police should act outside the law to produce order is thus a dangerous suggestion.

In any free society, there will always be forces of disorder. Disorder is normal and necessary in a free society open to change and renewal. The challenge for any free society is to balance the need for order with citizens' rights to freedom and liberty. Thus, police following this order-driven model frequently focus on groups of youth who are perceived to be rowdy and unruly. For example, a group of young persons may be listening to music that is perceived as either loud or annoying. The police, to promote order, are encouraged to crack down on these rowdy youth. These young people are engaged in normal, age-specific behavior, which may violate the norms of middle-aged to older adults but likely does not violate the norms for their age-group. These young persons are engaged in youthful behavior that defines their independence and their coming of age as adults in society. Such behavior may be problematic to some in society, but it is normal age-specific behavior!

If the police focus some of their resources on this sort of disorderly behavior, the society clearly will be more orderly, but the creativity and energy of change will be muted. In focusing on this disorderly behavior, the police have crossed a dangerous line that elevates the value of order over the value of freedom. Clearly, there will be times when valuing order over freedom of expression is the appropriate balance for the police to strike, for example, when a rowdy patron in a crowded theater shouts *fire* and creates a dangerous panic. In choosing to emphasize these order issues, police will focus more and more on social order issues, and police are therefore likely to increase their tendency to value order over freedom of expression. Therein lies the risk for our society. America has long valued the freedom and individuality of its citizens. Our values of freedom and liberty draw immigrants from all corners of the world, where order has been elevated above freedom and liberty.

Some years ago I worked with a former political prisoner from eastern Europe. She had fled Communism to come to the West in search of freedom. My friend described her first day in the United States with great joy. She was in New York in a relatively difficult section of the city. I expected that she would have second thoughts about having come to the United States given the apparent chaos and disorder of her surroundings, but to my surprise her eyes filled with tears as she describe the joy she felt in experiencing the absolute freedom of the people in this neighborhood. Yes, some played loud music, some dressed oddly, some were in fact criminal, and there was an apparent lack of order. Across all of these observations, one fact dominated all others: the citizens were free to be individuals, and against the backdrop of her orderly communal experience under communist rule, this freedom she experienced on the disorderly streets of New York was highly cherished.

Clearly no reasonable person would argue that the police do not have an important role to play in maintaining order in society. The problem with the Wilson and Kelling argument is in the balance they strike between the needs of society for order and rights of the individual. Wilson and Kelling recognize that their argument is not easily reconciled with American notions of individual justice and suggest that the answer is found in the concept of communalism. In this view the police have dual missions to protect communities as well as individuals. In the abstract this is an appealing argument, and it represents an emerging stream of thought in modern public affairs. A wide array of scholars and commentators have come to endorse this view, sometimes described as Communitarianism. Communitarianism seeks to shift the balance between individual rights and social responsibilities in the direction of greater emphasis on social responsibilities. This argument is not unlike the classical debate between Mill and Stephen over the balance between individual rights versus society's rights. This enduring debate reflects a fundamental tension in free societies, a tension between anarchy and totalitarian oppression at its extremes. Modern free societies constantly strive to find the correct balance between the needs of order and freedom. The way a society strikes this difficult balance defines its sense of justice, and in my view a just society cannot allow its police to be above the law, and we cannot value order above the rule of law.

The police must likewise be careful that they do not fall into the trap of becoming more isolated and intolerant in focusing on these issues of public disorder. Police officers face many difficult challenges in their work, one of which is the tendency of officers to close ranks and form a blue wall that isolates them from the public. In directing police officers to control disorder and to aggressively deal with disorderly persons, we run the risk that some police officers may become more isolated and more prone to abuse the power of their office. Although no systematic evidence exists to establish a direct causal link between aggressive campaigns on disorder and police misconduct, anecdotal evidence from some cities seems to indicate the potential for increases in police violence and distrust among minority communities when aggressive campaigns against public disorder have been implemented. For example, the anecdotal evidence out of New York seems to indicate that there is a direct link between the city's use of these order maintenance tactics and an increase in police violence and abuse of minorities. Wilson and Kelling explicitly worry about this type of difficulty and recognize the danger of police becoming agents of bigotry.

These problems are inextricably linked to Wilson and Kelling's notion that police should act outside the rule of law to promote order. This message is an exceedingly dangerous message to send to officers and the public. It values order over law and sets a dangerous precedent for an officer of the law. In the face of the difficult circumstances law enforcement officers are frequently placed in, we should never suggest that some tactical ends justify breaking the law. Once the department's official policy is that ends justify means, then all hope of maintaining order and discipline within the ranks is abandoned. We then leave the officer to pick and choose which rules to obey, and we set ourselves up for more significant ethical and legal dilemmas. For example, tell the truth and a known criminal may walk, shade the truth and sweeten the case and insure the good guys win? In reflecting on Wilson and Kelling approach to policing, I am reminded of a discussion with a veteran sergeant many years ago when I was a young officer. The officer was describing an incident with a known criminal that resulted in an arrest and a seemingly (at least to my eyes) unwarranted beating. The senior officer explained that he had administered justice because the courts would not, or to use Wilson and Kelling's phrase to describe similar behavior by Chicago police in reference to policing a housing project, he "kicked ass."

To their credit, Wilson and Kelling recognize that such behavior is not easily reconciled with American notions of individual justice, and they clearly do not intend to condone police abuse of citizens. The problem, however, is in their willingness to accept extralegal measures to produce order. They suggest that the justification for the use of these extralegal measures is found in their concept of communalism. In this view, the police have dual missions to protect communities as well as the rights of individuals. But once more we return to the question of how to accomplish such an incredibly complex regulatory task. In my view, police must be subject to the rule of law, and we cannot value order above liberty. We must be careful to recognize the rights of individuals in our society. Increasingly, under the banner of communalism or communitarianism, the individual's liberty and rights are being marginalized. Historically, our society has proved that individual liberty and freedom of action are the keys to progress. We have prospered as we have sought to free the spontaneous forces of a free society, and resorted as little as possible to governmental coercion.

REFERENCE

Wilson, J. Q. & Kelling, G. L. (1982, March) "Broken windows." *Atlantic Monthly.* 29–38.

Rejoinder to Dr. Norton   CRAIG FRASER

Those who espouse and practice the broken window approach to policing do not condone the police using illegal methods. On the contrary, the full legal tools police have available to them are mammoth and comprehensive. The system of laws that police enforce are not the product of police imagination or of a police wish for totalitarian control but are the product of federal, state, county, and municipal legislative bodies where the people's freely chosen representatives act on behalf of the common good. The issue is not whether police should use illegal tactics against disorder, thus curtailing liberty. In reality, it is about police selective enforcement of often little-used laws and ordinances. Police illegal behavior cannot be condoned.

There can be no doubt that in some American neighborhoods normal behavioral boundaries established by social control mechanisms have been lost. People become trapped by fear of becoming a victim of crime symbolized to them by rampant disorder. When such communities are plagued with apathy brought on by poverty, poor education, and perceived powerlessness, and are crippled by fear, a restoration process may need to begin with the police acting as external agents of social control until neighborhood social control can be reestablished.

The choice is not between the right of an individual and his or her desire for free expression versus the right of some abstract community. It is between one person's free expression manifested through illegal behavior versus the legitimate rights of others to live in peace.

The law is the guiding force in these choices. Some have characterized the New York Police Department's "zero tolerance" approach to fixing New York's seriously shattered windows of the early 1990s as a crackdown on mere aberrant behavior and free expression. Instead, it was zero tolerance for behavior that allegedly violated the law. It is important to remember that the police are not in this repair process alone. The police cannot long engage in strict enforcement without substantial community support or eruptions will occur. And, it is not a police officer who decides whether the law has been broken; the officer asserts that he or she has probable cause to believe the violation has taken place. Courts and juries decide whether the law has been violated.

The difficulty is that in many places, some laws and ordinances have been ignored and unenforced for many years. Police did not bother with the small stuff to concentrate resources to deal with serious crime. What we discovered was that this approach has led to spirals of escalating illegal behavior as unpunished violations of one set of laws resulted in the feeling among some that they could do whatever they wanted, that the law, and the social norms embodied in it, were irrelevant.

Strict enforcement tends to bring into the criminal justice system those who were acting with impunity one day and who are held accountable for their actions the next. It may also bring into the system those who had been so influenced by the neighborhood environment that they were unaware that the law could be used to control what seemed to have become normal behavior.

For the rule of law to succeed, civic responsibility is necessary. The rule of law depends on habitual voluntary compliance along with enough enforcement that those who fall into bad habits are reminded of the negative consequences of their lapses. When the rule of law loses deterrent power, when it is not enforced or when it is not observed because of convenience, individual preference, and "free expression," the result at some level is anarchy and chaos. Where do we draw the lines; do we all get to choose which laws we will obey and which we will not?

One of the many tactics police can use to repair broken windows is to maintain order through strict enforcement of existing laws and ordinances. But this approach will not work for long when faced with strong opposition from the community. It must be done in consultation and partnership with the community so the police help a neighborhood reestablish social norms that are, at a minimum, in keeping with our system of law. It is through community and police collaborative efforts that broken windows are repaired and then stay unbroken.

Should the Juvenile Justice System Get Tougher on Juvenile Offenders?

Sandra Stone is Assistant Professor of Criminology in the Department of Sociology/Anthropology at the State University of West Georgia. She received her Ph.D. from Emory University. Dr. Stone has worked in the field of social services for over twenty years with a primary emphasis on families and children. She has worked in and with a variety of agencies as a direct service provider, researcher, administrator, and teacher. Before her appointment at the State University of West Georgia, she served as the Director of Planning and Research for the Georgia Department of Juvenile Justice. Her current research interests include use of mediation in juvenile court, youth involvement in gangs, and collaborative agency involvement in prevention efforts with high-risk youth.

Robert M. Regoli is Professor of Sociology at the University of Colorado in Boulder. He received his Ph.D. from Washington State University. He is a member of Phi Beta Kappa, former President and Fellow of the Academy of Criminal Justice Sciences, and the author or coauthor of seven books and roughly one hundred scholarly articles. He is currently involved in research examining world views of children.

YES

SANDRA STONE

The future of the juvenile justice system has been a topic of much debate over the past few years. As juvenile violent and serious crime increased during the latter part of the 1980s and early 1990s, critics of the juvenile court argued that the underlying principle of treatment versus punishment on which that court was established was no longer appropriate for this new breed of juvenile offender. That view was generally supported by political leaders and the public, as state after state passed legislation making it easier to transfer certain juvenile offenders to adult criminal court and mandating changes in juvenile court such that the distinctions between the two systems have become increasingly blurred (see Feld 1992 for a discussion of the criminalization of the juvenile court and Torbet et al., 1996, for an overview of state responses to serious and violent juvenile crime). Whether these particular responses have improved the situation is certainly questionable (see Schwartz, Hsieh, & Kenagy, 1996, and Torbet et al., 1995, for discussions), but the fact that the juvenile justice system needs to get tougher on juvenile offenders is not what, ironically, brings the juvenile system full circle to grapple once again with one of the issues it was initially created to address—how to deal more effectively with juvenile offenders while taking into account that they are developmentally different from adults.

Until the 1800s, in this country as well as in other places and times, there was no distinction made between juveniles and adults in terms of their treatment by the criminal justice system if they were caught engaging in illegal behavior. Although separate prisons were built to house incarcerated juveniles as early as 1825, juveniles and adults were processed through the same courts. The Progressive movement of the late 1800s included a call for reform in the way children were treated by the courts. In the wake of the Industrial Revolution, a separate period of "childhood" had emerged, along with the belief that children were developmentally different from adults, with different needs, thus requiring different treatment. The thinking was that children's personalities were still being formed, and their lives were more amenable to change. Even though there was no separate court system for juveniles at that time, since the mid-1800s the courts had gained increasing authority over minor children such that judges could not only provide sanctions for juveniles who committed crimes, they could also remove children from their homes if their parents or their environments were deemed "unfit." Many children, both delinquent and deprived, were sent by the courts to a variety of institutions created for such purpose, where they were given a basic education, provided moral guidance, and, more often than not, used as a source of labor. These institutions did not turn out to be the hoped-for panacea for troubled, troubling, or unwanted children, however, and those concerned with child welfare eventually recognized that perhaps institutional placement resulted in more harm than good.

Thus, in response to public pressure for change, the first juvenile court was established in Chicago in 1899, further expanding governmental authority over the lives of children, particularly those children whose parents were considered inadequate. The legal doctrine under which the juvenile court was established is referred to as *parens patriae*, or "the state as parent." In addition to separating juveniles from adults in the criminal justice system, the juvenile courts were structured differently as well. The intent was to determine the source of the problem and provide an intervention that would be rehabilitative in nature. Thus, the guiding principle was the "best interest" of the child, precluding standardized treatment. Proceedings were determined to be civil rather than criminal, and the child's background and current situation guided dispositions more than the nature of the offense he or she had committed. In the spirit of being a surrogate parent, the court was informal and flexible to the point of dispensing with the procedural safeguards granted adults.

The juvenile court remained relatively unchanged until the 1960s and 1970s, when a series of cases challenging juveniles' lack of due process rights worked their way to the Supreme Court. Gradually, case law dictated changes in juvenile court procedures such that the juvenile court began to more closely resemble the adult criminal court in nature as juveniles were granted due process rights. Regardless of the procedural changes, however, the juvenile court maintained its basic philosophy of treatment and rehabilitation and its role as "parent" acting in the "best interest of the child." But as the nature of juvenile crime began to shift dramatically in the 1980s, the philosophy and role of the court began to be questioned as well. The lack of research findings documenting successful intervention programs, increasing violent and serious juvenile crime, and a shift in public sentiment to a more punitive stance against lawbreakers in general resulted in legislation being passed in several states to increase opportunities to waive juveniles to adult court (Parent, Dunworth, McDonald & Rhodes, 1997). To many, the juvenile court appeared to model the very parental characteristics it was designed to protect children against and was demonstrably as ineffective as the families on its caseload.

One of the primary responsibilities of parents is to socialize children, including teaching them appropriate behavior. According to behavioral/social learning principles, that goal is best accomplished through establishing clear rules and expectations, engaging in close supervision and monitoring of the child's behavior, intervening immediately and consistently when inappropriate behavior is displayed, providing negative sanctions for inappropriate behavior, and modeling and rewarding the behavior that is desired. Children typically initially appear in juvenile court on delinquency or unruly charges when one or more of those parental tasks is weak or lacking. If the court were truly a surrogate "parent," then it would compensate for those parental inadequacies; however, it has not done so in the past and does not do so today.

The juvenile court has not given clear rules and expectations. As stated earlier, because of the philosophies on which it was based, no provisions were made for standardized interventions. As a result, juveniles brought into court for the same offense(s) may receive different treatment, and even the same juvenile brought in for the same offense on different occasions may receive a different disposition. Often, if the offenses are not considered serious, a juvenile may appear several times before a juvenile court official and the cases be disposed of in such a way that the juvenile does not experience a negative consequence (e.g., voluntary probation, writing essays, suspended probation, etc.). Furthermore, the same offense may be handled differently in different jurisdictions, by different judges within the same jurisdiction, and differently on different days, depending on the availability of court personnel and other resources.

This method of processing allows for flexibility and individualized hand-ling of cases, which, to some extent can be desirable, but it does not provide clear standards for behavior, consistent intervention, or necessarily negative sanctions. Consequently, as most court service workers will agree, many youths consider ju-venile court "a joke," are not intimidated by it, and do not take it seriously. Even if a juvenile is placed under court supervision, traditional practices, and now, size of caseloads, result in little supervision and monitoring. Thus, there can be no im-mediate, consistent intervention if undesirable behavior persists. Further, with lax supervision, most desirable behavior goes unnoticed and unrewarded, resulting in a lack of reinforcement. And, although the court's philosophy is to deal with the problems underlying a child's misbehavior, courts generally do little in the way of assessment to identify what those problems are, and even those that do have never had adequate resources to address the problems once identified. Thus, the juve-nile court has little deterrent effect on repeat juvenile offending.

To complicate matters further, since 1980, juveniles have been coming to the attention of the court at younger and younger ages. Arrests for juveniles age twelve or younger increased 24 percent from 1980 to 1995, 54 percent for juve-niles ages thirteen and fourteen, and only 18 percent for juveniles age fifteen or older (Butts & Snyder, 1997). Although the younger juveniles tend to get the most lenient treatment by the court (Butts & Snyder, 1997), there is ample evidence to show that one of the strongest predictors of repeat offending is engaging in delin-quent behavior at a young age, and that the most serious, chronic, and violent of-fenders tend to be those youths who begin their delinquent careers early, often before the age of ten (Foote, 1997; Kelley, Huizinga, Thornberry & Loeber, 1997; Moffitt, 1993; Nagin & Land, 1993). It would seem reasonable, then, to recom-mend that young first- or second-time offenders be given more serious, intensive treatment rather than waiting until the juvenile is in his or her peak offending years as a middle adolescent before taking him or her seriously.

Take F. C., for example, a child who initially came to the attention of a metro-Atlanta juvenile court at the age of six for criminal damage to property. Over the next six years, he returned to court five times for charges ranging from criminal trespass to theft by receiving stolen property to theft by shoplifting to burglary to simple battery. For all these appearances, the most serious disposition he was ever given was twelve months' probation, which he violated twice within the year with no sanctions applied. Or there is the case of D.D., who was first seen in court at age thirteen for theft by shoplifting, and within the following three years was seen fifteen times for numerous theft charges, criminal damage to prop-erty, burglary, simple battery, criminal trespassing, and motor vehicle theft. Like F. C., the most punitive disposition he ever received was twelve months probation, until the last time, when he was involved in a hit and run accident while driving without a license, and he was then committed to the state. Similar cases are common fare in today's juvenile courts (Stone, personal research, 1997).

Even when the court finally does decide to get tough on young offenders, the ultimate intervention, incarceration, may not be experienced as a necessarily negative sanction for many juveniles. For youths who mostly live in the streets, incarceration can mean a level of safety otherwise unobtainable, regular and balanced meals, shelter, school, friends, and often adult staff members who genuinely care about them.

Transferring serious offenders to the adult court does not necessarily deliver the "get tough" message it is designed to, either. For example, in Georgia, after two years of implementing the new mandatory waiver legislation for juveniles, of 828 cases, 24 percent were dismissed, 33 percent were transferred back to the juvenile court, and 38 percent plea-bargained down to lesser offenses, most of whom then received probation. Only 6 percent of cases actually went to trial (Torbet et al., 1996). There are other problems with the transfer of juveniles to adult court as well. Data indicate that more youths are being transferred for property rather than violent crimes, and transfer decisions disproportionately affect minority youths. Further, whereas some youths may experience some years of incarceration as a result of being processed through the adult system, many are getting shorter sentences than they would have in the juvenile system, and some data indicate that they return to the system at a higher rate than comparable youths processed through the juvenile system (Frazier, Bishop, Lanza-Kaduce, & Winner, 1995; see discussion in Jones & Krisberg, 1994; Podkopacz & Feld, 1996; Schwartz, Hsieh, & Kenagy, 1996). So, waiving juveniles to adult court does not necessarily result in either more serious or more effective treatment.

The argument for getting tougher on juvenile offenders does not necessarily mean an increasing number need to be incarcerated; rather, it means immediate and effective intervention at the first sign of trouble. Some degree of negative sanction needs to be applied to give a clear message that the problem behavior is unacceptable, but this needs to be coupled with an intervention that teaches and rewards prosocial behavior. In addition, because juveniles do not live in a vacuum, intervention efforts need to involve the family, peer group, the school, and the larger community. This may appear to be an impossible task, but recent analyses of program effectiveness at different levels of intervention have documented programs that work (Howell, Krisberg, Hawkins, & Wilson, 1995; Sherman et al., 1997). Furthermore, the Office of Juvenile Justice and Delinquency Prevention has documented not only programs that work but also a sound strategy for implementing them (Coordinating Council on Juvenile Justice and Delinquency Prevention, 1996; Howell et al., 1995).

It is time to stop pretending we do not know what to do with juvenile offenders. We are still far from having all the answers, but we have ample evidence that there are some interventions that work. Ideally, prevention is most preferable and certainly the most cost-effective of all possible interventions. We do not live in an ideal world, however, so the next best thing is to seriously intervene when a juvenile first displays problematic behavior. One thing we have learned is that the earlier in the process, the more intensive and the longer in duration the intervention, the more positive the outcome. If getting tough with juveniles when they initially engage in delinquent behavior prevents them from further offending, then by choosing to do so the court will have made a wise decision, and like a good parent, will have truly acted in the best interest of the child.

REFERENCES

Butts, J. A., & Snyder, H. N. (1997, September). The youngest delinquents: Offenders under age 15. *Office of Juvenile Justice and Delinquency Prevention Juvenile Justice Bulletin*, NCJ # 165256.

Coordinating Council on Juvenile Justice and Delinquency Prevention (1996, March). Combating violence and delinquency: The national juvenile justice action plan. *Office of Juvenile Justice and Delinquency Prevention.* NCJ # 157105.

Feld, B. C. (1992). Criminalizing the juvenile court: A research agenda for the 1990s. In I. M. Schwartz (Ed.), *Juvenile justice and public policy: Toward a national agenda* (pp. 59–88). New York: Lexington Books.

Foote, J. (1997, October). Expert panel issues report on serious and violent juvenile offenders. *Office of Juvenile Justice and Delinquency Prevention Fact Sheet.* FS-9768.

Frazier, C. E., Bishop, D. M., Lanza-Kaduce, L., & Winner, L. (1995). *Juvenile justice transfer legislation in Florida: Assessing the impact on the criminal justice and correctional systems.* Report prepared for the Task Force for the Review of Criminal Justice and Correctional Systems and the Collins Center for Public Policy.

Howell, J. C., Krisberg, B., Hawkins, J. D., & Wilson, J. J. (1995). *A sourcebook: Serious, violent and chronic juvenile offenders.* Thousand Oaks: Sage.

Jones, M. A., & Krisberg, B. (1994). Images and reality: Juvenile crime, youth violence and public policy. *National Council on Crime and Delinquency.* San Fransisco. National Council on Crime and Delinquency, 1994.

Kelley, B. T., Huizinga, D., Thornberry, T. P., & Loeber, R. (1997, June). Epidemiology of serious violence. *Office of Juvenile Justice and Delinquency Prevention Juvenile Justice Bulletin.* NCJ # 165152.

Moffitt, T. E. (1993). Adolescence-limited and life-course-persistent antisocial behavior: A developmental taxonomy. *Psychological Review, 100,* 674–701.

Nagin, D. S., & Land, K. C. (1993). Age, criminal careers, and population heterogeneity: Specification and estimation of a nonparametric, mixed Poisson model. *Criminology, 33,* 111–139.

Parent, D., Dunworth, T., McDonald, D. & Rhodes, W. (1997, January). Key legislative issues in criminal justice: Transferring serious juvenile offenders to adult courts. *National Institute of Justice Research in Action.* NCJ # 161840.

Podkopacz, M. R., & Feld B. C. (1996). The end of the line: An empirical study of judicial waiver. *The Journal of Criminal Law and Criminology, 86,* 449–492.

Schwartz, I. M., Hsieh, C., & Kenagy, G. P. (1996). *Juveniles in adult prisons.* Center for the Study of Youth Policy, School of Social Work. Philadelphia: The University of Pennsylvania.

Sherman, L. W., Gottfredson, D., MacKenzie, D., Eck, J., Reuter, P., & Bushway, S. (1997). Preventing crime: What works, what doesn't, what's promising. *National Institute of Justice Report to the United States Congress.* NCJ # 165366.

Stone, S. S. (1997). Personal research in a metro-Atlanta juvenile court.

Torbet, P., Gable, R., Hurst IV, H., Montgomery, I., Szymanski, L., & Thomas, D. (1996, July). State responses to serious and violent juvenile crime. *Office of Juvenile Justice and Delinquency Prevention Research Report.* NCJ # 161565.

Torbet, P., Gable, R., Hurst IV, H., Montgomery, I., Szymanski, L., & Thomas, D. (1995, February). Tough responses to serious juvenile crime includes waiver to adult court—But is that the best answer? *Juvenile Justice Update, 1*(1)). Kingston, NJ: Civic Research Institute.

Torbet, P., Gable, R., Hurst IV, H., Montgomery, I., Szymanski, L., & Thomas, D. (1996, May). Juveniles charged as adults under SB440. *Georgia Indigent Defense Council.* Report # 14.

Rejoinder to Dr. Stone ROBERT M. REGOLI

A person is still a person, no matter how small he or she is.

—Dr. Seuss

Do you believe what Dr. Seuss says? Should people be treated equally? Should some people have more rights than others? At what age should people receive full constitutional rights? At conception? Birth? When does a human being become a person? These are important questions to ask yourself as you evaluate the arguments presented in the two essays.

After reading Professor Stone's essay, I allowed several weeks to pass before writing a response. During this time, I thought a lot about what she wrote and what I would say. I decided the most constructive way for me to reply to her essay was to identify for you the common ground in our works. So I decided to frame my reply inside of her paper. When I did, I discovered that Sandra and I are really not too far apart. Both of us want desperately to reduce the incidence and prevalence of juvenile delinquency. What separates us is what we believe is the point in the process that society ought to intervene. I think society needs to intervene in the lives of children's much sooner than does Professor Stone.

What we end up calling juvenile delinquency reflects the culmination of a process that begins at conception and evolves through adolescence. Characteristic of this process from the beginning of a child's life is society's failure to meet his or her needs in its systems of medical delivery, the economy, education, parenting, and the law. Thus, to my way of thinking, juvenile delinquents are manufactured; they are a product produced by a society that strongly reinforces the separate statuses of children and adults. Therefore, the only way to reduce the incidence and prevalence of delinquency is for society and its members to change in a permanent way what it believes children are in relation to adults. That is why I recommended a constitutional amendment granting children the same rights as those enjoyed by every other citizen.

In contrast, Professor Stone believes in the ability of the justice system to alleviate the conditions that produce juvenile delinquency. She thinks a good way of reducing the prevalence and incidence of delinquency is for the court to get tough on young offenders. I have at least two problems with that recommendation. First is that court intervention comes much too late in the child's life. It comes after he or she may have been denied prenatal and postnatal care, proper nutrition, or an opportunity to receive a first-rate education. Second, her recommendation implicitly assumes that juvenile delinquency is about the behavior of children. It is not. Juvenile delinquency is about that adult behavior that discriminates against children because of their age. Third, American society has never made a full-fledged effort to rehabilitate wayward children. At best, the institutions we have constructed to manage problem children provide a mixture of punishment and treatment. But most children are warehoused in custodial-type facilities, receive a very small amount of so-called treatment, typically from not-so-well-trained professionals.

There are differences in what Professor Stone and I recommend. You must carefully evaluate the merits of each argument, because both are meritorious. Which argument do you agree with? Explain why. What beliefs do you have that move you to favor one argument over the other? What sort of society do you imagine if Dr. Stone's recommendation is implemented? Professor Regoli's? What does the society you want to live in look like? Which model gets us closer to what you hope for?

In closing, I want to share with you a story I recently read. The storyteller was Dr. Jerry Weiner, former president of the American Academy of Child & Adolescent Psychiatry:

> A group of people were standing by the side of a fast-moving stream when one of them saw a baby floating in the rapids. The people quickly formed a

human chain, entered the stream and brought the baby to shore to a zone of safety. They looked back and saw three more babies and again locked arms, formed a human chain, and brought the three babies to shore, a zone of safety. They looked again and saw twelve babies floating to disaster and, as they formed the chain again, one of them walked away. The group was agitated and shouted at the departing person to return and save the imperiled babies. "No," the person replied. "You save these babies, I am going upstream to find out who is throwing them in."[1]

Policy recommendations that urge us to get tough on children are at the side of America's stream of life. There is an alternative: for each of us go upstream to prevent the trip in the first place.

NOTE

1. This story was told at a speech given by Dr. Weiner on being installed as President of the American Academy of Child & Adolescent Psychiatry in 1987.

NO

ROBERT M. REGOLI

"Should the juvenile justice system get tougher on juvenile offenders?" Unequivocally, no. But more interesting is how the editors of the text have framed this question for you. The way they have written the question diverts you from examining the more salient issue—the status of children in society. Only the editors know why they did this and what was their intention. However, once you take notice of what was done and reframe the question in terms of who and what children are in relation to adults, the original question becomes much easier to answer.

The Discrimination against Children

Children are the most discriminated-against group of people in society. They experience more discrimination than do any adults, regardless of whether the adult is a member of a racial or ethnic group or a woman. Children, for example, are the only group of people not protected by the U.S. Constitution. Most students are surprised when they learn the Constitution does not apply to children. But more important than their surprise are the consequences for children of not having inalienable protected rights. In addition to children not being able to vote or enter binding contracts, adults may hit children, refuse or subject them to medical treatment, establish curfews to regulate their movement, control their speech, determine what style of clothing they may wear, and much, much more (Gill, 1991).

It is unconscionable that now some policy makers and academicians are suggesting that society get tougher on children. Society is already tougher on children than it is on anyone else.

That is why:

- Children are nearly twice as likely as adults to live in poverty. Twenty-one percent of American children live in poverty, versus 11 percent of adults.
- Children living in the United States are two times more likely to be poor than children living in Great Britain, and three times more likely than those in France or Germany, even though the United States is the wealthiest of these nations and has lower unemployment levels.
- Children are ten times more likely to be victims of violence than to be arrested for violence. Of every twenty youths who are arrested, nineteen are arrested for nonviolent crimes (Children's Defense Fund, 1997).

The world we adults have created and maintain for our children is one in which a child drops out of school every eight seconds; is reported abused or neglected every ten seconds; is arrested every fifteen seconds; is born to an unmarried mother every twenty-four seconds, into poverty every thirty-four seconds, to a teen mother every minute, and at low birth weight every two minutes; is killed by a gun every ninety minutes; and commits suicide every four hours (Children's Defense Fund, 1997).

If living under these conditions is not sufficiently horrendous for our 65 million American children, now some policy makers and academicians want to seemingly add insult to injury. They believe society is too lenient with children. That children commit heinous crimes because society coddles them. In their view, it is imperative that state legislators pass laws that would require society to treat problem children with more firmness and rigidity. Only then will children straighten up. To implement these ideas, proponents of this new approach suggest resurrecting a type of thinking popular a hundred or so years ago. Then it was believed that children were miniature adults. If the day should ever come when proponents of the "miniature adult" philosophy are able to blur your vision regarding the developmental differences between children and adults, then taking the next step, treating children and adults alike, will be easy.

The Origin of "Get-Tough"

State statutes define the jurisdiction of the juvenile court. In thirty-seven states, persons under age eighteen who are charged with a law violation are considered juveniles. In ten states, the upper limit for original juvenile court jurisdiction is age sixteen, and in three states, the upper age limit is fifteen (DeFrances & Strom, 1997). However, numerous exceptions to the age criteria permit a prosecutor to proceed against a juvenile as an adult in criminal court. Such prosecutorial discretion raises questions, such as: Should children be held accountable for their behavior in criminal court? If children are tried in criminal court and are found guilty of their crimes, should they be sentenced as adults?

The idea to transfer children to criminal court is part of a conservative movement in juvenile justice sweeping across the nation. It is fueled by a Congress that is considering providing $500 million in grants to states who will allow youths age fifteen or older to be tried as adults for violent crimes. To qualify for the grants, states also will have to make their juvenile courts operate more like criminal courts, where repeat offenders are punished by increasing penalties (Willing, 1997).

Some readers may find it interesting to know there is nothing "new" or "tough" about the "get-tough" approach. In our past, children have been treated much more harshly by the legal system than what is being proposed today. Moreover, the current policy recommendations have their origin in revisionist thinking that can be traced to Northern Italy in the fourteenth century, when people started to believe they had free will, or the ability to make choices. This notion single-handedly changed what people thought about themselves and others. It also gave rise to the corollary belief that people should be held responsible for their behavior. Therefore, anyone who violates the law, including children, deserves to be punished.

This way of thinking is central to the Classical School of Criminology. Proponents of this perspective, in addition to believing people practice free will, also believe that people are rational and intelligent beings who weigh the costs and benefits of their behavior before they act. Participation in crime is voluntary. People commit crime because they imagine greater gains coming from crime than from conformity. Punishment is therefore justified on the grounds of retribution. Because the offender purposely violated another citizen's rights, he or she deserves to be punished. The punishment should be severe enough to deter the offender from committing future crimes (specific deterrence) and severe enough to send a strong message to anyone else who may be contemplating committing a similar crime (general deterrence).

Critics of the get-tough approach believe the reasoning on which the perspective is based is badly flawed. First, it is arguable whether people have free will. No one really knows. Because free will is a construct that cannot be scientifically measured, there is no way to determine whether people have it.

When advocates of free will are pressed as to how they know people have it, typically they tell you that free will is something people receive from God. Unfortunately, we know of no scientific evidence that indicates the presence or absence of God either. God, like free will, is an untestable notion. What there is scientific evidence of is that behavior is determined by antecedent conditions that precede it. To put it differently, behavior (juvenile crime) is the result of something that comes before it, and whatever the something is, is observable in the natural world (e.g., biological defect, psychological abnormality, social deprivation). That is why many criminologists do research: to discover the precise determinants of behavior. That the determinants of juvenile crime have yet to be discovered is not a reason to worry. Rather, what the absence of findings tell us is more research is needed.

Second, people may not be as rational as proponents of the get-tough approach think they are. If "rational" describes a state in which people always have full and accurate access to the potential outcomes of behavior, the theory on which the get-tough approach is based is patently false. If, however, "rational" describes a state in which people make decisions based only on the information available to them (the level and accuracy of such information being dependent on various situational and cognitive constraints), then we are left with a "limited," or "bounded," rationality. In this case, the emphasis on free will and autonomy, which is the unique quality of the perspective, is lost (Akers, 1990).

Third, it is not clear whether punishment deters unwanted behavior. Sometimes it does; sometimes it does not. Criminologists generally conclude that given the way punishment is carried out, it does not work. For punishment to be effective, it must be swift and certain. In the adult and juvenile justice systems the time between the crime, arrest, conviction, sentencing, and imprisonment is usually many months, sometimes years. Also, the likelihood of being arrested for committing a criminal offense is very low. The chance of an offender committing a crime and not getting caught is very good. Most crime is not detected, and when it is, few people are arrested, even fewer are convicted, and still fewer are sent to prison. Thus, the criminal law may have no deterrent effect until the likelihood of being arrested increases substantially, regardless of whether society gets tougher on juveniles (Reynolds, 1997).

There is only scant empirical evidence on whether transferring children to adult courts reduces recidivism. In fact, there is only one published research study on the topic. The results of the study may surprise you. Criminologists Lawrence Winner, Lonn Lanza-Kaduce, Donna Bishop, and Charles Frazier compared a group of 2,738 children whose cases were transferred to adult criminal courts with a matched sample of youths sentenced in the juvenile justice system. They found that 30 percent of the children who were transferred were arrested in the year after their release from custody, wheras only 19 percent of youths whose cases were handled in the juvenile justice system committed new offenses. They concluded that the transfer of juveniles to adult court had little (if any) deterrent effect. It was added, "Nor has it (transfer) produced any incapacitative benefits that enhance public safety. Although transferred youths were likely to be incarcerated for longer periods than those retained in the juvenile justice system, they quickly reoffended at a higher rate than the non-transferred controls, thereby negating any incapacitative benefits that might have been achieved in the short run" (Winner, Lanza-Kaduce, Bishop, & Frazier, 1997). The reason? Possibly, the children who were transferred had more associations with adult criminals, thereby exacerbating their own problem behavior on release.

An Alternative Policy Recommendation

Transferring children to adult court is a very bad idea. Not only is it based on badly flawed theory, it is not supported by existing research, although admittedly, there has only been limited research on the topic. At best the practice of transferring juveniles to criminal court will have a negligible deterrent impact on adolescent criminal behavior and may actually exacerbate the problem. Nor is it likely that any other quick-fix solution, such as instituting curfews or parent-liability laws, will do much good. The sad truth is, the programs and policies we use today to control and prevent juvenile delinquency do not work. Other criminologists have previously recognized this (Martinson, 1974; Lab and Whitehead, 1988; Romig, 1978; Whitehead and Lab, 1989; Palmer, 1991). The very best that can be said is that some of the programs and policies work some of the time for some children. For which children and when, no can say. The reason our programs and polices fail is because they are based an antiquated understanding of juvenile crime that delinquency is about the behavior of children. It is not. Delinquency is about the behavior of adults. Delinquency is a product produced by adults. If it is our intention to control and prevent delinquency, then we need to articulate a way to implement a strategy for teaching adults to think differently about who and what children are in relation to them. This can be done through the legal system.

The plight of children in the United States is in critical condition. The nation faces a national emergency, the origin of which can be traced to the maltreatment of children rooted in our collective benign neglect of their needs. How America treats children constitutes a moral disaster. Every year millions of children come face-to-face with relentless forms of maltreatment: They are starved and abandoned, burned and severely beaten, raped and sodomized, berated and belittled.... (United States Advisory Board on Child Abuse and Neglect, 1990). If America had solved the problem of polio using the same techniques it has used to solve child maltreatment, thousands of people would be wearing high-tech leg braces, scientifically advanced crutches and state-of-the-art, computer-age iron lungs. There also would be telethons to make sure each new victim could have the appropriate apparatus (Gill, 1991).

As alarming as the condition of children is, there is a way to correct it if Americans were willing to adopt a policy that would permanently change the status of children from one of chattel to full citizen. A way to do that is to provide children with inalienable protective rights. That would require amending the Constitution. We thus recommend a Children's Constitutional amendment as a vehicle for putting into action ideas expressed in 1930 by President Hoover, who, at the White House Conference on Children declared:

- For every child a home and that love and security which a home provides: and for that child who must receive foster care, the nearest substitute for his own home.

- For every child a school which is safe…and properly equipped. For younger children, nursery schools and kindergartens to supplement home care.
- For every child an education which, through the discovery and development of his individual abilities, prepares him for life; and through training and vocational guidance prepares him for a living which will yield him the maximum of satisfaction.
- For every child who is blind, deaf, or otherwise physically handicapped, and for the child who is mentally handicapped, such measures as will early discover and diagnose his handicap, provide care and treatment, and so train him that he may become an asset to society rather than a liability. Expenses of these services should be born publicly where they cannot be privately met.
- For every child protection from abuse, neglect, exploitation or moral hazard.
- For every child these rights, regardless of race, or color, or situation, wherever he may live under the protection of the American flag (Myers & Newton, 1936, pp. 458–461).

President Hoover's words represent an idea whose time has come…again. What was proposed in 1930 was not a radical idea then and it is not a radical idea today. Is it radical to propose that Americans guarantee to all of its children a constitutional right to health care, education, safety, and a nurturing environment? We think it is radical not to guarantee these rights. We believe this because "if we could have one generation of properly born, trained, educated, and healthy children, a thousand other problems of government would vanish" (Myers & Newton, 1936, pp. 456–457).

REFERENCES

Akers, R. (1990). Rational choice, deterrence, and social learning theory in criminology. *Journal of Criminal Law and Criminology, 81,* 654–676.

Children's Defense Fund (1997). *The state of America's children—Yearbook 1997.* Washington, DC: Children's Defense Fund.

DeFrances, C., & Strom, K.(1997). Juveniles prosecuted in state criminal courts. *BJS Bulletin,* NCJ-164265. Washington, D.C.: U.S. Department of Justice.

Gill, C. (1991). Essay on the status of the American child. *Ohio Northern Law Review, 17,* 543–579.

Lab, S., & Whitehead, J. (1988). An analysis of juvenile correctional treatment. *Crime and Delinquency, 34,* 60–83.

Martinson, R. (1974). What works—Questions and answers about prison reform. *The Public Interest, 35,* 22–54.

Myers, W., & Newton, W. (1936). *The Hoover administration: A documented narrative.* New York: Scribner's Sons.

Palmer, T. (1991). The effectiveness of intervention. *Crime and Delinquency, 37,* 330–346.

Reynolds, M. (1997). *The Reynold's Report: Crime and punishment in the United States.* NCPA Policy Report No. 209. Dallas, TX: National Center for Policy Analysis.

Romig, D. (1978). *Justice for our children.* Lexington, MA: Lexington Books.

United States Advisory Board on Child Abuse and Neglect. (1990). *Child abuse and neglect: Critical first steps in response to a national emergency.* Washington, D.C.: U.S. Government Printing Office.

Whitehead, J. & Lab, S. (1989). A meta-analysis of juvenile correctional treatment. *Journal of Research in Crime and Delinquency, 26,* 276–295.

Willing, R. (1997, September 18). House's bill tougher than Senate's. *USA Today,* p. 2A.

Winner, L., Lanza-Kaduce, L., Bishop. D., & Frazier, C. (1997). The transfer of juveniles to criminal court. *Crime & Delinquency, 43,* 548–563.

Rejoinder to Dr. Regoli SANDRA STONE

After reading Dr. Regoli's essay, it occurred to me that we basically agree on many points, although I did not specifically state some of them in my initial argument. Points on which we agree are as follows:

1. I fully agree that we as a society have miserably failed in providing adequate care for millions of our children. Dr. Regoli cites data to support this fact, and I will not repeat them here. I agree that it is essential for healthy growth and development for children to receive proper care and nurturing from conception forward. It is surely an indictment of us as adults that nearly three million cases of child abuse and neglect are reported annually in this country, and that many more children do not get their basic needs met but never come to the attention of any "official" agency. The long-term effects of child maltreatment have been documented, and they include, among other things, a higher likelihood of child victims to engage in delinquent/criminal behavior than children who were not mistreated. Child maltreatment is but one of many variables that contribute to delinquency, however, and not all children who are maltreated become delinquent, nor do all children who are treated well refrain from engaging in delinquent acts.

2. Expanding the position stated in point 1, I think that Dr. Regoli and I agree that all behavior, including delinquency, is the result of antecedent conditions. I do believe that we all make choices, but I also believe that our choices are limited by other conditions in our lives, be they biological, psychological, social, environmental, spiritual, or whatever. I do not believe, nor did I state in my essay, that we are totally free agents who always make rational decisions regarding how to behave. I do believe, though, that under certain conditions we may be more or less "free," and we may think and behave more or less rationally.

3. I agree with Dr. Regoli that heretofore little real effort has been made to rehabilitate delinquent children. He is correct in stating that most children who come into the custody of the justice system, especially those held in locked facilities, are, for the most part, warehoused. Little is provided in the way of treatment, and what treatment is available is often provided by inadequately trained staff. I think we would further agree that this is due primarily to a lack of true commitment to the well-being of children in our society.

4. I also agree with Dr. Regoli's argument that punishment, as now delivered, is not effective. That was, in fact, one of the main points in my essay. Punishment can be an effective means of shaping behavior, but it must be consistently delivered (swift and certain). And, as I argued, it is more effective if paired with reinforcement for desirable behavior. I am not arguing for being punitive just for the sake of showing children who's boss. I am arguing, though, for the administration of negative sanctions to give children a clear message that certain behaviors are not acceptable and for the installation of positive rewards for desirable behavior to teach them a better way.

5. Dr. Regoli and I are in agreement that the transfer of juveniles to adult court and adult corrections is not only ineffective but harmful. I did not advocate for the transfer of juveniles to the adult system. In fact, I argued in my original essay that if juveniles are dealt with effectively early on in their offending careers, far fewer of them will commit those more serious crimes that helped spark the recent "get tough" approach.

6. Finally, I agree wholeheartedly with Dr. Regoli that there is desperate need in this society for policy changes in terms of treatment of families and children that will result in a reallocation of resources. I, like him, am committed to work for long-term change that will improve the quality of life for all children, not just my own. This level of change will not occur overnight, however, and I am also committed to working for better solutions to the problems we face right now. Today's problems will not go away if not addressed; rather, they will just become worse.

There are other areas, however, where Dr. Regoli and I appear to have different perspectives. The main points with which I disagree are these:

1. I do not agree that children and adults should have equal status in society. I do believe that children deserve respect, guidance and care, but they are, after all, children. Even Dr. Regoli acknowledges in his original essay that children are clearly developmentally different from adults and that we should not revert back to the "child as miniature adult" philosophy. Children by definition do not have the same decision-making abilities as adults. They are still learning and developing cognitively, emotionally, and morally through adolescence. It is for this reason we do not allow children to drive, vote, see "R"-rated movies, and engage in many other behaviors until they reach a certain level of maturity. It is also for this reason that we as adults are legally charged with providing for childrens' basic needs until they reach a certain age. That is why we have a juvenile court, because children are different and need to be treated accordingly. Again, I am not arguing for the transfer of juveniles to adult court and adult corrections; I am arguing for the juvenile court to do its job more effectively.

2. Dr. Regoli argues that the intervention of the juvenile court comes too late, after the damage to a child has already been done. While I would agree that the ideal situation is for each child to get his or her needs met at each stage of his or her life, preferably in his or her family, in reality that is not always the case. It is then better for some third party to intervene as soon as possible to attempt to prevent further damage rather than for no one to intervene at all. If we truly believe that people can change and that rehabilitation works, then it is never too late to offer assistance.

3. I do not fully agree with Dr. Regoli that delinquency is about the behavior of adults, not children. I would agree that a primary source of delinquent behavior is the failure of adults to adequately care for children; I would not agree, however, that delinquency is a result of discriminatory behavior against children on the part of adults simply because of their age. Whatever the cause, the truth is that sometimes children behave in ways that are harmful to themselves, others, or property, and they need to be held responsible. If we do not establish clear expectations about appropriate behavior and hold them responsible, then we, the adults, are, once again, contributing to the problem. Furthermore, whatever the causes of delinquency may be, understanding them does not negate the need to address the unacceptable behavior. As Dr. Regoli discusses in his textbook, *Delinquency in Society,* one of the primary functions of the family is to socialize children. Socialization includes teaching children appropriate behavior, which requires that parents provide some type of discipline. If parents fail in this task, it then becomes the role of other social entities, such as the juvenile court.

4. Dr. Regoli makes the point that children's behavior is determined by antecedent conditions; in other words, children do not have free will. Although I do not believe that any of us totally have free will, I do believe that we make choices within our own particular limitations (see #2 in the previous section). Children make choices just like everyone else, and they will often admit after the fact that sometimes they make poor ones. Children, just like adults, need to learn to deal with the consequences of their choices. How can we teach children to be responsible adults if we do not first teach them to be responsible children?

5. I both agree and disagree with Dr. Regoli regarding his point that there is scant empirical evidence that programs for delinquent children are effective. Past programs and past research findings have not been very encouraging. This is due in part, however, to the fact that there was little monitoring to ensure proper implementation of programs, many programs did not stay in existence long enough to determine whether they worked, and program funders have not historically required any systematic evaluations, and many that were conducted were not methodologically sound. This has begun to change, and in recent years the ability to obtain funding for many programs has been contingent partly on the recipient's agreement to allocate a certain amount of the budget to evaluation. This has been particularly true for programs that are funded through federal, state, and local government agencies. As program quality controls increase and rigorous evaluations are conducted, researchers are beginning to identify programs that do work (see the new Office of Justice Programs' recent research report, *Preventing Crime: What Works, What Doesn't, What's Promising*). Consequently, that argument is no longer valid. Findings do suggest, though, that programs are more effective the earlier in the child's life they can be implemented. Furthermore, many of the programs that work with delinquents will require a reallocation of resources, at least in the short-term. So, we can no longer dismiss intervening with delinquent juveniles because "nothing works;" instead, the new question becomes, "Are we willing to pay for positive results?" In addition, just because a system has not worked properly in the past does not necessarily mean we should eliminate it. Rather, we need to identify where the weak points are and attempt to make repairs. Families, schools and even our government have many flaws, yet we commit to making them better, not abolishing them altogether.

In closing, I would encourage you, the reader, to give this issue serious thought. We are all affected, directly or indirectly, by juvenile delinquency, and at some point in the future, you will be the ones to decide what needs to be done. The issue is complex, and we are continuously gaining a better understanding of all its many facets. Yes, we need to work long-term to make the world a better place for children, but we also need to address the short-term realities of the world we live in now, including how to deal effectively with juvenile delinquents. We cannot simply ignore delinquent behavior because adults have failed to meet children's needs; if we do, we fail them once again.

Chemical Corrections: Is Medical Treatment a Useful Way to Deal with Criminal Offenders?

Diana Fishbein, Ph.D., is Research Faculty at the University of Maryland's HIDTA Research Program, which is funded by the White House Drug Policy Office, where she implements and evaluates drug abuse prevention programs. Previously, Dr. Fishbein was a Senior Researcher with the U.S. Department of Justice, Professor at the University of Baltimore, Staff Scientist with the National Institute on Drug Abuse, and Research Faculty at the University of Maryland Medical School.

Joyce Carbonell, Ph.D., is Professor of Psychology at Florida State University and is licensed as a psychologist in Florida and Georgia. She received her doctoral degree from Bowling Green University in 1978. Dr. Carbonell's main research interests concern incarcerated populations and the prediction of violent and criminal behavior. Her current research is on the correlates of violent and criminal behavior in women. She has authored numerous journal articles and book chapters and has presented her research at national and international conferences. In addition, she performs forensic assessments in civil and criminal cases.

YES

DIANA FISHBEIN

Pharmacological approaches to treatment intervention, otherwise known as pharmacotherapy, are increasingly used in clinical settings for the modification of behaviors often associated with crime and violence. Several studies provide support for the notion that pharmacotherapy, combined with conventional psychosocial treatments, produce more favorable treatment outcomes than traditional therapies alone or simple incarceration (Kristiansson, 1995). Although no medications are approved by the Food and Drug Administration specifically for criminal or antisocial behavior, several drugs have been approved for use in patients with behavioral and personality disorders related to criminality (e.g., violence, drug abuse, impulsivity, negative affect, and angry temperament) with significant success; i.e., by improving the disordered behavior of individuals who attract the attention of the criminal justice system (Nemeroff, 1995). Pharmacological treatment of certain offenders is predicated on research that finds that violence and aggression, drug addiction, and other excessive and compulsive behaviors are often present in those with underlying disorders of the brain. Medication in these cases may lead to behavioral improvements by stabilizing a neurochemical imbalance or physiological disturbance that would otherwise increase risk for offending behaviors. As a result, the individual becomes more in control of his or her own behavior, minimizing the need for external controls.

Because the chemical correction of antisocial behaviors is multifaceted and controversial, it is critical that several key issues be addressed by both research and public policy experts before incorporating pharmacotherapy into correctional policies: (1) identification of underlying mechanisms in certain forms of antisocial behavior potentially responsive to chemical corrections; (2) identification of individuals or subgroups appropriate for pharmacological treatments; (3) identification of specific medications that alter underlying mechanisms for antisocial behavior; and (4) identification of ethical, social, and legal ramifications. The last issue recognizes the need for further research and regulations before implementation of policies to incorporate this approach, particularly with respect to voluntary versus coercive treatment.

Underlying Mechanisms in Antisocial Behavior

Although certainly social factors such as poverty and discrimination play a major role in violence and crime, not everyone so afflicted engages in these behaviors. Thus, individual differences in neurochemistry and physiology likely play a determining role in these outcomes. Considerable evidence indicates that there is a neurobiological basis for the pharmacological treatment of certain subgroups of criminal offenders. In particular, neurochemical and physiological abnormalities have been associated with the pathological traits of personality-disordered patients, including aggressiveness, impulsivity, sensation-seeking and risk-taking, drug abuse, anxiety, and cognitive-perceptual distortions (Fishbein, 1990; Raine 1993; Volavka, 1995), all of which are considered to be risk factors for antisocial behavior. Dysfunctions of neurotransmitter systems that control brain activity (Brown et al., 1982; Coccaro & Murphy, 1991; Linnoila et al., 1983; Linnoila et al., 1994) and aberrations in sex hormone responses (see Ellis, 1988, and Fishbein, 1992) have been consistently linked with risk for antisocial behaviors. Also linked with antisocial behaviors are abnormalities in the PET scan (positron emission tomography) and electroencephalogram (EEG), low heart rate and skin conductance, and neuropsychological deficits that reflect problems with brain function (see Raine, 1993).

Origins of the various personality disorders that increase risk for criminalization vary widely, from head injury to childhood trauma to genetically determined neurotransmitter imbalances. Nevertheless, whether these traits are a function of environmental circumstances or of underlying genetic vulnerabilities, they are often amenable to pharmacological treatment (Treastman, de Veguar, & Silver, 1995). With appropriate assessment of underlying biomedical conditions in antisocial behaviors, as well as with well-informed pharmacological management of their symptoms, internal self-controls over their otherwise disruptive behaviors can be achieved in many cases.

Appropriate Recipients of Pharmacotherapy

Whether an offender is a candidate for pharmacotherapy and will respond favorably are a function of both the presence of an underlying condition that is amenable to medication and the likelihood that the offender will comply with the treatment regimen. Only a subset of offenders are appropriate for medical treatment, and there are indications that these offenders may contribute to the base rate for serious, violent crime. There is a high prevalence of aggression and violence among psychiatric patients (Yudofsky, Silver, & Hales, 1995) and numerous studies implicate mental illness and personality disorders in the development of antisocial and aggressive behavior within offender populations (Pallone, 1991; Teplin, 1983). Conversely, estimates of prevalence are sketchy and indicate that a significant number of offenders do not suffer from a psychopathological condition; rather, their criminal activity is often a result of rational choice, learning experiences, or social opportunities (Clarke, 1985; Clarke & Felson, 1993). Certainly, in the absence of documented evidence for cognitive deficits, head trauma, physiological abnormalities, neurochemical imbalances, or other treatable psychological or psychiatric syndromes, pharmacotherapy should not be considered an option.

Several types of personality, psychiatric, and behavioral disorders are both prevalent among offenders and amenable to pharmacotherapy. The most common types of disorders, as categorized by the *Diagnostic and Statistical Manual* (APA, 1994), in offender populations are of the personality and include Antisocial Personality Disorder, Borderline Personality Disorder, Substance Abuse, and Post-Traumatic Stress Disorder. Psychiatric disorders commonly seen in this population are Bipolar Disorder (manic–depression), Anxiety, and Paranoid Schizophrenia (other forms of schizophrenia are not significantly associated with criminality). It is also instructive to assess the presence of a history of Conduct Disorder, Oppositional Defiant Disorder, and Attention-Deficit/Hyperactivity Disorder, because they are each more prevalent among offenders, substance abusers, and individuals with antisocial behavior problems.

Even in the absence of a standard psychiatric diagnosis, several behaviors and personality characteristics linked to risk for antisocial conduct are prevalent in offenders and will potentially improve with appropriate medication. Aggressiveness and the other correlates of offending behaviors, such as impulsivity, negative affect, or cognitive deficit, can be a symptom or consequence of an overriding psychiatric disorder, or aggressiveness can be a primary criterion for a psychological disorder. For example, paranoid schizophrenics are often aggressive and sometimes violent along with a complexity of other symptoms that are even more prominent in the diagnosis. Conversely, aggressiveness is a primary diagnostic trait of Antisocial Personality Disorder or Conduct Disorder. A trained clinician must employ a precise nosology (typology of symptoms) to specify for each patient/offender the diagnosis or traits to be targeted that, in turn, would lead to specific and effective treatment. Without an in-depth assessment, it is less likely that pharmacotherapy will be effective or properly monitored. Furthermore, offenders should never be categorized into groups on the basis of their offense; rather, they should be assessed on an individualized basis for clinical signs and symptoms of a pathological condition that would indicate a medical approach to treatment.

Before attempting to assess and treat an offender, several determinations are necessary. It is critical, for example, to determine whether he or she has a drug or alcohol abuse history. Many of the symptoms delineated are alleviated once substance abuse or dependence is resolved, negating the need for pharmacological treatment of their antisocial behavior. Only when a clinician is certain that no other treatable physical illness is present and that substance abuse or dependence disorders are under control should pharmacological interventions be considered (Treastman et al., 1995). In addition, there must be a willingness to comply with the regimen, maintain use of the medication over time, and discuss potential problems with the prescribing physician. This prerequisite is especially pertinent when the offender may receive reduced criminal justice supervision as a condition of their treatment.

Potentially Effective Medicinal Regimens

Several medications have been used extensively in clinical populations and offenders to ameliorate underlying behavioral and psychological disorders. It is important to distinguish between various disorders in determining which medicinal regimen would be most efficacious. And as indicated, isolation of primary and secondary symptoms or manifestations of psychopathology is needed to avoid the use of medications just to alleviate bothersome symptoms that do not stem from the underlying disorder, leaving the disorder unaffected or producing unwanted side effects. The table below provides a simple chart delineating medications frequently used for syndromes common in offender populations.

Syndrome	Medication
Sex offending	Depo-Provera (chemical castration)
Substance abuse	Antidepressants and opiate antagonists
ADHD and conduct disorder	Stimulants and anticonvulsants
Intermittent explosive disorder	Anticonvulsants (Elliott)
Alcoholism	Naloxone and serotonergic agonists
Paranoid schizophrenia	Psychotropics or antipsychotics
Obsessive compulsive disorders (e.g., gambling)	Serotonergic agonists
Violent behavior	Lithium, antipsychotics, and beta-blockers

Psychological, neurochemical, and physiological tests are recommended to identify individuals with abnormalities amenable to medical treatment and are useful in the choice of medication. For example, an electroencephalogram may show signs of central nervous system instability or actual epileptic seizural activity, which would suggest a regimen of anticonvulsants. Or an increase in noradrenergic metabolism (a neurotransmitter), which has been correlated with pathological gambling, impulsivity, and risk taking (Stein et al., 1996; Roy, De Jong, & Linnoila, 1989), may suggest that noradrenergic agents would be helpful. Unfortunately, such testing can be expensive and certainly is not routinely accorded offenders processed through the criminal justice system.

Several medications are preferred in the treatment of aggression because of their specific effects on brain processes implicated in aggression and its associated attention deficits and negative mood states. Because a large body of evidence shows that diminished serotonin (a neurotransmitter) function in the brain is linked to aggressive behavior, treatments that increase serotonin activity are often used to reduce aggression and impulsivity (Fuller, 1996). As mentioned previously, attention-deficit/hyperactivity disorder is prevalent in the childhood histories of individuals with antisocial behavioral patterns. Various medications with stimulant properties have been used successfully in these individuals as adults to decrease anxiety, impulsiveness, and other untoward symptoms that tend to be otherwise resistant to treatment (Dulcan, Bregman, Weller, & Weller, 1995; Ratey, Greenberg, & Lindem, 1991). In the past, neuroleptics and benzodiazepines have been used extensively to treat aggressiveness, but they have grave side effects and unpredictable results. Instead, current approaches with psychiatric patients who exhibit extreme aggressiveness and explosive personality disorders include beta-blockers, which have consistently proved safer and more effective in enhancing self-control (Ratey et al., 1992; Ratey & Gordon, 1993). Also, a combination of pharmacotherapy and cognitive behavior therapy has shown promising results in psychopathic, criminal men generally considered to be "incurable" (Kristiansson, 1995). And a few clinics that treat sex offenders, known to be difficult if not intractible to treat, have used depo-provera (a male hormone antagonist) with some success (Berlin, 1983; McConaghy, Blaszczynski, & Kidson, 1988; Murray, 1988; Uphoff, 1983). These medications are obviously expected to have more efficacy in syndromes that are biological in origin. Notwithstanding, even disorders with social origins, such as histories of severe childhood trauma, may respond to a serotonin agonist given the effects of extreme, chronic stress on the serotonin system (Corrigan, Garbutt, Ekstrom, & Golden, 1992; Higley, Suomi, & Linnoila, 1991).

Issues and Implications

In light of increasing recognition that biological factors contribute to various aspects of antisocial behavior and may be amenable to pharmacological treatment, the need to address and resolve several additional relevant issues is critical. Questions that arise include: (1) What defines "undesirable" versus "functional" behavior in the context of an individual offender's environment? (2) Is coercive or mandatory treatment warranted, effective, and properly regulated? (3) Can criminal justice supervision be safely withdrawn or reduced in offenders involved in pharmacotherapy? and (4) Importantly, will pharmacotherapy in appropriate offenders reduce recidivism? These questions cannot be fully addressed in this short chapter, but brief attention is paid to each.

What is "undesirable" behavior? Obviously, behaviors are antisocial by virtue of their consequences; they either psychologically, financially or physically harm others. But there may be dimensions of antisocial conduct, such as forms of aggression, that the CJS or lay public sees as undesirable that may actually be functional in an offender's environment. Do we have the right to suppress these responses, which may actually be adaptive in a hostile and violence-ridden neighborhood? The same may be true for certain property offenses, which may be functional responses to limited opportunities. Granted, these behaviors are unacceptable. Nevertheless, the question remains as to whether we are simply adhering a band-aid to disguise an open wound that would be better treated by attending to the macro-level ills in our society. One point must be made clear: The use of pharmacotherapy should not replace or detract from larger social programs to ameliorate these global ills. Conversely, there is a substantial offender population that suffers from brain dysfunction manifested as depression, anxiety, personality disorders, or other psychological and psychiatric dysfunctions, which, if left, untreated, jeopardize personal well-being and public safety. It is critical that those in need of treatment are distinguished from those who simply live in environments in need of treatment.

Should pharmacotherapy be coerced or strictly voluntary? There is widespread recognition that drug-addicted offenders require treatment and are more likely to recidivate in its absence. As a result, many states have enacted statutes that permit the courts to mandate treatment for drug-involved offenders. Studies of coerced treatment provide evidence for its efficacy (Anglin & Hser, 1991; Leukefeld & Tims, 1990). In a similar vein, can we mandate treatment for violent offenders when a treatable disorder is established? The answer may be "yes" to this question when cause and effect can be established, that is, that the underlying disorder is responsible for the violence, and when there is evidence to substantiate the effectiveness of treatment in reducing violent behavior. Certainly, the methods to treat violence used in the criminal justice system, which is largely restricted to tranquilizers, intermittent group encounter sessions, or incarceration only, do not show efficacious results. Thus, standards for treatment need to be better established overall in the system to determine what will work and for whom. And while society strives to punish those who are violent, the high recidivism rates amongst these offenders suggest we need to look elsewhere for an answer. Once again, do we ask violent offenders to consent to imprisonment, a technique that is notoriously unsuccessful? No. Then perhaps mandatory treatment in appropriate cases can be considered, given the alternatives. The answer to this set of questions may be contingent on the extent to which pharmacotherapy works, can be instituted and monitored properly, and can be maintained by the offender for purposes of protecting public safety. In any event, current techniques and regulatory statutes must be revamped to reflect current knowledge.

Another related issue pertaining to volunteerism versus coercion concerns the pervasive discrimination in our system. We must take steps to ensure that not only the privileged or whites have access to treatment; the means to evaluate, treat, and monitor must be equitably distributed throughout the offender population regardless of affluence or race. However, we must take precautions against the use of pharmacotherapy in certain classes or ethnic groups as a means to control or oppress them. Although this is more of a concern with the tranquilizers often prescribed in prisons to control inmates, medications that target specific problems in brain function work not by tranquilizing, but by enabling the individual to become more fully functional.

Can criminal justice supervision be safely reduced in offenders receiving pharmacological treatment? This question raises a host of related issues, including, first and foremost, whether the medication is effective in suppressing antisocial responses. To make that determination, offenders must be intensively monitored, preferably within the confines of a secure institution, because measurements of change are taken to establish that the pharmacotherapy is working. On release, monitoring must continue on a regular basis in the same way that clinical populations are supervised. Given that the system generally releases offenders with minimal to no monitoring and often no treatment, this may be a tremendous improvement. Another consideration mentioned previously is ability to ensure that the offender maintains the medical regimen over time; an activity that requires the creation of realistic procedures for monitoring.

Will pharmacotherapy reduce recidivism? The answer to this question enters into unexplored territory and is at the root of all of the issues raised. Although numerous studies of psychiatric populations provide evidence for the effectiveness of this method in conjunction with more traditional therapies in treating various forms of antisocial behavior (see Volavka, 1995), no study has yet been done with an offender population undergoing pharmacotherapy. As with other clinical treatment approaches, each offender must be treated as an individual with unique traits and needs in determining an appropriate course of treatment. Studies to assess the effects of pharmacotherapy on recidivism must evaluate a sample of offenders receiving treatment as a group, but with varying medicinal regimens. Only then will these questions be answerable.

Closing Remark

Individuals who engage in serious criminal activity are considered to be worthy of punishment and are routinely incarcerated and sometimes even executed. The conditions of prisons are not conducive to positive behavioral or attitudinal change and often worsen the prognosis. Some protest that the conditions of most prisons are cruel and inhumane and cannot be justified on the basis of crimes that most offenders commit,[1] particularly in light of their increased risk for offending after imprisonment. Eventually, offenders are nearly always released back into the community in this worsened state, and many are destined to commit new offenses; recidivism rates are astronomical. Do we ask offenders whether they want to be imprisoned or executed? No. The argument could be made that we also need not ask if they want to be treated. Perhaps we owe it to society to examine the issues and consider the medical treatment of certain offenders under appropriate conditions and with proper regulations intact. The bottom line question is, which is more effective, more justifiable, and more protective of public safety—imprisonment or treatment? Further research must be conducted before an informed opinion can be shaped. The next generation of criminal justice officials and policy makers may be charged with these decisions.

NOTE

1. The majority of offenders convicted and incarcerated commit petty crimes and drug offenses.

REFERENCES

American Psychiatric Association. (1994). *Diagnostic and statistical manual of mental disorders* (4th ed.). Washington, D.C., American Psychiatric Association.

Anglin, M. D., & Hser, Y-I. (1991). Criminal justice and the drug-abusing offender: Policy issues of coerced treatment. *Behavioral Sciences and the Law, 9,* 243–267.

Berlin, F. S. (1983). Sex offenders: A biomedical perspective and a status report on biomedical treatment. In Greer, J. G., and Stuart, I. R. (Eds.), *The sexual aggressor.* New York: Van Nostrand Reinhold Company.

Brown, G. L., Ebert, M. H., Goyer, P. F., Jimerson, D. C., Klein, W. F., Bunney, W. E., & Goodwin, F. K. (1982). Aggression, suicide and serotonin: Relationships to CSF amine metabolites. *American Journal of Psychiatry, 139,* 741–746.

Clarke, R. V. (1985). Delinquency, environment, and intervention. *Child Psychology and Psychiatry, 26,* 505–523.

Clarke, R. V., & Felson, M. (1993). Criminology, routine activity, and rational choice. In R. V. Clarke, and M. Felson (Eds.), *Routine activity and rational choice: Advances in criminological theory.* New Brunswick, NJ: Transaction Publishers, pp. 1–14.

Coccaro, E., & Murphy, D. L. (1991). *Serotonin in major psychiatric disorders.* Washington, D.C.: American Psychiatric Press.

Corrigan, M., Garbutt, J. C., Ekstrom, D., & Golden, R. N. (1992). Serotonergic function in trauma victims. *Biological Psychiatry, 31,* 12.

Dulcan, M. K., Bregman, J. D., Weller, E. B., & Weller, R. A. (1995) Treatment of childhood and adolescent disorders. In A. Schatzberg and C. Nemeroff (Eds.), *The American Psychiatric Association textbook of psychopharmacology.* Washington, D.C.: APA.

Ellis, L. (1988). Neurohormonal bases of varying tendencies to learn delinquent and criminal behavior. In E. Morris and C. Braukmann (Eds.), *Behavioral Approaches to Crime and Delinquency.* New York: Plenum.

Fishbein, D. H. (1990). Biological perspectives in criminology. *Criminology, 28,* 27–72.

Fishbein, D. H. (1992). The psychobiology of female aggression. *Criminal Justice and Behavior, 19,* 99–126.

Fuller, R. W. (1996). The influence of fluoxetine on aggressive behavior. *Neuropsychopharmacology, 14,* 77–81.

Higley, J. D., Suomi, S. J., & Linnoila, M. (1991). CSF monoamine metabolite concentrations vary according to age, rearing and sex, and are influenced by the stressor of social separation in rhesus monkeys. *Psychopharmacology, 103,* 551–556.

Kristiansson, M. (1995). Incurable Psychopaths? *Bulletin of the American Academy of Psychiatry and Law, 23,* 555–562.

Linnoila, M., Virkkunen, M., Scheinin, M., Nuutila, A., Rimon, R., & Goodwin, F. K. (1983) Low cerebrospinal fluid 5–hydroxyindoleacetic acid concentration differentiates impulsive from nonimpulsive violent behavior. *Life Sciences, 33,* 2609–2614.

Linnoila, M., Virkkunen, M., Eckardt, M., Higley, J.D., Nielsen, D., & Goldman, D. (1994). Serotonin, violent behavior and alcohol. *EXS, 71,* 155–163.

Leukefeld, C. G., & Tims, F. M. (1990). Compulsory treatment for drug abuse. *International Journal of Addictions, 25,* 621–640.

McConaghy, N., Blaszczynski, A., & Kidson, W. (1988). Treatment of sex offenders with imaginal desensitization and/or medroxyprogesterone. *Acta Psychiatria Scandanavia, 77,* 199–206.

Murray, J. B. (1988). Psychopharmacological therapy of deviant sexual behavior. *The Journal of General Psychology, 115,* 101–110.

Nemeroff, C. (1995). *The APA textbook of psychopharmacology.* Washington, D.C.: APA.

Pallone, N. (1991). *Mental disorder among prisoners.* New Brunswick, NJ: Transaction Publishers.

Raine, A. (1993). *The psychopathology of crime.* New York: Academic Press.

Ratey, J., Greenberg, M. S., & Lindem, K. J. (1991). Combination of treatments for attention deficit hyperactivity disorder in adults. *Journal of Nervous and Mental Disorders, 179,* 699–701.

Ratey, J., Sorgi, P., O'Driscoll, G. A., Sands, S., Daehler, M. M. L., Fletcher, J. R., Kadish, W., Spruiell, G., Polakoff, S., & Lindem, K. J. (1992). Nadolol to treat aggression and psychiatric symptomatology in chronic psychiatric inpatients: A double-blind, placebo-controlled study. *Journal of Clinical Psychiatry, 53,* 41–46.

Ratey, J., & Gordon, A. (1993). The psychopharmacology of aggression: Toward a new day. *Psychopharmacology Bulletin, 29,* 65–73.

Roy, A., DeJong, J., & Linnoila, M. (1989). Extraversion in pathological gamblers correlates with indexes of noradrenergic function. *Archives of General Psychiatry, 46,* 679–681.

Schatzberg, A. F., & Nemeroff, C. B. (1995). *The American Psychiatric Association textbook of psychopharmacology.* Washington, D.C.: APA Press.

Stein, D. J., Trestman, R. L., Mitropoulou, V., Coccaro E. F., Hollander, E., & Siever, L. J. (1996, Fall). Impulsivity and serotonergic function in compulsive personality disorder. *Journal of Neuropsychiatry and Clinical Neuroscience, 8,*(4), 393–398.

Teplin, L. (1983). The criminalization of the mentally ill: Speculation in search of data. *Psychological Bulletin, 94,* 54–67.

Treastman, R. L., deVeguar, M., & Siever, L. J. (1995). Treatment of personality disorders. In Schatzberg, A. and Nemeroff, C. (Ed.), *The American Psychiatric Association textbook of psychopharmacology.* Washington, D.C.: APA.

Uphoff, R. J. (1983). Depo-Provera for the sex offender: A defense attorney's perspective. *Criminal Law Bulletin, 22,* 430–439.

Volavka, J. (1995). *Neurobiology of violence.* Washington, D.C.: American Psychiatric Press.

Yudofsky, S., Silver, J. M., & Hales, R. E. (1995). Treatment of aggressive disorders. In Schatzberg, A., & Nemeroff, C. (Eds.), *The American Psychiatric Association Textbook of Psychopharmacology.* Washington, D.C.: APA.

Rejoinder to Dr. Fishbein

JOYCE CARBONELL

Dr. Fishbein makes several arguments for the use of chemical correction for criminal offending. She argues that there is a substantial population of brain-damaged offenders in which the brain damage is manifested as depression, anxiety, and multiple other psychiatric diagnoses. She also argues that trained clinicians can accurately diagnosis disorders such as antisocial personality disorder, which has "aggressiveness as a primary diagnostic trait." Dr. Fishbein also points to a high rate of aggressiveness among psychiatric patients as part of her argument. There are serious faults with these and other arguments on behalf of chemical correction, which are outlined here.

The basic problem is that there is no evidence that the majority of criminal behavior is caused by brain damage. Nor is there any evidence that criminal behavior is likely in people with disorders such as depression and anxiety. In fact, the group mentioned most frequently in relation to criminal behavior are those diagnosed as antisocial personality disorders, whose hallmark tends to be a lack of anxiety and remorse, rather than anxiety and depression. There is of course a certain amount of anxiety and depression associated with being caught and incarcerated, which may be mistakenly seen as part of the disorder.

Yudofsky, Silver, and Hales (1995) are cited as support for the fact that patients in mental hospitals are aggressive, and as Yudofsky et al. point out, the demented elderly are aggressive. Although this may be true, these are hardly considered criminal justice problems. Few people fear the demented elderly, nor do they consider chronically hospitalized schizophrenics as a crime problem. But somehow we are then led to presume that because psychiatric patients may be violent in institutions (which may be for a host of other reasons secondary to the institutional environment), criminals are therefore mentally ill. I would argue that criminals are rarely demented elderly people, nor are they the chronically hospitalized schizophrenics whose behavior is too disorganized to form the necessary intent for a crime. Studies of criminal behavior and aggression in psychiatric patients indicates instead that drug and alcohol abuse account for a large part of the variance in violence among psychiatric patients (Rasmussen & Levander, 1996).

And, as Dr. Fishbein stated, "many symptoms are alleviated once substance abuse or dependence is resolved."

Leaving the hospitalized patients and the demented elderly behind, we can turn to a group that is more likely to be associated with criminal behavior. Fishbein also argues that certain diagnoses such as antisocial personality disorder (APD) have "aggression as a primary trait." This is simply incorrect. It is not in any way a primary characteristic of APD, and it is not even required for a diagnosis of APD (American Psychiatric Association, 1994), Aggressiveness is not a required trait for borderline personality disorder or conduct disorder either. Whereas criminal activity may be common in such diagnoses as conduct disorder, it is a disorder of childhood or adolescence and may simply involve property crime. In addition, although criminal behavior may not be unusual in APD, it tends to decrease with age, leading one to suspect that it is not secondary to brain dysfunction, because there are few brain dysfunctions that are cured by turning forty.

Dr. Fishbein correctly argues that we must precisely diagnosis each patient/offender to specify effective treatment. Unfortunately, this is not possible. We have at best a categorical system that does not imply anything about cause and "makes no assumption that all individuals having the same disorder are alike in all important ways." The DSMIV specifies that "nonclinical decision makers should also be cautioned that a diagnosis does not carry any implications regarding the cause of the individual's mental disorder or its associated impairments." It further states that even in disorders in which diminished control is a feature of the disorder, having the diagnosis does not indicate that a particular individual "is (or was) unable to control his or her behavior at a particular time."

Fishbein also suggests that a regimen of anticonvulsants would be useful for those with epileptic seizure activity that would be revealed by an electroencephalogram (EEG). Although I wholeheartedly agree that those with epileptic seizures benefit from anticonvulsant medication, there is no evidence that seizure activity leads to crime. Although Jack Ruby's lawyers argued that he was in the throes of a psychomotor seizure when he shot Lee Harvey Oswald, "a person having partial complex seizures will not engage in structured, purposeful and sequential activity. . . . In general, the incidence of violent behaviors in psychomotor seizures is quite low" (Berg, Franzen, & Wedding, 1994). Even if psychomotor seizures could somehow be held responsible for violent behavior, the diagnostic problem looms again. Unless the seizure is actually occurring at the time of the EEG, the EEG will be normal in "at least 50 percent of the bona fide seizure patients."

An additional concern in the use of pharmacological agents in treating offenders is that there is a racial and cultural bias in diagnosis and decision making. Dr. Fishbein expresses concern that such treatments must not be limited to "not only the privileged or whites" and that it must not be used as a means of social control. And, yet, the diagnostic system used to categorize individuals as in need of such interventions is biased. There is a race bias in the differential diagnosis of certain disorders such as schizophrenia and psychotic affective disorders, and a gender bias in the diagnosis of the personality disorders (Garb, 1997). Perhaps of more concern to this discussion is that there is a race bias in the prediction of violence and a social class bias in terms of who is referred to psychotherapy. Although there is no difference in the violent behavior of inmates based on their race, case managers and psychologists predict more violence for American Indians and black inmates (Cooper & Werner, 1990). Even more disturbing is that when the presence of a psychotic disorder, severity of disturbance, dangerousness, psychiatric history, and need for physical restraints are controlled, African American patients receive a significantly larger number of psychiatric medications, a significantly larger number of doses of antipsychotics, and a significantly larger number of injections of antipsychotic medications (Segal, Bola, & Watson, 1966, cited in Garb, 1997). Thus, chemical correction may be more likely to be erroneously prescribed for those who come from minority populations simply by virtue of their race.

There is literature that supports the role of social and family variables in the development of aggressive and deviant behavior. High parental monitoring, for example, is related to lower deviance in adolescents regardless of race (Forehand, Miller, Dutra, & Chance, 1997). And, childhood exposure to violence in the family of origin is consistently correlated with later domestic violence (Feldman, 1997), a problem of epidemic proportion. It would be best to turn our attention to these important social issues and to the development and use of empirically supported nonchemical treatments for problems that are primarily social in origin.

In her summary, Fishbein makes an arguments that treatment should perhaps be coerced and likens it to imprisonment. But this argument confuses treatment with punishment. Incarceration and execution are punishments; treatment is not punishment. And, although there is no strong evidence that the use of medication is useful for violent criminal behavior, there is no evidence at all that chemical correction is appropriate for the majority of inmates who are imprisoned for "petty crimes and drug offenses." Although it may be true that conditions in prisons are not conducive to positive behavioral or attitudinal change, coerced chemical intervention would certainly not improve attitudes or behavior in the inmate population. Although beyond the scope of this rejoinder, the ethical issues posed by the notion of coerced treatment are serious.

In spite of many difference in our positions, Dr. Fishbein and I do agree on perhaps the major issue at hand., We need to find more effective ways to provide social programs to ameliorate the problems that lead to criminal behavior. And we need to focus more attention on the development of criminal behaviors and develop programs that will both counteract these influences on development and provide intervention for those who are already embarked on a course of criminal or violent behavior. But chemical intervention, although seemingly neat and easy, is not the answer; the real answer is far more complex and yet to be determined. As H. L. Mencken said, "There's always an easy solution to every human problem—neat, plausible, and wrong" (quoted in Peter, 1977).

REFERENCES

American Psychiatric Association. (1994). *Diagnostic and statistical manual for the mental disorders* (4th ed.). Washington, D.C.: Author.

Berg, R. A., Franzen, M., & Wedding, D. (1994). *Screening for brain impairment* (2nd ed.). New York: Springer Publishing.

Cooper, R. P., & Werner, P. D. (1990). Prediction violence in newly admitted inmates: A lens model of staff decision making. *Criminal Justice and Behavior, 17,* 431–447.

Feldman, C. M. (1997). Childhood precursors of adult interpersonal violence. *Clinical Psychology: Science and Practice, 4,* 307–334.

Forehand, R., Miller, K., Dutra, R., & Chance, M. W. (1997). Role of parenting in adolescent deviant behavior: Replication across and within two ethnic cultures. *Journal of Consulting and Clinical Psychology, 65,* 1036–1041.

Garb, H. (1997). Race bias, social class bias, and gender bias in clinical judgment. *Clinical psychology: Science and practice, 4,* 99–119.

Peter, L. J. (1977). *Peter's quotations: Ideas for our time.* New York: William Morrow.

Rasmussen, K. & Levander, S. (1996). Crime and violence among psychiatric patients in a maximum security psychiatric hospital. *Criminal Justice and Behavior, 23,* 455–471.

Yudofsky, S., Silver, J. M., & Hales, R. E. (1995). Treatment of aggressive disorders. In A. Schatzberg & C. Nemeroff (Eds.), *The American Psychiatric Textbook of Psychopharmacology.* Washington, DC: American Psychiatric Association.

NO

JOYCE CARBONELL

Chemical or pharmacological correction is not the answer to violent criminal behavior. Although some violent and criminal behavior may be a function of brain lesions and other neurological impairment, there is no evidence that most aggressive or violent behavior is related to a physiological dysfunction or problem. And, it is certainly not the case that criminal behavior is always secondary to anger. Although anger is a common emotion, it is not necessarily related to aggressive acts of a physical nature. Aggression and violent criminal acts are best understood in the context of individual learning, group influence, and the impact of community standards on behavior. Intervention must span all of these areas, and although in some specific cases, intervention may be biological in nature, familial, social, and cultural pathways that lead to aggression must be addressed. Chemical correction may act as a form of "incarceration" in that it may, for the time of the incarceration, inhibit the behavior, but it does nothing to prevent it's reoccurrence, nor does it teach a new behavior to replace the old. By seeing chemical correction as the answer to complex social problems, we are providing only a palliative solution. The multiple determinants of aggression and violence, the problems in treating and defining "anger," and the diagnostic issues involved are discussed.

The Multiple Determinants of Aggression

Just as there is no simple or single cause for criminal behavior and violence, there is no single solution. In fact, offenders represent many different groups, and it is hard to imagine that there is a single solution for the varied problems that they present. As Megargee described in 1982, there are many different groups of offenders, ranging from the normal, adequately socialized people exposed to situational factors that are extremely provocative or whose inhibitions are lowered by alcohol, to those who are instrumentally violent as means to an end. There are those who are violent secondary to overcontrol of hostility, whose violence erupts after consistently inhibiting the normal expression of angry behavior. And there are those whose developmental patterns are disturbed to the point that they fail to develop adequate inhibitions against violent behavior or those who are violent because the subculture in which they live reinforces violent and aggressive behavior.

Thus, criminal and violent behavior have many determinants. Additionally, in a given individual, a behavior is multiply determined and may be a function of individual, social and group factors. Chemical correction ignores all factors other than biological ones and does not appreciate the complexity of any given behavior, failing to take into account the individual decisions that enter into all behavior. In almost all situations, there are choices to be made. When committing a crime, there are choices to be made, such as whether to take a weapon, whether to enter a home where people are present, and whether to use the weapon when faced with that choice. Megargee (1982) describes a convenient algebra for examining the multidimensional complexity of violence. He has suggested an "algebra of aggression," which includes four factors, the instigation to aggression, the habit strength of a given behavior, the inhibition against aggression, and the stimulus factors. When the motivating factors exceed those that act to inhibit the behaviors, then the aggressive act becomes a possibility, but a final factor is needed, the influence of competing responses. In most all situations, there are several options or possible responses available, and this "response competition" is another factor in determining a particular behavior at any given time. Even those with brain lesions or mental illness still have multiple response options that are a function of their history on a personal and social dimension. Violence is not a single entity, and neither are people simply violent or nonviolent; they are responsive to their situation, and their internal and external motivations, making a simple solution such as chemical correction an overly simplistic solution to a complex problem. Even attempting to treat and define anger or aggression, a far simpler problem than dealing with the complexities of criminal behavior, is beyond a simple solution.

Anger, Aggression, and Attempts at Control

Chemical correction has frequently been aimed at controlling anger, although it is not at all clear that anger motivates criminal behavior, and the kind of "anger" presented in most studies bears little relationship to the criminal and aggressive behavior that is of primary social concern. Research on controlling anger often presents case studies of anger that do not involve criminal or violent aggression, but cases of those with anger that, although uncontrolled, does not involve criminal behavior or violence. Mattes (1985) presents two case studies of control of intermittent explosive disorder, controlled by medication, but brain damage was suspected in both, and such cases are not related to criminal behavior. Other studies (Yudofsky, Williams, & Gorman, 1981) note that patients with brain lesions can be controlled with medication, but once again, this does not deal with typical anger or criminal behavior. Aggression against mental health professionals when dealing with mentally ill clients and aggression among the elderly is also treated with pharmacological intervention, but as a social problem, aggression in nursing homes has little relationship to criminal violence and behavior. Few people consider the angry outbursts of demented elderly or brain-damaged as a crime problem, or even as a major social problem. Other studies that purport to deal with the treatment of "aggressive" patients (Lion, 1979) deal with the treatment of anxiety, not anger. Even a review of the pharmacological treatment of aggression deals not with criminal aggression, but with aggression among the mentally ill (Yudosfky, Silver, & Schneider, 1987). Even when chemical control is used to control anger and aggression in prison, it is used with mentally ill inmates, not those individuals whom we typically consider as dangerous criminals. Even in psychiatric patients, aggression inside and outside the institution is related to drug abuse, alcohol abuse, and psychopathy (Rasmussen & Levander, 1996), not disorders such as schizophrenia and manic depression that are frequently the object of chemical control.

There is an underlying issue that complicates matters even further, involving the relationship between anger and aggression. Although anger and aggression may be related, anger does not cause aggression, nor is aggression always accompanied by anger. Anger is a common emotion, with people reporting frequent angry feelings, but the angry feelings result in direct physical aggression only 10 percent of the time (Kassinove & Sukhodolsky, 1995). Thus, examining drugs that help decrease anger is limited in scope, because anger is not a precursor to violence in most situations. But, even if the use of drugs is advocated for those mental disorders that include aggression, there are serious problems in diagnosis, and we once again must remember that mental illness is not the cause of crime.

Problems in Diagnosis

Even if anger or some psychiatric disorder were the root of criminal and violent behavior, the ability to define anger or diagnose mental disorders is limited. There are general problems related to diagnosing mental disorders, and very specific problems associated with diagnosing those disorders that might be considered the "anger" disorders.

Diagnosing and categorizing mental disorders is not an exact science. The most common method of classification, the Diagnostic and Statistical Manual IV (DSMIV, 1994) is a set of guidelines that is informed by clinical judgment. It is a categorical classification system, rather than a dimensional system, which by its nature results in lower reliability and communicates less information than a dimensional system. Although a categorical system would seem to imply that there are discrete members of each class, this is not true. In fact, in the DSMIV specifically notes that there is no "assumption that all individuals described as having the same mental disorder are alike in all important ways." Individuals sharing a diagnosis are likely to be a heterogeneous group and may not share what could be considered to be the major characteristic of a disorder. The diagnostic criteria for a personality disorder, for example, indicate that the person must have only three of a list of seven criteria to qualify. A diagnosis of a disorder, although providing a common language, may not describe people with overlapping characteristics. An examination of some specific diagnoses typically associated with aggression may help clarify why prescribing chemical treatment based on such diagnoses is inappropriate.

Intermittent explosive disorder (IED) and the personality disorders are the two most obvious disorders that relate to anger and aggression and do not have a known organic cause (such as organic personality syndrome, explosive type). IED is a diagnosis that requires "several discrete episodes of failure to resist aggressive impulses that result in serious assaultive acts or destruction of property" and also includes the notion that the aggressiveness is out of proportion to any psychosocial stressors that might be present. There are several problems with the diagnosis itself. It requires aggression, but not anger, and seems to imply that at times the aggressive impulses are resisted successfully, which in turn implies that aggressive impulses are present at other times. Although a convenient way of describing aggression we do not otherwise understand, it is a diagnosis that is lacking in any information about age of onset, course, or prevalence. The DSMIV notes that "Reliable information is lacking, but Intermittent Explosive Disorder is apparently rare." It is a poorly defined disorder that does not provide information about cause, course, or prevalence. And, because the impulses are at times resisted and at other times indulged, chemical correction seems an unlikely answer.

Although antisocial personality disorder (APD) is another example of a diagnosis typically associated with aggressive behavior, it does not require aggressive behavior as part of its diagnostic criteria. As with IED, it is a rare diagnosis, occurring in approximately 3 percent of males and 1 percent of females. Aggressive or assaultive behavior is not required for a diagnosis. Those with APD are manipulative to gain profit, power, or material gratification, generally not a problem amenable to chemical correction. To further complicate matters, two people with APD may look entirely different. For example, one person may have the characteristics of impulsivity, lack of remorse, and reckless disregard for the safety of self and others. Another person may have APD and have characteristics of deceitfulness, consistent irresponsibility, and reckless disregard for the safety of self and others. Both of them would have the underlying characteristic of a "pervasive pattern of disregard for others and violation of the rights of others" but would look entirely different, and neither has the characteristic of "failing to conform to social norms with respect to lawful behavior...." Both meet the criteria for APD, but they are radically different. Thus, proposing a chemical correction based on diagnosis makes little sense. Other personality disorders, often the object of supporters of chemical correction, have the same lack of homogeneity. Whereas pharmacological intervention has long held a place in the treatment of schizophrenia and other major mental health disorders, it does not have a place in the correction of criminal behavior, which is not a mental illness.

Summary

The use of chemical correction or pharmacological correction for violent and criminal behavior is not appropriate. Chemical correction ignores the totality of experience that leads to behavior, does nothing to address the causes of such behavior, and attempts to correct a problem that is poorly defined. Diagnostic categories classify disorders that people have, not the people themselves, and conflicts that are primarily between individuals and society are neither classified as disorders nor are they amenable to a simplistic chemical intervention. Those disorders that do appear to have genetic markers, such as schizophrenia, have been amenable to chemical intervention, but people with these labels are not usually criminal perpetrators. And, even in disorders such as schizophrenia, the genetic markers do not provide a full account for cases of schizophrenia.

Although the influence of genetic and environmental factors is unclear in most disorders with elements of aggression, there is ample literature that suggests that developmental influences are clearly important in the development of aggressive and violent behavior. Chemical correction does nothing to address the cause of violent and aggressive behavior, nor does it help us to prevent children from developing into violent and aggressive adults. As Szasz (1961, 1970) suggested, we have taken "problems in living" and labeled them as mental health issues.

To use chemical correction as the answer to a social problem is simplistic and dangerous. It treats not the problem, but the symptom. By dealing only with the symptom and not the underlying problem, we will continue to have a societal problem with crime and aggression that is palliated, not treated. And, even among those who regard chemical correction as an answer, there is at least the recognition that developmental influences may be "beyond the reach of pharmacotherapy" (Soloff, Siever, Cowdry, & Kocsis, 1994).

Although chemical correction may seem to be an easy and simple solution, it is not a solution at all. It is easy, and it is simple, but it fails to deal with the cause of the problem, provide a long-term solution, or even provide the impetus to further search for the causes of aggressive behavior. Although the body temperature of a patient with a fever may be lowered by the application of cold, the solution is temporary unless the underlying cause of the fever is addressed. Likewise, the administration of a tranquilizer may calm an angry and aggressive person, but it provides only a temporary solution, an incarceration for the mind.

We must continue to examine the individual, social, and cultural influences that create violent and aggressive behaviors. We must look cross-culturally to better understand the roots of aggression and violence, and we must avoid simplistic solutions to a complex and growing social problem. Antisocial behavior is not a disease and not a mental disorder; it is a social and cultural problem that needs to be addressed as such.

REFERENCES

American Psychiatric Association. (1994). *Diagnostic and statistical manual for the mental disorders (4th ed.)*. Washington, D.C.: Author.

Kassinove, H., & Sukhodolsky, D. (1995). Anger disorders: Basic science and practice issues. In H. Kassinove (Ed.), *Anger disorders:* Definition, diagnosis, and treatment. Washington, D.C.: Taylor and Francis, pp. 1–26.

Lion, J. R. (1979). Benzodiazepines in the treatment of aggressive patients. *Journal of Clinical Psychiatry, 40,* 70–71.

Megargee, E. I. (1982). Psychological correlates and determinants of criminal violence. In M. Wolfgang & N. Weiner (Eds.), *Criminal violence.* Beverly Hills, CA: Sage, pp. 81–170.

Mattes, J. A. (1985). Metoprolol for intermittent explosive disorder. *American Journal of Psychiatry, 142,* 1108–1109.

Rasmussen, K, & Levander, S. (1996). Crime and violence among psychiatric patients in a maximum security psychiatric hospital. *Criminal Justice and Behavior, 23,* 455–471.

Szaz, T. S. (1961). *The myth of mental illness.* New York: Harper & Row.

Szasz, T. S. (1970). *The manufacture of madness.* New York: Harper & Row.

Soloff, P., Siever, L. Cowdry, R., & Kocsis, J. (1994). Evaluation of pharmacologic treatments in personality disorders. In R. F. Prien & D. S. Robinson (Eds.), Clinical evaluation of psychotropic drugs: Principles and guidelines. New York: Raven Press.

Yudofsky, S. C., Silver, J. M., & Schneider, S. E. (1987). Pharmacologic treatment of aggression. *Psychiatric Annals, 17,* 397–404.

Yudofsky, S., Williams, D., & Gorman, J. (1981). Propranolol in the treatment of rage and violent behavior in patients with chronic brain syndromes. *American Journal of Psychiatry, 138,* 218–220.

Rejoinder to Dr. Carbonell Diana Fishbein

Dr. Carbonell presents four primary arguments in her chapter against the use of pharmacotherapy for criminal offenders: (1) that criminal or violent behaviors are multiply determined and complex phenomena, frequently not associated with brain dysfunction; (2) that chemical correction is not the sole answer to a complex problem; (3) that anger does not always underlie violence or criminality; and (4) that diagnosing and categorizing mental disorders is an equivocal art, not an exact science.

There is no question that criminal behavior is characterized by multiple generators of both biological and social origins and encompasses a variety of psychological, behavioral, and historical traits. And not all forms of criminality are equally amenable to pharmacotherapy, as emphasized in my chapter. Nevertheless, there is ample evidence to suggest that certain types of offenders, who tend to persist in their criminality and are characterized by impulsivity, cognitive deficits, substance abuse, family history of similar problems, and negative affect, possess underlying neurological dysfunctions that increase susceptibility to criminal and sometimes violent behavior (Raine, 1993; Reissk, Miczek, & Roth, 1994; Volavka, 1995).

Current research in genetics and neurobiology is identifying "vulnerability" genes and neurological substrates that may help us to develop new, more specific medications to reduce impulsive criminality, including violence (see Ciba Foundation, 1996). Identification of these markers could facilitate early detection of individuals at risk and implementation of preventive behavioral and environmental interventions (Reiss et al., 1994). Double-blind studies are now in progress to determine whether habitually violent behavior and impulsivity can be reduced using pharmacotherapy. Thus, perhaps even the prevention of so-called incurable psychopaths may in the future enter the realm of medical treatment, at least when there is evidence of abnormal neurobiological function.

Dr. Carbonell's argument that there is no evidence for a high prevalence of mental disturbance and brain dysfunction amongst adult and juvenile offenders is unfounded. The literature is replete with reports showing organic defects and mental illness in offenders, particularly recidivistic criminals, to be more common than in the general population (Elliott, 1992; Pallone & Hennessy, 1997). Behavioral disorders such as intermittent explosive disorder, episodic dyscontrol syndrome, conduct disorder, and antisocial personality disorder are often characterized by underlying biological or genetic dysfunctions. And although the origins may vary, from genetic susceptibility to environmentally inducements (e.g., head injury, child neglect, or prenatal drug exposure), they are oftentimes amenable to pharmacotherapy. It is accurate to note that most uses for pharmacotherapy have traditionally been with mentally ill offenders and for anger management, but the purpose of my review was to highlight research suggesting that repeat offenders with impulse control disorders may similarly benefit from medical treatment. Thus, in the same way that aspirin was developed for the relief of acute pain and subsequently found also to be helpful in the prevention of heart attacks, certain medications initially developed for mental illness or other disorders also may have import to an appropriate subgroup of offenders. And although much literature deals with the use of pharmacotherapy for anger disorders, in offender populations, impulse control disorders and related neurological dysfunctions are more prevalent and potentially also responsive to particular medications, particularly drugs that act at relevant neurotransmitter sites.

I am in full agreement with Dr. Carbonell that pharmacotherapy should never be considered in isolation of other approaches. It is critical that a complete assessment be conducted in each individual to determine the underlying generators of the behavioral problem before a treatment can be considered. Situational and circumstantial information must be collected to determine whether the sources of the problem can be ameliorated with lifestyle changes, social skills training, or counseling. Pharmacotherapy, to reiterate my initial argument, should only be employed when there is clear evidence and justification for its utility. And even then, it should be accompanied by supportive counseling and other indicated services, and no individual should receive only medication when a complex behavioral problem exists. Because antisocial behavior, violence, and substance abuse involve multidimensional manifestations and causes, a comprehensive approach to treatment must be used. As stated previously, research shows that pharmacotherapy is an effective approach when used in combination with other forms of therapy.

Dr. Carbonell's point that diagnosis and categorization of personality and psychiatric disorders are controversial is well taken. DSM-IV diagnoses (APA, 1994), for example, are much too vague, have overlap between categories, and are not predictive of treatment response. Instead, the focus of an assessment should be on primary psychological and behavioral traits that are often associated with underlying genetic and biological conditions, which can be measured in physiological and biochemical indicators. And although it is important to note that disorders often observed in offenders are not exclusively attributable to genetic and biological conditions, stabilizing the individual with medications that target disturbances that are present enhances responsivity to behavioral and social therapies that the individual may otherwise be unresponsive to. Moreover, measurement of these indicators during the course of treatment will provide essential information as to whether the individual is responding appropriately to treatment without having to wait for noticeable behavioral change, which can take months. Assessment of underlying indicators (e.g., as seen in an electroencephalogram or brain chemistry measures) that shows a trend toward improvement provides further justification for the use of that particular treatment.

Taking into account both the arguments Dr. Carbonell has stated and the cautionary notes delineated in my chapter, it becomes apparent that stringent checks and balances must be well thought out before treatment can be considered in correctional populations. Given that our criminal justice system is understaffed, underfunded, and undertrained, the difficulties in providing the comprehensive assessments, rigorous monitoring, and supportive services necessary in a medical treatment model are somewhat daunting. System-wide changes in philosophy and operations must occur before such a model could be applied. Nevertheless, evidence is compelling for the efficacy of treatment in reducing problematic behaviors and the rate of recidivism, particularly among drug abusers (Hubbard et al., 1989), sex offenders (Berlin, 1983; McConaghy, Blaszczynski, & Kidson, 1988; Murray, 1988) and those with underlying psychiatric disturbances (Volavka, 1995). Perhaps it would be criminal to deny treatment to offenders, both for the sake of public safety and for their own mental health. After working with hundreds of offenders over the years, I can confidently argue that most violent offenders do not willfully commit crimes or intentionally behave in ways that reflect a lack of self-control. If treatment would reduce the odds of their offending, as suggested by recent scientific advances, society should consider establishing the appropriate guidelines so that treatment can be a viable option. So far, the alternatives have been unsuccessful.

REFERENCES

American Psychological Association. (1994). *Diagnostic and statistical manual of mental and emotional disorders* (4th ed.). Washington, D.C.: American Psychiatric Press.

Berlin, F. S. (1983). Sex offenders: A biomedical perspective and a status report on biomedical treatment. In J. G. Greer and I. R. Stuart (Eds.) *The sexual aggressor.* New York: Van Nostrand Reinhold Company.

Ciba Foundation. (1996). *Genetics of criminal and antisocial behaviour.* Chichester: Wiley.

Elliott, F. A. (1992). Violence: The neurologic contribution: An overview. *Archives of Neurology, 49,* 595–603.

Hubbard, R. L., Marsden, M. E., Rachal, J. V., Harwood, H. J., Cavanaugh, E. R., & Ginzburg, H. M. (1989). *Drug abuse treatment: A national study of effectiveness.* Chapel Hill, NJ: University of North Carolina Press.

McConaghy, N., Blaszczynski, A., & Kidson, W. (1988). Treatment of sex offenders with imaginal desensitization and/or medroxyprogesterone. *Acta Psychiatria Scandanavia, 77,* 199–206.

Murray, J. B. (1988). Psychopharmacological therapy of deviant sexual behavior. *The Journal of General Psychology, 115,* 101–110.

Pallone, N. & Hennessy, J. (1997). *Tinder-box criminal aggression: Neuropsychology, demography, phenomenology.* New Brunswick: Transaction Publishers.

Raine, A. (1993). *The psychopathology of crime: Criminal behavior as a clinical disorder.* San Diego: Academic Press.

Reiss, A., Miczek, K., & Roth, J. A. (Eds.). (1994). *Understanding and preventing violence, Vol. 2: Biobehavioral influences.* National Research Council. Washington, D.C.: National Academy Press.

Volavka, J. (1995). *Neurobiology of violence.* Washington, D.C.: American Psychiatric Press.

Is the "Three Strikes and You're Out" a Useful Sentencing Policy?

Mike Reynolds is the father of the two toughest, most effective crime laws in America: "Three Strikes and You're Out" and "Ten, Twenty, Life." Of most importance, he is the father of an eighteen-year-old murdered daughter, Kimber, whom he loves and misses.

Dr. John Kramer is Staff Director of the United States Sentencing Commission. He is also Professor of Sociology and Criminal Justice at Pennsylvania State University. For the past eighteen years he has served as Executive Director of the Pennsylvania Commission on Sentencing. As well as working with the development of sentencing guidelines, Dr. Kramer's research focuses on sentencing and sentencing disparity. His most recent articles appeared in *Criminology* and *Justice Quarterly.*

YES

MIKE REYNOLDS

Throughout history, many devices, treatments, inventions, and solutions have come from necessity. They have also come from someone's basement, garage, or workshop and from people who were never expected to be an inventor or creator. The airplane, penicillin, and the personal computer all came from such humble beginnings. Most importantly, they happened without the support of the established institutions of learning, power, or policy. In some cases, these institutions hindered development and implementation. California's Three Strikes and You're Out, the toughest repeat offender sentencing law in the nation, also came from such humble beginnings. I am a photographer who has spent thirty-five years photographing weddings. My wife, Sharon, is a nurse. On the last day of June 1992, our world changed forever when two men with long criminal records murdered our eighteen-year-old daughter, Kimber, in cold blood.

The shooter had been out of prison for only three months. My wife and I were left with pain, sadness, and an unanswered question: How was it possible that criminals were being turned back to society when there was obvious certainty that they would re-offend? I looked up California crime statistics in "The Corrections Yearbook, Criminal Justice Institute Inc. South Salem, NY," and my worst fears were confirmed:

Average prison sentences	48 months
Average time served	22 months
Recidivism rate	56 percent every two years

From these numbers, it was easy to see why California had earned a reputation for having a revolving door prison policy. Less than one month after Kimber's murder, I asked a select group of people to meet with me around an old redwood Bar-B-Q table in my backyard. Joining me were three judges, one defense attorney, a police officer, a high school superintendent, two businessmen, a prosecutor, and several others, people who work with both the criminals and the laws that affect them.

It was a hot summer night, the dress was casual, and the conversation was candid. Two questions were before us that night. How come violent criminals were being released from prison only to re-offend again, and what could be done to put an end to it? The sincere, frank comments voiced around the table that night were truly informative and insightful. By speaking openly of problems in their own areas of expertise, this group identified three doors that criminals were using to walk out of California's "revolving door" prisons.

Door 1: California criminals were receiving as much as a fifty-percent reduction in their prison sentences in time credits for good behavior.

Door 2: Ninety-four percent of all cases were plea-bargained by the county district attorneys in return for guilty pleas. That meant that criminals were being charged with, and pleading guilty to, charges less severe than the crimes they were committing.

Door 3: Judges were sentencing convicted felons to probation or diversion programs in lieu of prison.

To shut these doors, we came up with the concept of a three-time loser law. We knew this was not a new concept, so some research was necessary before we could proceed. At that time, my son was a law student at UCLA and was working in a downtown federal court over the summer. He was given access to a computer that contained every law that every state had ever passed. In his spare time, my son searched for examples of the concept we had in mind.

The data he produced were fantastic. We had laws that went clear back to the 1800s. We even found that California had passed such a law in 1982, referred to informally as "the habitual felon law," that would provide life without parole for anyone convicted of three violent crimes.

But why, if California already had this law on the books, were the two men responsible for murdering my daughter free to commit this horrible crime? The California Attorney General's Office conducted some research on the law and its implementation. They found it had been used only forty-two times in ten years. That is an average of 4.2 criminals per year that were being affected. In a state of 33 million people, 4.2 criminals per year would not clean up a city block, let alone the entire state.

California has two separate lists of crimes labeled serious felonies and violent felonies. The original concept of the law we were contemplating was for all three strikes to be violent felonies. From our research, however, it was abundantly clear that a law with that formula would not work. So, while making all three strikes violent may have been politically correct (insofar as the criminal justice "establishment" was concerned), in practical application the impact on crime would be minimal.

Therefore, we redefined our concept to make the first and second strikes violent or serious, while the third strike could be any felony conviction. This cast our net wide enough to work. During our research phase, we found one common denominator that nearly all criminals share; criminals re-offend at a rate of nearly nine out of ten during their late teens and into their twenties and thirties. When they are over age forty, only one of ten came back with new convictions.

Why is anyone's guess. It could be something as simple as a good dose of common sense. But my question was not "why?" My question was "how?" How do we get offenders from twenty-something years old to forty-something years old without locking them up for life? The answer was a second strike that doubled the time served. This, combined with a truth in sentencing clause that mandates 80 percent of the term must be served in prison with no parole or diversion programs, was precisely what we needed. It has since become the least talked about and yet most effective part of the law. It locks up violent criminals on their second offense during the most prolific part of their criminal career. It locks them up during a time that in many cases, had they been on the streets, they would have committed a crime or crimes that would have resulted in life sentences. In short, it locks them up for the least amount of time and money and turns them loose near the forty-year age mark.

When attempting to enact a law, implementation language is very important. Too often we see laws that, once made, often go uninforced. This becomes a bit like yelling at your kids. After a while no one responds because they know that yelling has no consequences.

Another major consideration for us was that this law be written in the simplest, shortest, and easiest to understand language possible. The three things that I believe make laws work are:

1. They are tough enough to stop or deter.
2. They are certain to be implemented.
3. They are easy to understand.

California's Three-Strikes law is only 1½ pages of typewritten language. When a law is simple and straightforward, it is also hard to misinterpret by the courts or the defendants.

During the fight to implement Three Strikes, many detractors made predictions of everything from budget-busting prison construction costs to, incredibly, an increase in violent crime. With some time since implementation now having passed, we can compare the projections with facts.

Projection:	Twenty new prisons by 2005
Actual:	Two or three new prisons by 2005
Projection:	$5 billion per year budget increase, with a prison population doubling in three to four years
Actual:	Ten percent increase in prison population, a rate of increase smaller than before passage of Three Strikes
Projection:	No decrease in crime
Actual:	Four-year drop of 40 percent in murder and 30 percent drop in overall crime statistics

In fact, the state has registered the greatest drops in crime since the Attorney General's Office began keeping track of the annual crime statistics. California's crime rate has fallen to the mid-1960s level in only four years. Keep in mind that the magnitude of these drops is far above the national average. One sixth of all crimes occur in California, and as California crime rates drop, it has a tremendous effect on the national averages.

Once crime rates in California began to fall, the detractors were quick to claim that Three Strikes could not be credited with the decline. The question is, then, has Three Strikes had any effect on these falling crime statistics?

Cause and effect have always been hard to prove. Just ask the tobacco companies. For many years we have known that smoking causes a variety of lethal diseases. Yet, for just as many years, the tobacco companies were able to duck conclusive evidence in court. Time, however, has a way of bringing out the truth, and time will leave a clear trail of evidence. What has become apparent is that paroled felons are leaving California in record numbers.

We are also seeing fewer arrests despite the fact that many cities have actually added officers to their police forces in the last four years. Ordinarily, as the number of police increase, so do the number of arrests. As the arrests increase, the crime rate drops. What we have seen in California, in the few years since the implementation of Three Strikes, is a drop in crime without an increase in arrest rates. This would suggest that something else is causing those crime statistics to drop—maybe Three Strikes?

Those who argue that crime is dropping because baby boomers are turning forty, and thus their active crime years are in decline, have only two problems. First, World War II ended in 1945. Baby boomers began turning forty in the 1980s, a time when crime rates were not recording significant drops. Second, demographics cannot possibly come close to explaining the size of the drops in crime. If there is a 30 percent drop in overall crime in 4½ years, demographics should show a 30 percent drop in population of the group most likely to commit crime. This has not occurred.

The most obvious indicator of the effectiveness of Three Strikes comes from the people who are most intimately involved in the criminal justice system: the police, judges, prison guards, and the inmates themselves. They have all indicated that Three Strikes has had the biggest impact on the reduction of crime that they have ever seen. During the fight to enact Three Strikes, the one factor that was never acknowledged by those opposed to the law was its deterrent effect. A law with a strong deterrent effect produces the best kind of results—no police investigation, no court cost, no probation cost, no incarceration cost and, most importantly, no victim.

Until recently, the war on crime in this country was fought in much the same manner as the Vietnam War—a long, protracted war with no intention of winning. Unlike Vietnam, however, this war is being played out on our city streets. Where can we retreat? To the suburbs? Not for long.

This war must be fought with the will to win. We must prosecute the war on crime in the same manner that we prosecuted Desert Storm and get this conflict behind us.

With this in mind, California has recently passed a law to stop gun violence using the 1-2-3 formula inspired by Three Strikes. It is called 10-20-Life. Pull a gun during the commission of designated serious or violent felonies, and there is an automatic addition of ten years to any prison sentence. Pull the trigger—twenty years extra. Shoot someone and, whether they live or die, it will result in an automatic life sentence for the perpetrator. This applies from the age of fourteen up. A judge cannot stop it, and the felon must serve 85 percent of the sentence. This new law became effective on January 1, 1998. Its impact on gun violence should follow closely and quickly. In closing, it should be noted that the designing, research, and drafting of effective laws is not hard. What is hard is to get them on the books. The actual process of implementation of an effective law can be further studied in the book *Three Strikes and You're Out—A Promise to Kimber* published by Quilldriver Books.

Rejoinder to Mr. Reynolds

JOHN KRAMER

"Bad cases make bad laws." This common saying captures the essence of the driving force behind three-strikes legislation. Mike Reynolds's family was the victim of a tragedy that we all want to prevent. But a tragedy such as Mr. Reynolds and his family suffered may blind us from good public policy. Mr. Reynolds makes many strong arguments in favor of California's Three Strikes legislation, and although I favor attempting to prevent such crimes, I disagree that California has taken a major step forward, and I think the data support my case. And it is data that will ultimately be the test of the effectiveness of the legislation. In responding to Mr. Reynolds, I will take his major points and provide my view and what evidence I am aware of to shed light on the accuracy or the limits of his claims.

California's Revolving Door

Mr. Reynolds presents the fact that his daughter was murdered by two men with long criminal records, and the shooter had been out of prison for only three months. Obviously, if the offenders had been incarcerated, they would not have been able to commit the offense. However, treat Mr. Reynolds' data with caution. He reports that the average prison sentence was 48 months, with the average time served of 22 months. Furthermore, he reports that 56 percent recidivate within two years. From these data he concludes that California had earned a reputation for having a revolving door prison policy. In my paper, I point out that California had developed relatively serious penalties for repeat violent offenders after adopting determinate sentencing in 1978. My point is that the information from which Mr. Reynolds concludes a revolving door in fact tells us little. To be informative for this discussion, we would have to know the sentences being given for offenders similar to those who murdered his daughter, whether they were being given prison sentences, and the length of those sentences. Moreover, a 56 percent recidivism rate tells us very little. We need to know the recidivism rate for violent offenders and the offenses they commit. These statistics and the linkage with Kimber's murder suggests that serious violent offenders are getting out of California's prisons in 22 months and that their recidivism is for serious violent crimes. The data presented by Mr. Reynolds represents sentencing data for all California offenders sent to prison and released in a particular year (I assume 1992). It does not reflect the sentences for repeat violent offenders.

Three Doors

Mr. Reynolds indicates that they identified three "doors" from which offenders escaped the system. Door 1 is excessive good time. I agree with Mr. Reynolds that 50 percent is excessive, because 50 percent good time provision undermines the honesty of the system.

Door 2 is that 94 percent of all cases were plea bargained and that this means that they pled guilty to less severe crimes than they were committing. Just two brief comments on this issue. First, the statistic that 94 percent of offenders plead guilty does not mean that 94 percent are plea bargains. Second, when an offender does plea bargain, this does not necessarily mean that they plead to a less severe crime than they actually committed. This is one common form of plea bargaining. Space does not permit going into detail here, but the reader who studies plea bargaining will find that there are many forms of bargains, and often the offender gets no "bargain" at all. Thus, plea bargaining is not as he describes, and it is not closed by Three Strikes, as my paper suggests. Second, Mr. Reynolds uses misleading data once again to support inadequate sentences pre–Three Strikes. Yes, habitual offender laws were often ignored, and many states abandoned them in recent history because they were poorly crafted. Bad laws are often corrected by nonapplication or plea bargains, and this was the way that many courts responded to habitual offender laws.

Door 3 was the judiciary's excessive use of probation for felons. It is important to understand that incarceration has been used in California for a much higher percentage of offenders than was true before the determinate sentencing law going into effect. I do not have the data necessary to test the implication of this third door, but I doubt that California judges were using probation for repeat felons before Three Strikes, and Mr. Reynolds does not provide support that they were.

In fact, California has increased the extent of incarceration both in terms of the proportion of offenders who are incarcerated and the length of incarceration over the past twenty years since it adopted determinate sentencing. Its prison populations have risen from 18,113 on December 31, 1976 to 115,573 on December 31, 1993 (right before the Three Strikes legislation went into effect). This reflects severe increases in sanctions being levied against California offenders before the implementation of Three Strikes legislation. My point is that the door may have been more open than some wished, but the data suggest that California was sentencing offenders much more harshly then Mr. Reynolds suggests. Although I do not have the data to substantiate my caution in accepting Mr. Reynolds claim, I know that the data that he presents shed little light on the issue. Yet once again, he makes claims using data that are not relevant to the particular conclusion that he apparently reached and that he wants the reader to reach.

I agree with Mr. Reynolds that the second-strike provisions of the statute are probably the most likely to be effective because he correctly identifies the relationship between age and risk of re-offending. However, once he reached this conclusion it of course illustrates that incarcerating Three Strike offenders for at least twenty-five years and up to life are poorly conceived laws from a crime reduction perspective and from a cost-effectiveness perspective, particularly in view of the fact that any felony serves as a strike to trip the twenty-five-to-life sentence.

Interestingly Mr. Reynolds' interpretation of the projections data that he presents is quite different then mine. He views the dire predictions of twenty new prisons by 2005 and the reality of two or three new prisons by 2005 as an indication of the extreme dire and inaccurate predictions. It is not clear why the projections were so out of line with the reality; however, I suspect that one of the major reasons is the fact that many jurisdictions are not implementing the Three Strikes legislation as written. I document this in my paper and will not repeat it here, but it reinforces my view that the bill has not eliminated prosecutorial and judicial discretion in the application of the act. Furthermore, the RAND corporation in fact projected a decrease in crime rates of from 25 to 33 percent. Again, Mr. Reynolds misrepresents facts to imply the ignorance of the criminal justice system.

My final comment focuses on the drop in crime rate in California during the past four years. In my paper, I cite a very recent study looking at the potential impact of the Three Strikes legislation on crime rates in ten California cities. That study concluded that the crime rates had started falling before the implementation of Three Strikes legislation, and therefore they could not conclude that the legislation caused the decline in the crime rates. The issue of cause is very difficult to make, as Mr. Reynolds notes, but there is little to support Three Strikes legislation as the cause. I suspect that the decline in crime rates, and violent crime rates in particular, results from many contributing factors, including (1) decline in young male adults over the past decade; (2) the settling of the drug trade so that the turf battles have diminished; (3) improvements in policing, such as those recently evidenced in many urban areas such as New York City and Boston; and (4) the greater use of incarceration to incapacitate offenders. This last point started in California and almost all other states long before the Three Strikes fad, and clearly increasing the use of incarceration removes from the pool of potential offenders some who are high-rate offenders. However, it also removes from the pool those who have ended their criminal career and for whom we get little return on our incapacitation investment. All extremely long sentences incapacities offenders for much longer than necessary to protect society.

Conclusion

I agree that we should attempt to protect the public. However, we must do so intelligently and not with misleading and unfair policies. Three strikes is both misleading and unfair. It misleads by suggesting that offenders who have serious criminal histories and commit serious felonies do not receive severe penalties. Are they severe enough? Sometimes not. But it is misleading to suggest that we as a country do not incarcerate a significant population of offenders. We have increasingly relied on incarceration as the response to crime, and the new wave arguments such as Three Strikes is like the habitual offender laws of several decades ago, another panacea to a crime problem that cannot be addressed by eliminating those who have reached the latter stages of their criminal careers. I agree that such offenders deserve significant punishment because of what they have done. But twenty-five years to life probably provides little incapacitation value beyond California's determinate sentencing legislation.

Three Strikes is a good headline but poor policy.

NO

JOHN KRAMER

"Three Strikes and You're Out" became popular during the last decade as legislators and the public became frustrated with repeat offenders committing violent crimes. Furthermore, our frustration was fueled by social scientists such as Marvin Wolfgang's (Wolfgang, Figlio & Sellin, 1972) research at the University of Pennsylvania, who found that only 6 percent of Philadelphia juveniles with frequent prior arrests accounted for the vast majority of the serious offenses committed by the cohort. For example, these offenders accounted for 73 percent of the rapes, 71 percent of the homicides, and 82 percent of the robberies committed by members of the cohort. Complementing Wolfgang's work was Greenwood and Abrahamse's (1982) self-report research of incarcerated adult offenders in California, Michigan, and Texas. These researchers found a few offenders reported committing a great number of offenses. The conclusion from these important studies was that there are a relatively small percentage of offenders who commit the vast majority of serious offenses. The policy conclusion was that if we can identify these repeat violent offenders and incapacitate them while they are in the active years of their criminality, we will protect the public by reducing crime significantly, particularly serious crime.

Thus, we entered the 1990s armed with not only media examples of serious career offenders preying on the public, but with social science research confirming the severity of some career offenders. The response was to reach back to an old vehicle, historically called habitual offender laws, now labeled "three strikes and you're out" legislation, to mandate long prison sentences for such offenders.

Legislative Diversity in Three Strikes

To conduct a reasoned discussion of three strikes legislation, we must understand what we mean by three strikes. Legislation across the country uses the same term to describe very different legislation. However, to provide a common benchmark, I will use the three strikes term to mean the 1994 legislation passed in California. There are several reasons for selecting this legislation as the working definition for this paper. First, it was one of the first three-strikes bills passed. Second, there has been some preliminary evaluation of its enforcement and its impact. Third, California's three-strikes legislation drew national attention, and it has become the focus of debate among scholars. Thus, it defines for most what the term *three strikes* means. Fourth, California served as the model for many other states as they drafted their own version of three strikes. Finally, the California legislation is broadly defined compared with many states, and this makes it more likely to affect the crime rate.

California's Three Strikes legislation contains three very important ingredients. These ingredients are the offenses included as strikes, the prescribed sentences, and the eligibility for release. California specifies a relatively wide range of felonies as "strike" offenses, including murder, rape, robbery, any felony resulting in bodily harm, burglary of an occupied dwelling, drug sales to minors, any felony with a deadly weapon, and any felony in which a firearm was used. If an individual is convicted of any felony and has two strikes from the list of enumerated strike offenses, then the offender is subject to a mandatory indeterminate life sentence, with no parole eligibility for twenty-five years. California also has a two-strike provision that doubles the term for the current felony conviction if the person has a previous conviction for one of the "strike" offenses. The legislation limits good time to a maximum of 20 percent, whereas regular good time in California is up to 50 percent.

There are a couple of points to highlight in California's Three Strikes legislation. First, the second and third strikes may be any felony, not just those enumerated as strike offenses. Second, California adopted a determinate sentencing statute in the late 1970s that was intended to set fixed terms of incarceration and limited good time to 50 percent for participation in prison treatment programs and good behavior. As part of this legislation and subsequent amendments, the California legislature increased the severity of penalties for repeat offenders, and repeat violent offenders in particular. Thus, the Three Strikes legislation supplemented previous attempts to set determinate repeat offender penalties that were severe compared with the penalties in the 1970s.

Expected Impact

Peter Greenwood and his colleagues at RAND (1996) estimated that if fully implemented the law would reduce serious felonies by from 22 percent to 34 percent and that one third of these prevented offenses would be violent felonies. These effects were based on Greenwood's estimate of the offenses prevented by incarcerating the offenders falling under the Three Strikes law beyond their incarceration under current law. A part of this "incapacitation effect" is that offenders will serve longer periods of confinement then under current law and that offenses that they would commit after release will not be committed if their incarceration is extended.[1]

A second potential impact is deterrence. The deterrence impact may take two forms. First, deterrence may be specific, in which offenders are punished or threatened with potential future punishment and therefore decide not to engage in further crime. Under the three strikes goal of deterrence, it might be expected that individuals with one strike may decide not to engage in future eligible three-strikes offenses because of the threat of serious penalties. A second form of deterrence, general deterrence, occurs when potential punishments dissuade members of the public from committing three-strikes offenses because of the perceived risk of severe and certain (due to mandatory nature of penalties) punishment if convicted.

Recent Sentencing Reform

Sentencing has undergone serious reform during the past three decades, shifting from highly discretionary, unstructured sentencing systems to more structured and less discretionary systems. California and many other states and the federal system reformed their sentencing process and the types of sentences given. One purpose of these reforms was to institute fair, more certain, and more honest sentencing systems. These systems replaced sentencing systems that few understood and allowed offenders committing similar sentences to be sentenced very differently. This latter system was generally known as the indeterminate sentencing model. Its goal was to individualize sentences to allow for the most rehabilitative sentence, depending on the needs of the offender. The duration of incarceration was based on when the offender was rehabilitated and thus a good risk for release. Recent reforms focus on addressing what many viewed as very unfair results from this individualized model such that offenders who had committed similar offenses were punished very differently. Also, many thought that this individualized model allowed judges to use characteristics such as race, gender, socioeconomic status, education, and employment status in sentencing. As a consequence, many believed that sentencing was biased against minorities, men, lower classes, the less educated, and unemployed offenders. To reduce or eliminate unwarranted disparity, many states and the U.S. Congress passed sentencing reform legislation creating sentencing commissions to provide the courts guidance in setting sentences. This movement to create fairness in sentencing incorporated the philosophy of just punishment wherein punishments were set commensurate to the severity of the offense and to the prior criminal conduct of the defendant. One question we need to ask of the Three Strikes legislation is whether it sets fair and equitable penalties. If it treats dissimilar offenders similarly, then it is creating disparate and unfair results.

Critical Analysis of California's Three Strikes Legislation

There are many issues to be raised regarding California's Three Strikes legislation. I will limit my focus to two basic issues. First, I will raise the question of whether the legislation is fair. Second, I will discuss whether it is likely to be effective.

Fairness

There are several perspectives from which to question fairness. For purposes of my discussion, I assume that one of the major concerns in sentencing is that sentences are fair. By fair, I mean that the sentences are commensurate with the severity of the crime, and for three-strikes offenders, whether the punishments are commensurate to the risk of the offender committing a serious crime in the future.

One of my operating principles is that punishment should primarily be commensurate to the severity of the offender's culpability and the injury or risk of injury to the victim. Criminal statutes define what is criminal and in the definition take important steps in defining the culpability of the offender in committing the crime and the injury to the offender. For example, homicide statutes generally specify two or three degrees of murder and then also provide for voluntary and involuntary manslaughter. For each of these offenses, a victim is dead, but there are important differences in the culpability of the offender in committing the crime. For example, under Pennsylvania's Crimes Code (1997), first-degree murder is intentional or premeditated murder, and second-degree murder is killing during the commission of a felony. Voluntary manslaughter is homicide in the sudden heat of passion, and involuntary manslaughter is the unintentional killing of another while acting in a "reckless or grossly negligent manner." For each of these offenses, statutes specify a maximum penalty, and these maximum penalties reflect the legislature's interest in limiting the punishment for the worst case that might meet the statutory requirement. Other offenses are scaled based on the degree of injury, amount of property loss, and other factors reflecting the degree of injury to the victim. The purpose of this excursion into criminal statutes and setting penalties linked to the culpability of the offender and the injury to the victim is to contrast this with California's Three Strikes legislation. California's Three Strikes legislation sets the three strikes penalties for a broad range of offenders, thus treating them as equally culpable and serious. The point is that the Three Strikes legislation favors treating widely different offenders in terms of their culpability and victim injury as equal.

Mandatory minimums are often criticized as treating dissimilar offenders similarly, and this fundamental fairness issue is one of my most serious concerns with most three strikes legislation and with the California legislation in particular. Under the California Three Strikes provisions, offenders who have committed any of the specified crimes and who are currently convicted of any felony are subject to the mandated penalties. Thus, offenders like the example often cited of the offender who for his third strike stole a piece of pizza from children and who had two prior strike-eligible offenses received a sentence of twenty-five years to life. Juxtapose this with an offender, with two prior strike-offenses, who murdered someone. It is hard to argue that these offenders are similarly culpable or similar risks for future violence. This is a justice issue, and although the focus of Three Strikes is on prediction of future criminality and dangerous criminality in particular, it is one of the basic principles of law that penalties should be fair. Three

Strikes legislation, and many other forms of mandatory minimums, often lose the principle of fairness in favor of uniformity for a broadly defined class of offenders. In the long run, the value of the legislation may well be undermined by prosecutors who view it as unfair and a public who comes to expect manipulation of the administration of "three strikes" in clandestine decisions by prosecutors and judges. This is not, however, a system of justice that will be widely respected.

Effectiveness

Effectiveness can be viewed in several ways, and in this section I want the reader to consider the purpose of the legislation as to prevent serious offenders from harming the public in the future. This is an appropriate goal and an appropriate sentencing goal. My criticisms of California Three Strikes legislation is not whether incapacitation is an appropriate criminal justice goal, but with the particular manner in which it is implemented in California's Three Strikes provisions. I will focus my discussion first on the cost-effectiveness of the legislation and second on the most recent data suggesting the impact of the legislation on crime rates.

Cost Effectiveness

The concept of incarcerating offenders for the rest of their lives with the goal of protecting the public is a poor investment. The cost of incarceration rises with age, and one assessment of the cost of confining an offender in California is projected at $21,000 per year. But the cost of confining someone in California between the ages of fifty and sixty is $60,000 and for offenders over the age of sixty, the costs exceed $69,000 (Skolnick, 1995). Research indicates that criminal behavior declines significantly as offenders move into their thirties and offenders who are active in their thirties have an expected crime life expectancy of approximately ten years (Blumstein, Cohen, Roth, & Visher, 1987). Investment in incarcerating such offenders beyond their crime-prone years brings diminishing returns in terms of incapacitation. By the time the offender reaches fifty years of age, he or she has in general a minimal risk of committing a violent crime, and the cost of incarceration has risen to $60,000 a year. Moreover, to the degree that the Three Strikes offenders begin to crowd the prisons, they may well force out offenders who are a greater risk because of overcrowding or reluctance to invest more in incarceration on the part of the state legislature. Thus, my first concern is that Three Strikes legislation such as that in California is poorly conceived, in that the long-term incapacitation investment is of minimal value and may have a negative effect if the correctional system becomes overcrowded and growing proportions of the correctional investment is spent on offenders whose criminal behavior has ebbed or ceased entirely.

Effectiveness

It is an operating premise that unfair legislation will be undermined by plea bargaining and other avoidance techniques by the court system. It may be that such practices in California will correct the fairness concerns I raised earlier, but only if the selective prosecution is uniformly developed and applied throughout the state. If selective prosecution occurs such that, in some jurisdictions in California the Three Strikes legislation is applied as specified in the legislation, and in others where it depends on what the prosecutor thinks is appropriate, then California will find itself with a serious disparity problem. This disparity of differential application will undermine the intent of the structured sentencing reform implemented in the late 1970s, when it passed determinate sentencing to increase certainty and fairness in sentencing. There are early signs that there are serious problems in equitable implementation across the state. First, the projections that were made by the California Department of Corrections estimating the likely impact of the legislation have had to be reduced (Clark, Austin, & Henry, 1997). While this may be due to a change in the types of offenders who are being convicted in California, it appears to result from two adjustments not built into the projections. One of these adjustments is that judges are sentencing in lower parts of the ranges provided by statute. A second reason for the lower impact of the legislation than anticipated appears to be the result of management by the system. Clark and his associates have found that there is widely discrepant application of the law. San Francisco and Alameda rarely apply the law, while San Diego and Sacramento use the law relatively vigorously. There are no data that suggests that these differences reflect different types of offenders in the jurisdictions; rather the differences most likely rest in the policies of the prosecutors and the courts in the jurisdictions. This is expected based on research in other jurisdictions that indicate that courts often adapt to legislation by plea bargaining and manipulation to achieve what they view as fair (Eisenstein et al., 1988). In some respects these adjustments may make the legislation more effective. If the prosecutor narrows the targeting of offenders so that the least serious offenders (the pizza robber) may be "managed" out of the coverage of the Three Strikes legislation, then such manipulation may increase the fairness and the cost-effectiveness of the legislation.

Finally, it is too early to tell the long-term impact of the legislation on crime rates, but there is a very recent study by Lisa Stolzenberg and Stewart D'Alessio (1997) examining the impact on crime rates in ten California cities. Stolzenberg and D'Alessio conducted a time series study in these ten cities to see whether the implementation of the law made any difference in the serious crime rate (referred to as CCI or the California Crime Index[2]) or in petty crimes. The authors conclude that: "The results generally indicate that the three-strikes law did not decrease the CCI rate below that expected on the basis of pre-existing trends (p. 464)." The only city of that ten that they studied that showed a significant decline in crime rate greater than that expected from preexisting trends was Anaheim. The authors explore why the law seems to have had no impact on crime rates, and their observations provide important suggestions as to what is often ignored in the politicalization of such legislation. First, California had serious penalties for repeat offenders before Three Strikes, and the additional severity brought about by Three Strikes should not necessarily be expected to have a significant effect. Second, they note that criminal careers decline with age and that Three Strikes offenders are captured at the very age when their criminality is ending. Thus, we should not expect a significant impact of Three Strikes legislation. Third, juvenile crime accounts for a large percentage of serious crime committed in the United States, and Three Strikes legislation focuses on the older offender, ignoring this important contributing group to crime rates.

Conclusions

Protection of the public is a worthwhile goal of the criminal justice system, and it is clear that the criminal justice system has not done a perfect job of protecting the public. The recent attempt to enhance public safety through Three Strikes legislation has an admirable goal, but it is poorly executed. It fails to achieve credibility by virtue of treating a broad range of offenders as though they were equal in terms of their risk and in terms of their culpability and their injury to victims. It fails to protect the public by imposing unnecessary incapacitation on offenders who are late in their criminal careers. We can do better for less.

Notes

1. There are two basic ways in which incapacitation incarceration works and that is to incarcerate those who would not otherwise be incarcerated or to extend the term of incarceration. The biggest benefit of incapacitation results in California will be the extension of incarceration because most offenders falling under the "three strikes" legislation were expected to get an incarceration sentence under already existing law.

2. The California Crime Index is the number of reported willful homicides, forcible rapes, robberies, aggravated assaults, burglaries, and motor vehicle thefts divided by the city population and multiplied by 100,000.

References

Clark, J., Austin, J., & Henry, D. A. (1997). *"Three strikes and you're out": A review of state legislation.* Washington: National Institute of Justice.

Blumstein, A., Cohen, J., Roth, J., & Visher, C. (1986). *Criminal careers and career criminals.* Washington, D.C.: National Academy Press.

Eisenstein, J., Flemming, R. B., & Nardulli, P. (1988). *Contours of justice.* Boston: Little Brown.

Greenwood, P. W. & Abrahmse, A. (1982). *Selective incapacitation.* Santa Monica: RAND Corp.

Greenwood, P. W., Rydell, C. P., Abrhamse, A. F., Caulkins, J. P., Chiesa, J., Model, K. E., & Klein, S. (1996). Estimated benefits and costs of California's new sentencing law. In *Three strikes and you're out.* In D. Shichor and D. K. Sechrest (Eds.). Thousand Oaks, CA: Sage, pp. 53–89.

Skolnick, J. H. (1995). What not to do about crime. *Criminology, 33,* 1–15.

Stolzenberg, L. & D'Alessio, S. J. (1997). "Three strikes and you're out": The impact of California's new mandatory sentencing law on serious crime rates. *Crime and Delinquency* 43: 457–469.

Wolfgang, M. E., Figlio, R. M., & Sellin, T. (1972). *Delinquency in a birth cohort.* Chicago: University of Chicago Press.

Rejoinder to Dr. Kramer MIKE REYNOLDS

Let me respond to Mr. Kramer's focus on two issues: whether the "three-strikes" law is fair and whether it is effective.

Fairness

Mr. Kramer defines "fairness" in sentencing as whether "the sentences are commensurate with the severity of the crime, and for third strike offenders, whether the punishments are commensurate to the risk of the offender committing a serious crime in the future." This definition avoids emphasis on the offender and focuses on the magnitude of the crime the offender is charged with. Punishment always considers the offender in terms of his or her record measured against the crime itself.

The primary considerations in punishment are rehabilitation, deterrence, retribution, and isolation. The emphasis given to each of these considerations changes depending on the crime and the offender. Furthermore, three strikes seeks to avoid the future commission of serious crime, but it does so by considering that the offender has already demonstrated the capacity to commit a serious or violent crime, otherwise he or she would not qualify under the Three Strikes law. And to qualify as a "third strike," the offender must have committed at least two serious or violent felonies. Therefore, any person subject to "three strikes" has demonstrated a propensity to commit crimes with a high risk of death or bodily injury and has been charged with committing a new felony.

Under basic concepts of punishment, the third-strike offender (1) has not been rehabilitated by previous punishment; (2) has not been deterred by previous punishment; (3) society's standard of retribution has been unable to sufficiently restrict the offender from further commission of felonies. Therefore, isolation becomes an appropriate consideration. The Three Strikes law addresses "isolation" by a mandatory twenty-five-years-to-life term. Because three strikes limits time credits to a maximum of 20 percent, third-strike offenders can be assured of a minimum twenty-year prison term. Isolation is an appropriate response to the refusal of the offender to conform his or her conduct to society's requirement. In effect, the offender is isolated because his pattern of past criminal activity and his commission of a new felony is the best predictor of future criminal activity.

Mr. Kramer would simply say that the past is not a fair predicator of the future. His position is contrary to every judgment we make in society about probable behavior. And while it may be true that one cannot say with certainty that every third strike felon will commit another violent or serious crime in the future or another felony in the future, it certainly can be said that it is probable that he or she will based on past patterns of behavior. I do not believe society should have to continuously accept the risk of new criminal conduct to be certain that the offender gets another chance to prove he or she has reformed. At some point, society is entitled to say we will no longer accept the risk and we conclude individuals who have at least two prior serious or violent felonies and continue to commit new felonies are, as a matter of policy and common sense, an unacceptable risk.

Mr. Kramer says "three strikes favors treating widely different offenders in terms of their culpability and victim injury as equal." This is not correct. Three Strikes attempts to treat their basic threat—continued felony criminal conduct—as equal. In other words, it does not seek to differentiate between the threat of committing another violent crime or another felony. It responds to the probable threat of continued felonious conduct.

Effectiveness

Mr. Kramer considers the cost of incarceration as a factor in determining effectiveness. I agree, but with a different perspective. Current costs of prison incarceration are approximately $21,000/year. That cost arguably goes up for some older offenders. However, such costs must be measured against not incarcerating them for long periods. There is a significant economic cost to crime, and it is substantially higher for society while a career criminal plies his trade before he is caught. In other words, you must weigh the economic cost of incarceration against the economic cost to society of a pattern of criminal activity that is only interrupted by short ineffective periods of incarceration. Of course, there can be no financial price placed on the misery of future victims.

What is certain, however, is that if a law is strong enough to deter crime, the cost of prosecuting and incarcerating the criminals who would have committed those crimes is saved. In the sixteen years before the implementation of Three Strikes, the California prison population expanded at a rate of 400 percent, or, 100 percent every four years. In the four years after implementation of Three Strikes, the prison population grew by only 50 percent. This represents a 50 percent reduction in the incarceration rate in California prisons since Three Strikes became law.

Although there is a certain amount of inherent optimism in the objective of deterring the commission of crimes by the existence of punishment, it is an express goal of our system. Although the reports are largely anecdotal, the consistent comment from probation officers, parole officers, and district attorneys is that individuals subject to the Three Strikes law are aware of it and are afraid of it. Nothing in our past punishment system has clearly demonstrated that the existence of punishment has served as an effective deterrent. I believe this is largely because punishment is uncertain and not recognized as a real threat. I attribute part of the present downturn in criminal activity to deterrence and project larger downturns due to the consequences of removal of those who are not deterred.

This downturn in crime is statistically demonstrated in reports issued by the California Department of Justice representing the first three years since the enactment of Three Strikes. Following is a table that uses these statistics, which, based on 1993, the last year before enactment of Three Strikes, gives an actual representation of the drop in crime, not in percentages, but in real victim numbers.

Violent Crimes

Murder

Fewer Crimes

1993	Before Three Strikes	4,095				
1994	One year after Three Strikes	3,699	=	396 × 3yr	=	1,188
1995	Two years after Three Strikes	3,530	=	169 × 2yr	=	338
1996	Three years after Three Strikes	2,888	=	642	=	642

Three-year total: 2,168 Fewer Murders

Rape

Fewer Crimes

1993	Before Three Strikes	11,754				
1994	One year after Three Strikes	10,960	=	794 × 3yr	=	2,382
1995	Two years after Three Strikes	10,550	=	410 × 2yr	=	820
1996	Three years after Three Strikes	10,097	=	453	=	453

Three-year total: 3,655 Fewer Rapes

Robbery

Fewer crimes

1993	Before Three Strikes	126,347				
1994	One year after Three Strikes	112,149	=	14,198 × 3yr	=	42,594
1995	Two years after Three Strikes	104,581	=	7,568 × 2yr	=	15,136
1996	Three years after Three Strikes	93,182	=	11,399	=	11,399

Three-year total: 69,129 Fewer Robberies

Aggravated Assault

Fewer Crimes

1993	Before Three Strikes	193,904			
1994	One year after Three Strikes	192,138	=	$1,766 \times 3yr$ =	5,298
1995	Two years after Three Strikes	186,337	=	$5,801 \times 2yr$ =	11,602
1996	Three years after Three Strikes	165,654	=	20,683 =	20,683

Three-year total: 37,583 Fewer Aggravated Assaults

Total Fewer Violent Crime Victims = 112,535

Property Crimes

Burglary

Fewer Crimes

1993	Before Three Strikes	413,671			
1994	One year after Three Strikes	384,441	=	$29,257 \times 3yr$ =	87,771
1995	Two years after Three Strikes	353,817	=	$30,597 \times 2yr$ =	61,194
1996	Three years after Three Strikes	308,529	=	42,288 =	42,288

Three-year total: 194,253 Fewer Burglaries

Auto Theft

Fewer Crimes

1993	Before Three Strikes	319,225			
1994	One year after Three Strikes	308,303	=	$10,922 \times 3yr$ =	32,766
1995	Two years after Three Strikes	280,317	=	$27,986 \times 2yr$ =	55,972
1996	Three years after Three Strikes	239,672	=	40,645 =	40,645

Three-year total: 129,383 Fewer Auto Thefts

Total Fewer Property Crime Victims = 323,636

Total Fewer Violent Crime Victims = 112,535

Total Fewer Crime Victims = 436,171

We already know what happened before we had such a law. Why would we want to return to what we know was not effective in significantly reducing serious and violent crime?

Allyn & Bacon Order Form

The Controversial Issues in Criminal Justice Series
Steven A. Egger, Series Editor

Complete your set of books in the Controversial Issues in Criminal Justice Series with these additional titles—only $24.00 each*!

Available Now!

**Controversial Issues
in Corrections**
by Charles B. Fields
Order No. 0-205-27491-9

**Controversial Issues
in Criminology**
by John R. Fuller and Eric W. Hickey
Order No. 0-205-27210-X

**Controversial Issues
in Policing**
by James D. Sewell
Order No. 0-205-27209-6

Available Fall 1999*

**Controversial Issues
in Criminal Justice**
by Frank Horvath
Order No. 0-205-29214-3

**Controversial Issues
in Gender**
by Donna Hale
Order No. 0-205-29215-1

*Prices and Titles are subject to change

To Place an Order:

MAIL:
Allyn & Bacon Publishers
111 10th Street
Des Moines, IA 50309

CALL:
Toll-Free: 1-800-278-3525
Fax: 1-515-284-2607
WEBSITE: www.abacon.com

Name: _____

Address:_____

City: _____ State: _____ Zip Code: _____

Phone: _____ E-Mail:_____

Charge my: _____Amex _____Visa _____Mastercard _____Discover

Card # _____ Exp. Date _____

Enclosed find my: _____Check _____Money Order

*Shipping and handling charges will be added unless order is prepaid by check or money order.